BIOGRAPHY

OF

THE BLIND

W. Radcliffe. sc. Birming.

HOMER.

BIOGRAPHY

OF

THE BLIND:

INCLUDING THE

LIVES OF ALL WHO HAVE DISTINGUISHED

THEMSELVES AS

POETS, PHILOSOPHERS, ARTISTS,

&c. &c.

BY JAMES WILSON,

WHO HAS BEEN BLIND FROM HIS INFANCY.

COLLECTED AND EDITED BY KENNETH A. STUCKEY
FROM THE FOUR ORIGINAL EDITIONS OF 1821–38.

———

*Friends of Libraries for Blind and Physically
Handicapped Individuals in North America*
AND
*National Library Service for the Blind
and Physically Handicapped.*

———

LIBRARY OF CONGRESS, WASHINGTON.

———

1995.

LIBRARY OF CONGRESS
CATALOGING-IN-PUBLICATION DATA

Wilson, James, 1779–1845.
    Biography of the blind: including the lives of all who have
distinguished themselves as poets, philosophers, artists, &c.,
&c., / by James Wilson : collected and edited by Kenneth A.
Stuckey from the four original editions of 1821–38.
       p.   cm.
    "Published by the Friends of Libraries for Blind and Phys-
ically Handicapped Individuals in North America, Inc., and
the National Library Service for the Blind and Physically
Handicapped, the Library of Congress."
    Includes bibliographical references.
    ISBN 0–8444–0880–8
    1. Blind—Biography. I. Stuckey, Kenneth A. II. Title.
    HV1584.W5   1995
    362.4′1′0922—dc20   95–16368
    [B]   CIP

CONTENTS

CONTENTS

FOREWORD

STORIES recounting the accomplishments of blind achievers have long been circulated formally and informally. Among the first books to detail the courage and accomplishments of blind people was the work of a nineteenth-century American, James Wilson. Blind himself, Wilson collected short biographies of other blind people, historical and contemporary, who had achieved renown. His work, first published in 1821, proved to be so popular that it went to four editions.

Since James Wilson's time, perceptions and language regarding blind people have changed, thanks to the educational and organizational work of blind people and to their success in challenging historically imposed limitations. This reissue of the four editions of Wilson's book in one volume offers perspective on those changes and demonstrates that some attitudes and perceptions about blind people have been entrenched throughout history. It recalls for our inspiration and encouragement the stories of blind people who defied social expectations and successfully pursued careers and achieved goals.

It is noteworthy that with this reissue the book will, for the first time, be published in braille and recorded formats. No longer is James Wilson a biographer of blind individuals for the sighted. He is now the blind author of a book about blind individuals for blind individuals.

FRANK KURT CYLKE

Ex Officio member, Friends of Libraries for Blind and Physically Handicapped Individuals in North America

Director, National Library Service for the Blind and Physically Handicapped, Library of Congress

PREFACE

In preparing to give the banquet address to the National Federation of the Blind in 1973, I researched the role that blind people have played in history. I suspected that their accomplishments had been greatly underreported, but I was short on facts. It was then that I found *Biography of the Blind* by James Wilson (1779–1845). That book, along with William Artman and L. V. Hall's *Beauties and Achievements of the Blind* (1853), was exactly what I needed. It surprised and delighted me. I had spent most of my adult life trying to educate both the blind and the sighted public about the capabilities of the blind. Yet here were detailed accounts of illustrious careers and wide-ranging achievements that I had never before encountered.

The speech that resulted, "Blindness: Is History against Us?," would not have been possible without Wilson's book. I thus am glad that the book (long since out of print) is now being reissued. This composite facsimile edition is particularly in keeping with the spirit of the organized blind movement and the Friends of Libraries for Blind and Physically Handicapped Individuals in North America, both of which maintain active roles in the community.

Experts in the field of blindness, as well as members of the general public, have differed greatly as to what the future holds for the blind. Some see us blundering on forever in roles of economic dependence and second-class citizenship. Others predict a slow but steady progress toward independence, equality, and full membership in society. My view is that this is not a matter for prediction but for decision. I believe that neither of these outcomes is certain or foreseeable, for the simple reason that our choices and actions are the factors that determine our future. In short, we the blind (like all people) confront alternative futures: one future in which we will live our own lives, or another future in which our lives will be lived for us.

If the future is open and contingent, surely the past is closed and final. Whatever disputes people may have about the shape of things to come, there can be no doubt about the shape of things gone by. Or can there be? Is there such a thing as an alternative past?

The popular historical record tells us that until recently blind people were completely excluded from the ranks of the sighted community. In early societies they were abandoned, exterminated, or left to fend for themselves as beggars on the lunatic fringe of society. Beginning in the late Middle Ages, almshouses and other sheltered institutions provided for their care and protection. Only lately have blind people begun to move in the direction of independence and self-sufficiency.

The message commonly derived from historical accounts is that the blind have always been dependent

on the will and mercy of others. We have been the people things were done *to*—and, occasionally, the people
things were done *for*—but never the people who did
things for themselves. In effect, according to these accounts, we have no history of our own—no record of
active participation or adventure or accomplishment,
but only an empty and unbroken continuum of desolation and dependence. It would seem that the blind
have moved through time and the world not only
sightless but faceless—a people without distinguishing
features, anonymous and insignificant—not so much as
rippling the stream of history.

In reality the accomplishments of blind people
through the centuries have been disproportionate to
their numbers. There are repeated instances of genius, fame, adventure, and enormous versatility of
achievement. To be sure, there is misery also—
poverty and suffering and misfortune aplenty—just as
there is in the general history of humanity. But what
sighted historians often misrepresent is the chronicle
of courage, conquest, and glory that should accompany the history of the blind.

The accomplishments of many active blind figures
are set down in James Wilson's *Biography of the Blind*.
Prominent on Wilson's list of characters are blind military leaders as well as scientists, doctors, teachers,
lawyers, mathematicians, and other professionals. An
inspirational example is Zisca, the fifteenth-century
leader of Bohemia, who was completely blind when he
won his greatest battles and was offered the crown of
his country.

Perhaps the most persistent and destructive myth

concerning the blind is the assumption of our relative inactivity and immobility—the image of blind people who are glued to rocking chairs and, at best, sadly dependent on others to guide or transport them in their daily routine. "Mobility," we are led to believe, is a term that has just begun to have meaning for the blind. To be sure, many blind people have been cowed by the myth of helplessness into remaining in their sheltered corners. But there have always been others—like James Holman, Esquire, a solitary traveler of a century and a half ago, who gained the great distinction of being labeled by the Russians as "the blind spy." Holman traveled alone through much of Europe and, as he traveled across the steppes of Greater Russia to Siberia, was so close an observer of all about him that he was arrested as a spy by the czar's police and conducted to the borders of Austria, where he was ceremoniously expelled.

Other blind travelers in our own time have been as intrepid as James Holman. Yet Holman's story is important for its demonstration that blind people could wear such seven-league boots almost two centuries ago, before braille or the long cane, before residential schools or vocational rehabilitation, and before the myriad of special agencies and new devices that now abound.

Wilson does not limit his examples to the members of high society or the educated. He tells of ordinary citizens who are simply able to walk and run, to mount a horse, and to engage in the regular tasks of daily living. In this respect, perhaps no one has shown the way with more flair than a stalwart Englishman of the eighteenth century named John Metcalf. Totally blind from childhood, he was, among other things, a successful builder of roads and bridges, a racehorse rider, a bare-knuckle fighter, a card shark, a stagecoach driver, and, on occasion, a guide to sighted tourists through the local countryside.

Wilson is truly a pioneer with his biographical sketches, but they are only samples. Probably the best known of history's blind celebrities are Homer, Milton, and Helen Keller. These legendary figures—each in its own sentimentalized, storybook form—have come to represent not the abilities and possibilities of blind people but the exact opposite. Supposedly these giants are the exceptions that prove the rule that the blind are incompetent. Each celebrated case has an explanation: Homer was allegedly not a single person but a composite of poets; Milton is dismissed as a sighted poet who became blind in later life; and Helen Keller was the peculiarly gifted and lucky beneficiary of a lot of money and a "miracle worker" (her tutor and companion, Anne Sullivan).

These justly famous cases of accomplishment are not mysterious, inexplicable exceptions—they are only remarkable. Although Homer has become a legendary figure, thousands of other blind people have also mastered the art of storytelling. Milton composed great works while he was sighted, and greater ones (including *Paradise Lost)* after he became blind. Helen Keller's life demonstrates dramatically what great resources of character, will, and intellect may live in a human being beyond the faculties of sight and sound.

Despite the examples of Homer, Milton, and Keller—and despite the evidence amassed by Wilson—many people will try to maintain their outworn notions about the helplessness of the blind as a group. It is true that most blind people throughout the ages have lived humdrum lives, achieving neither fame nor glory, and were soon forgotten, but the same is true for the sighted.

Doubters may claim that a larger percentage of the blind than of the sighted has experienced failure. As in the case of other minorities, this is true because we tend to see ourselves as others see us. We have accepted the public view of our limitations and thus have done much to make those limitations a reality.

If Wilson were alive today, he would revel in the accomplishments and struggles of the organized blind movement. He would doubtless write a new biography of the blind and be a principal participant in it—especially because he was blind, as was William Artman. In our own time we have found leaders as courageous as Zisca and as willing to go into battle to resist tyranny. But we are no longer to be counted by ones and twos, or by handfuls or hundreds. We are now a movement, with tens of thousands in the ranks. Napoleon is supposed to have said that history is a legend agreed on. If this is true, then we the blind are in the process of negotiating a new agreement, with a legend conforming more nearly to the truth and the spirit of human dignity.

What legends will future historians agree on concerning the blind of the late-twentieth century? How will they describe our movement? It all depends on

what we do and how we act—for future historians
will write the record, but we will make it. Our lives
will provide the raw materials from which their legends will emerge.

While no one can predict what lies ahead, I feel
confident that certain contemporary leaders of the
blind will be recognized by future historians. Among
that number will be Newel Perry, pioneer of the organized blind movement in California and precursor
of the subsequent national movement. His brilliant
student, the renowned scholar Jacobus tenBroek,
will also be on the list for founding the national organized blind movement, the National Federation of
the Blind. Our dreams are also part of the historical
fabric, reaching forward to the next generation as a
heritage and a challenge and back through time to
keep faith with James Wilson and others like him.
History is not against us: the past proclaims it, the
present confirms it, and the future demands it. Let
the republication of Wilson's book be a symbol of
the progress we have made and a reminder of what
we still must do.

KENNETH JERNIGAN

President, Friends of Libraries for Blind and Physically Handicapped Individuals in North America

President Emeritus, National Federation of the Blind; Baltimore,
Maryland

EDITOR'S INTRODUCTION

———————

JAMES WILSON'S *Biography of the Blind* is one of the first books to record the lives of blind people who, "from Homer down to the present day, have distinguished themselves as poets, philosophers, artists, etc." The first of Wilson's four editions of this book was published in 1821 and the last in 1838. Although seldom found in libraries today, even those associated with organizations or schools for the blind, the *Biography* still merits study. It offers insights into the lives of blind people before the great emancipators of the blind, such as Valentin Haüy, Louis Braille, Samuel G. Howe, and Sir Francis Campbell, who influenced the education, welfare, and rehabilitation of the blind throughout the nineteenth and twentieth centuries. Wilson provides glimpses into the lives of blind men and women who vary in age, abilities, and status in life, from the legendary Homer and the mathematical genius Nicholas Saunderson to Adam Mond, the blind miser.

"I thought if these were collected together," Wilson wrote, "and molded into a new form, it might not only become an amusing, but a useful work, so far as it would show what perseverance and industry could do, in enabling us to overcome difficulties apparently insurmountable."

Wilson was also a remarkable person, and his own biography is an interesting addition to his book. Wilson's contemporary John Bird, a member of the College of Surgeons and also blind, says in his 1856 *Essay on the Life, Character, and Writing of Blind James Wilson* "... it is impossible for me to do justice to the memory of James Wilson and the value of his writings, in any degree proportionate to the esteem and gratitude I myself, in common with other blind, feel for his character and labors." Many authors of later works on the history of the blind have drawn from Wilson's compilation.

Wilson's is not a scholarly work researched, documented, and arranged by historical order or significance, like, for example, Alexander Mell's *Encyklopädisches Handbuch des Blindenwesens*, published some fifty years later in 1900, or William Artman and L.V. Hall's *Beauties and Achievements of the Blind,* published fifteen years after Wilson's fourth edition. Artman and Hall's book groups notable blind people in categories such as "Memoirs of Eminent Blind Authors" and "Achievements of the Blind in the Learned Professions." Wilson's work is more like a scrapbook, a collection of disparate pieces on one subject.

To make *Biography of the Blind* more accessible to modern readers, this edition takes the liberty of arranging Wilson's biographies into groups by field of interest and introducing each group with an essay giving additional information and historical perspective. This edition combines under one cover all the biographies found in each of the four Wilson editions. Within this framework, the individual biographies are

reprinted exactly as Wilson published them but in
chronological order.

Because people mentioned in *Biography of the Blind*
are sometimes referred to in several ways, both in the
book and in other literature, this edition includes as
Appendix A an index of names with cross-references.
For example, "John, the Blind King," is also known
as "John of Luxembourg" and the "Blind King of
Bohemia." When available, life dates for each person
are given. Appendix B reproduces Wilson's introduction to the second, third, and fourth editions of
the *Biography*. Appendix C provides a bibliography
of related works.

In the years since Wilson published his books, the
education, welfare, and rehabilitation of blind people
have changed significantly. In 1821 few schools or organizations for blind people existed outside Europe.
The first school in the United States (Perkins School
for the Blind) was not established until 1829. Later
in the nineteenth and twentieth centuries, many
schools, organizations, and rehabilitation centers
opened throughout the world. Today most visually
impaired children are integrated into regular
schools, and growing numbers of blind workers are
entering the labor market. Yet, while society is often
willing to provide the training, skills, and technology for blind people to be fully integrated, changes
in attitudes toward blind people have not been as
significant. The full benefits of training and technology await the opening of employment opportunities
for blind workers that equal those of their sighted
coworkers, an event that may be hastened by legisla-

tion such as the Americans with Disabilities Act of 1990.

In looking at the past as portrayed by Wilson, we glimpse the road society traveled up to the nineteenth century in Europe and America. His work also gives us perspective on changes since then as well as on today's challenges. *Biography of the Blind* was recognized in the past as a significant work, enlightening the world to the achievements of blind individuals in all walks of life. This reprinting makes the book once again accessible to the general public and researchers.

KENNETH A. STUCKEY
Research Librarian, Samuel P. Hayes Research Library, Perkins School for the Blind, Watertown, Massachusetts

BIOGRAPHY

OF

THE BLIND

BIOGRAPHY

OF THE

B L I N D,

INCLUDING THE LIVES OF ALL THOSE, FROM HOMER
DOWN TO THE PRESENT DAY, WHO HAVE DIS-
TINGUISHED THEMSELVES, AS

POETS, PHILOSOPHERS,

ARTISTS, &c. &c.

BY JAMES WILSON,
Who has been blind from his infancy.

TO WHICH IS PREFIXED
A MEMOIR OF THE AUTHOR.

———————————" But not to me returns
Day, or the sweet approach of ev'n or morn ;
Or sight of vernal bloom, or summer's rose ;
Or flocks, or herds, or human face Divine ,
But clouds instead, and ever-during dark
Surround me, from the chearful ways of men
Cut off, and for the book of knowledge fair
Presented with an universal blank."

BELFAST:
PRINTED BY D. LYONS, 23, SMITHFIELD

1821.

TO THE READER.

When perusing the productions of the Philosopher, the Divine, or the Biographer, there is no inquiry more natural to the human mind, whether ignorant, or intelligent, than, 'who is the Author of this production.' If therefore a Memoir of the writer accompanies a pleasing, or interesting work, the account is read with avidity ; and although, there be nothing extraordinary in the narrative,—nothing in which the individual is peculiarly distinguished from his contemporaries, yet, the outlines of his life are calculated to gratify the the curiosity which his works have excited.

I have not the vanity however, to suppose, that any of my readers will have their curiosity so strongly excited in relation to the Author, or rather compiler, of the succeeding articles, neither do I vainly imagine that they would sustain an irreparable loss, by remaining ignorant of the particulars that are to follow. No, but as it is pleasing to a rational mind, to contemplate the footsteps of an all-directing Providence, to trace the progress of the human mind, in various relations, and to get acquainted with the actions of individuals, who have laboured under great difficulties, so the present Memoir is presented to the reader, as distinguished by these features, as a simple unvarnished tale, and as calculated to awaken those sentiments which are common to the Peasant, and to the Philosopher.

Persuaded from the kind encouragement I have experienced, that this narrative will fall into the hands of many of my most distinguished and disinterested friends, I would consider myself ungrateful, should I not declare, that no length of time, no change of circumstances, shall ever be able to efface from my memory, those pleasing recollections of unmerited kindness, so long experienced.—Recollections which are stamped in indelible characters upon my heart.]

JAMES WILSON.

INTRODUCTION.

....

The branch of Biography which the following pages contain, has not until now been entered on as a distinct subject. In all preceding works the lives of the blind have been classed, and confounded with those of others; and though individuals have been pointed out as objects of admiration and astonishment, yet, no work has appeared, in which they have been considered in a proper point of view, as a class of men seemingly separated from society, cut of as it were from the whole visible world, deprived of the most perceptive powers that man can possess; yet, in whom, perseverance, industry, and reflection, have in many instances overcome all those difficulties which would have been thought insurmountable had not experience proved the contrary.

In the pursuit of knowledge the blind have been very successful, and many of them have acquired the first literary honours, that their own, or foreign Universities could confer. In the different branches of Philosophy, if they have not excelled, they have been equal to many of their contemporaries; but more particularly in the science of mathematics, many of them having been able to solve the most obstruse problems in algebra. In poetry, they have been equally distinguished. Two of the greatest men that ever courted the muses, laboured under the deprivation of sight.—Homer the venerable father of epic poetry, and the inimitable author of Paradise Lost. These two illustrious Bards will live in the minds of every true lover of poetry, as long as learning and learned men shall have a place in the page of history. In Philosophy, Saunderson and Euler appear in the most conspicuous point of view;—the former lost his sight when only twelve months old, but was enabled by the strength of his comprehensive genius to delineate the phenomena of the rainbow, with all the variegated beauty of colours, and to clear up several dark and mysterious passages, which appeared in Newton's Principia; and though the latter did not lose his sight until he arrived at the years of manhood, yet, from that period, he was able to astonish the world by his labours in the rich fields of science where he earned those laurels which still continue to flourish in unfaded bloom. He had the honour of settling that dispute which had so long divided the opinions of the Philosophers of Europe, respecting the Newtonian and Cartesian systems, by deciding in favour of Newton, to the satisfaction of all parties. The treasures of his fertile genius still enrich the Academies of Paris, Basle, Berlin, and St. Petersburg.

In mechanics, the blind have gone to a considerable length, almost to surpass the bounds of probability, were the facts not supported by evidence of unquestionable authority. Here we find Architects building bridges, drawing plans of new roads, and executing them to the satisfaction of the commission-

ers.   These roads are still to be seen through the
counties of York and Lancaster, where they have been
carried through the most difficult parts of the country,
over bogs and mountains.   Indeed, there are few
branches of mechanics in which the blind have not
borne a part; as the reader will find demonstrated
in the following pages.

SOME PARTICULARS OF

THE

LIFE OF THE AUTHOR.

_____

"But what avails it to record a name,
That courts no rank among the Sons of fame."

_____

I WAS born May 24th, 1779, in Richmond,
State of Virginia, North America. My father, John
Wilson, was a native of Scotland. His family was
originally of Queen's-ferry, a small village in Fifeshire, about eleven miles from Edinburgh; he had an
uncle who emigrated to America when a young man,
as a mechanic, where, by honest industry and prudent
economy, he soon amassed a considerable property.
He wrote for my father, who was then about eighteen
years of age, and promised to make him his heir in
case he would come to America. My grandfather
hesitated for some time, but at length consented, and
preparations were accordingly made for my father's
departure, who sailed from Greenock, and arrived
safely at Norfolk, in the United States; from whence
he was forwarded by a merchant of that place, and

soon reached Richmond, where he was gladly received
by his uncle. This man being in the decline of life,
without a family, and bowed down by infirmities, now
looked upon his nephew as the comfort of his life, and
the support of his declining years, and therefore entrusted him with the entire management of his affairs,
which he had the happiness of conducting to the old
man's satisfaction. Thus he continued to act till the
death of his uncle in 1775, when he found himself in
possession of £3000 value, in money and landed
property.

Prior to this event, my father, on a visit to Baltimore, became acquainted with my mother, Elizabeth
Johnson. To her he was introduced by an intimate friend, a Mr. Freeman, whom I may have
occasion to mention hereafter. His uncle, on hearing this, could not bear the idea of a matrimonial
connexion during his own life, and so stood as a grand
barrier to the completion of his wishes ; but, at the
decease of the old man, being left to think and
act for himself, as soon as his affairs were settled, he
hastened to Baltimore, where the long wished for union
took place.

Shortly after his marriage he returned again to
Virginia. His whole mind was now bent on the
improvement of his plantation, and the acquiring of
a paternal inheritance for his offspring. Flushed
with the hope of spending the eve of life on a fertile
estate that amply rewarded the hand of industry, of
spending it in the bosom of his family, and of tasting
the pleasures which domestic retirement affords, he

followed his avocation with alacrity, and could say in the midst of his employments,—

> " The Winter's night and Summer's day
> Glide imperceptibly away."

But, alas, how uncertain are human prospects and worldly possessions ! How often do they wither in the bud; or bloom like the rose, to be blasted when full blown ! How repeatedly do they sicken, even in enjoyment, and what appears at a distance like a beautiful verdant hill, degenerates on a closer survey into a rugged barren rock ! This moment the sky is bright, the air is serene, and the sun of our prosperity beams forth in unclouded splendour; in the next, blackness and darkness envelope us around, the cloud of adversity bursts upon our devoted heads, and we are overwhelmed by the storm. It was so with my father, and, of course, the misfortune was entailed on me.

The disturbance which took place at Boston at the commencement of the revolutionary war, was at first considered only a riot; but it shortly began to assume a more formidable aspect. The insurgents were soon embodied throughout all the Colonies, and the insurrection became general. Between them and the loyal party no neutrality was allowed, and every man was under the necessity of finally joining one side or the other. For some time, indeed, my father strove to avoid taking an active part, but he was soon convinced that this was totally impossible. Many of his early friends had embraced the cause of the revolutionists and were very anxious that he should join their party. To induce him to do this, several advantageous offers were made to him, and when this expedient failed,

threats were resorted to.   Exercising the right which
belongs to every man, in politics, as well as in religion, I mean the right of private judgment, he, in
conjunction with a number of his neighbours, enrolled
himself in a corps of volunteers, for the joint purpose
of defending private property, and supporting the
royal cause.   The iron hand of war was now stretched
out, and unrelenting cruelty towards each other, had
taken possession of the hearts of those persons, who
were formerly united by the ties of neighbourly affection; consequently, a band of enraged incendiaries,
about 150 in number, mostly black slaves belonging
to the neighbouring planters, and, no doubt excited
by their masters, attacked my father's house in his
absence, plundered it of every valuable article, and
finally burned it to the ground.   From this alarming
catastrophe, my mother and a few domestics narrowly
escaped with their lives, and were obliged to seek
shelter in the neighbouring woods, where they were exposed to the inclemency of the weather during a severe
winter night.   It would indeed be painful to me to
enter minutely into the sufferings of my parents at
this eventful period; suffice it to say, they were stript
of their all, and were left destitute and forlorn.

Down to the period of which I am now speaking,
no political question had ever given rise to more controversy than the American war.   It is not my business to enter into discussion of the subject; all that
remains necessary for me to say, is, a word or two in
relation to my father's political conduct.   That man
who would not rejoice in being able to speak well of

a departed parent, is not entitled to the name of man, and cannot be characterised by the feelings common to our nature. It affords me, then, a degree of pleasure to reflect, that my father must have acted throughout from principle. On this point I am perfectly satisfied, when I consider him rejecting emolument, despising threats, volunteering in the royal cause, forsaking his own home, and thereby leaving his family and property exposed, braving every danger, serving during five campaigns, and continuing active in the cause he had espoused, as long as he could be useful to it.

Being attached to that part of the army under the immediate command of Lord Cornwallis, he was taken prisoner when that gallant General was compelled to surrender to a superior force. His health, during these disasters, was much impaired, and on being liberated, he thought of returning to Europe, in hopes that the air of his native country would restore him to his wonted state of health and vigour. My mother was now residing near New-York, in the house of a friend, and thither he directed his steps. There he abode for a year, and found his health so much improved, that he determined to lose no more time in America, but prepared to re-cross the Atlantic,—

" And anxious to review his native shore,

" Upon the roaring waves embarked once more."

Bound for Liverpool, the vessel set sail, under the guidance of Capt. Smith, and my parents bade a final adieu to the shores of Columbia ; what my father's feelings were at this crisis, it would be difficult to

describe. Separated from that country in which his
best hopes centred—cut off from the enjoyment of
his lawful possessions, without a probability of ever
regaining them—impaired in his constitution, and
crossed in all his former prospects, we may view him
mourning over his misfortunes, and devising plans for
his future exertions. It is true, he might have consoled himself with the pleasing reflection, that he was
now about to revisit his native land, to meet with his
nearest relations and best friends, and to spend the
remainder of his days in the place of his nativity, in
peace and safety; but how vain and transient are the
hopes of mortal man ! All his joys and sorrows, hopes
and fears, anxious cares, and premature plans, were
shortly to terminate with himself, and I was to be
left at four years of age, destitute of a father. They
had scarcely lost sight of land when his disease returned with increased violence, and twelve days after
the vessel left New-York, he expired. The reader
will not consider my situation utterly deplorable, while
he thinks that still I had a mother to take care of me,
and to assist me in my childish years. True, I had
a mother, and a mother who survived my father; but
it was only for twenty minutes !—for being in the
last stage of pregnancy, the shock occasioned by his
death brought on premature labour, and terminated
her existence. Thus, on a sudden, I lost both father
and mother, saw them sewed up in the same ham-
mock, and committed to a watery grave !

> " My mother, when I learned that thou wast dead,
> Say, wast thou conscious of the tears I shed ?

Hover'd thy spirit o'er thy sorrowing son,
Wretch even then, life's journey just begun ?
Perhaps thou gav'st me, though unfelt, a kiss,
Perhaps a tear, if souls can weep in bliss,—
Ah ! that maternal smile, it answers YES."

Here my misfortunes did not end ; I was seized by the small pox, and for want of a mother's care, and proper medical aid, this most loathsome disease deprived me of my sight. After a long and dangerous voyage, it being a hurricane almost all the time, the Captain was obliged to put into Belfast harbour, as the ship had suffered much in her masts, rigging, &c. and the crew were nearly exhausted. When we arrived there, I had not recovered from the effects of my late illness, the symptoms of which were at one period so violent, as to threaten instant dissolution ; to make me the more comfortable, I was sent immediately to Belfast. The following circumstance is still fresh in my recollection : the vessel was four miles from the town, and one of the seamen, who had been my nurse from the time of my mother's death, and who, during the passage, rendered me all the assistance which his situation allowed, kept me on his knee in the boat, and this kind hearted individual administered the only cordial he possessed, which was rum and water.

There was no time lost by Captain Smith in applying to the church-warden in my behalf, and, in order to prevent me from becoming a charge to the parish, he deposited in his hands a sum of money, sufficient to pay the expense of supporting me for five years, and I was soon provided with a nurse.

The reader, by this time, will be curious to know

how I came by the information contained in the preceding pages. I am indebted for these particulars,
at least so far as they concern my family's misfortunes
in America, to the kindness of Mr. Freeman, who
came passenger in the same ship. With this worthy
gentleman, my mother had remained during my
father's absence, and as I have already observed, she
was received as one of the family, and treated with
all that humanity and attention which her forlorn situation required. Mr. Freeman had been the sincere
friend of my father from a short time after he landed
in America ; their age and their pursuits were the
same, and their habits, tastes, and dispositions were
congenial. Under these circumstances, a friendship
was commenced, which, through a long series of
vicissitudes and misfortunes, remained unbroken—a
friendship which only ended with my father's life.
Although, at one time, party politics ran high, and
although my father joined the royal standard, while
Mr. Freeman was a zealous republican, such were the
liberal sentiments of this gentleman, that he never
entertained towards his friend the least hostile feeling ;
and when my father was injured in his property, and
persecuted for his opinions, he was always sure to
find an asylum under the roof of this good and worthy
man. While the vessel in which I came to Ireland
was under repair, he and his family resided at Palmer's Hotel, Belfast, where, in the hearing of Mrs.
Palmer, he related the particulars of his early acquaintance with his deceased friend, and he subsequent misfortunes which befell him in America, till

the time of the mournful catastrophe which I have already described; this he did in such a simple and affecting manner, as not only caused him to shed tears himself, but also produced the same emotion in those who heard him. Some important papers belonging to my father were preserved by Mr. F., and given to the church warden. They consisted of old letters, and a journal which my father had kept from the time of his departure from Scotland till he left America, in which every particular connected with his history, during that eventful period, was carefully noted; but Mr. Scott, the church warden, without examination, pronounced them totally useless, and they were sent home to my nurse in the trunk with my clothes. The poor old woman was unable, herself, to ascertain their contents, nor did she ever think of shewing them to any intelligent person who could turn them to my advantage; she considered them mere waste paper, and used to light her pipe with them, and roll her flax, while spinning. A little playfellow of mine, who sought my company after school hours, for the purpose of getting me to tell stories to him, (for I was at that time famed over the neighbourhood for my legendary tales,) would occasionally read to me such scraps of my father's letters and journal, as he found scattered about the room. From this circumstance, I still remember the names of Generals Howe, Clinton, and Robinson, which occasionally occurred, and with whom my father had corresponded, during the course of his military services in America. Much blame has been attached to Mr. Robert Scott, for not having

had my case more narrowly enquired into, while
Captain Smith and Mr. Freeman were in Belfast.
From the testimony of two such respectable individuals, and the information the above documents would
probably have afforded, my claims might have been
substantiated, and a compensation obtained for me
in lieu of my father's services, and the losses he sustained during the revolutionary war. But Mr. Scott,
being a man of the world, thought he had fulfilled his
duty when he had provided me with a nurse, and
seen me comfortably lodged. Some years after, on
being spoken to respecting his conduct in this affair,
he replied, "that he had enough business of his own
to attend to, without giving himself unnecessary trouble." Thus was I neglected, at a time when something might have been done for me, by those whose
duty it was to take care of me; but I was an infant,
an orphan, and a stranger, and there was no one to
step forward on my behalf. Mr. Freeman, to whom
I owe so much, and whose memory I shall always
cherish with the most grateful recollection, was so ill,
during his stay in Belfast, that he was confined to his
room. As soon as the vessel was refitted, he proceeded
with his family to England, promising Mr. and Mrs.
Palmer, on his departure, to write concerning me,
and to take me back with him to America, having
only come for the benefit of his health, and being
about to return as soon as a change should take place
for the better. His intention, he said, was to place
me under a proper master, and have me taught music; but I never heard from him after, and from

the state of his health, when he parted with me, I conclude that he has long been dead.

The ship being now completely repaired, the benevolent Captain and kind-hearted crew left me in Belfast, a total stranger. No one knew me, or had ever heard any thing of my family. My situation at this time was truly pitiable, as I was deprived of my parents at the time I most required their care; still, however, I was under the protection of a merciful Providence, "who can temper the wind to the shorn lamb." In His word He has promised to be a father to the fatherless, and to me this gracious saying has certainly been fulfilled. Many of the first families in the kingdom I can rank among my kindest friends; and to nothing can I attribute this, but to the influence of His Providence, who inclines the hearts of men to that which is pleasing in His sight.

My nurse was a good-natured old woman, and the anxiety which she shewed for my recovery, was much greater than could have been expected from a stranger; night after night she sat by me, attended to my calls and administered to my wants, with all that maternal tenderness which a fond mother manifests to the child of her bosom. The prayers which she offered up in my behalf, and the tears of sympathy which stole down her aged cheek, bespoke a heart that could feel for the miseries of a fellow-creature. Contrary to all expectation, I recovered, and in the course of a few months I was able to grope my way through the house alone. Shortly after this, my right eye was couched by the late Surgeon Wilson, and in consequence of this operation, I could soon discern surrounding objects and their various colours. This was certainly a great mercy, for, though the enjoyment did not continue long, yet the recollection of it affords me pleasure even to the present day.

One day, when about seven years of age, as I crossed the street, I was attacked and dreadfully mangled by an ill-natured cow. This accident nearly cost me my life, and deprived me of that sight which was in a great degree restored, but which I have never since enjoyed. Thus it was the will of Providence to baffle the efforts of human skill, and to doom me to perpetual blindness ; and it is this reflection which enables me to bear my misfortune without repining.

> ————————— " Fond memory here revives
> " Each dream-like image of the days gone by ;
> " What time on other shores,   *   *   *   *
> " I chased the scaly brood, or mid the throng
> " Of giddy school-boys, sported in the waves,
> " Or with young triumph saw the tiny ship,
> " Fair miniature of such as bear afar
> " The thunder of Britannia, in the race
> " Shoot past her rivals."

When I was about eight or nine years of age, I was not only projector, but workman, for all the children in the neighbourhood. I amused myself occasionally in constructing little windmills, cars, and ships. A kind friend made me a present of a little ship, a perfect model of the Royal George, which was lost at Spithead, and this toy was esteemed by me as one of the most precious gifts I could possibly receive. Having made myself perfectly acquainted with its structure, I thought of making one for myself, upon the same principle. I procured a piece of wood, and with no other tools than an old knife, a chisel, and a hammer, completed (not, however, without the loss of some blood,) my first attempt at ship-building. This pleased my juvenile companions so well, that I had every day numerous applications for ships. They procured me the wood, and my ambition was not a little augmented, when I found that I was applied to by boys considerably my seniors, and possessing many advantages of which I never had to boast; before I resigned this trade, I completed my fourteenth ship. There was in the neighbourhood a piece of water, about one hundred feet in circumference, appropriated to the accommodation of some flocks of ducks and geese. In the evening we were accustomed to dispossess these hereditary occupiers of their native element, and form our fleet into two divisions; the English were distinguished by red and blue streamers— the French, by white. Two boys, with their breeches rolled up to their knees, were generally employed to direct the movements of each squadron, he on the right being distinguished by the name of Admiral, and the boy on the left by that of Commodore. The plan of attack was, that each ship should be so far from her companions, as to preserve the regular sailing distance, and at the commencement of the action, the English vessels were so placed as always to have the weather-gage of the enemy. Each English ship formed a triangle with her two French opponents, and so, when the wind blew, she passed between them, and this was called breaking the line. It was

the duty of the Admiral and Commodore of each fleet,
at this alarming juncture, to restore order, and form
the lines anew. The English were drawn up in the
same position which they occupied at the commencement of the action ; the French were placed about
two feet in advance, with their sterns towards the
English, and the wind filling the sails of both equally,
caused the French to fly and the English to pursue.
At this moment the shout of triumph was raised, and
the joyful cry of victory ! victory ! burst forth from
the infant multitude who were witnesses of our naval
exploit.

"Loud shouts of triumph from the victors rise,
"Roll o'er the main, and echo to the skies."

I have been somewhat particular in my details of
these Lilliputian engagements, hoping that it may
prove useful, in case this little book should chance
to fall into the hands of any benevolent person, who
might read it to some blind boy, to whom it might
serve as a stimulus to spur him on to similar amusements. It could not fail to produce, to such a boy,
a two-fold advantage, as the exercise would be con-
ducive to his health, (which he could not expect to
enjoy sitting in the chimney-corner, brooding over
his misfortunes,) and it would effectually destroy that
timidity and melancholy which are generally the fruits
of a sedentary life, and would inspire him with a confidence and courage, which he could not expect to attain in an inactive state.

A few years after this event, my foster-mother died,
and again I was left forlorn and without a friend. In
this precarious state, the only means I had of obtaining subsistence were apparently ill-suited to my

situation. The reader may, perhaps, smile when I inform him, that at this time I was considered by many as a man of letters, and that I earned my bread in consequence of my practical engagements in relation to them. This, indeed, was the case; for I was employed to carry letters to and from the offices of the different merchants in the town and neighbourhood. My punctuality and dispatch in this respect were much in my favour, so that I was generally employed in preference to those who enjoyed the use of all their senses. In the course of time my sphere was enlarged, and often, on important business, I have borne dispatches to the distance of thirty or forty miles. This was certainly not a little extraordinary, in a place where the confusion and bustle of business subjected me to so many dangers.

Being advised to attempt the study of music, I made an almost hopeless effort, as I had no person to instruct me; but, although I could only scrape a few tunes which I had learned by ear, this did not prevent me from being called on occasionally to officiate at dances. For no matter how despicable the musician, or insignificant his instrument, the sound operates like an invisible charm—elevates the passions of the lower orders—makes them shake their grief and their cares off at their heels, and, moving "on the light fantastic toe," causes them to forget the bitterness of the past, and prevents them from brooding over the prospect of future evils.

> " And happy, though my harsh touch, falt'ring still,
> But mock'd all time and marr'd the dancer's skill;
> Yet would the village praise my wondrous power,
> And dance, forgetful of the noon-tide hour."

I soon found, in consequence of this avocation,
that I was exposed to numerous vices. I was obliged to associate with the dregs of society, to witness
many scenes of folly and great wickedness, and to
stay out late at nights, and thus expose myself to
dangers of different kinds. As my feelings were continually at variance with this occupation, which I
adopted more from necessity than from choice, I soon
gave it up, and composed a farewell address to my
fiddle.

The family in which I lived was both poor and il-
literate, and hence I was a considerable time before I
acquired any taste for knowledge. They were generous and humane to all who required their help, and
were also strictly honest in their dealings, and would
not defraud on any account whatever. I am happy
to have it in my power to notice these traits of character, which certainly reflect credit on their memories;
yet, praiseworthy as these may appear, they were deficient in their duty to me, so far as the improvement
of my mind was concerned. It was painful, indeed,
in my youth, to behold both in towns and villages, the
ignorance and wickedness which prevailed among
children of both sexes—swearing, lying, and throwing
stones; and the feelings of the passengers, while
walking along, were not only pained by their profane
language, but their personal safety was also in danger,
from the stones which were carelessly and mischiev-
ously flung around. But, thanks be to God, this evil
is at length disappearing; the remedy applied has
been successful, and that remedy is the Sunday
School. In the districts where these institutions are

established, the children, both in their appearance
and manners, have undergone a great change for the
better. Instead of injuring their neighbours, and
breaking the Lord's Day, they are now taught to read
the Scriptures, which, under the Divine blessing,
qualifies them to fill the various situations of society.
They are here taught that stealing is sinful, and that
lying, swearing, and bearing false witness, subject
them to the wrath of Heaven. They are also taught
to honour their parents, that they may obtain the
blessing which God has promised unto the children
of obedience, "and that their days may be long in
the land, which the Lord their God giveth them;"
and they are likewise strictly enjoined to observe the
Sabbath-day. These doctrines may be lightly looked
upon by some, but it is in a breach of these laws, and
a disregard of these truths, that all the crimes origi-
nate, which disgrace the character of man, and degrade
him below the beasts of the field.

I present these circumstances to my reader, that
he may know the kind of society in which I mingled
during the first fifteen years of my life. It cannot be
imagined that much information could be derived from
such a source as this.

About this time I began to pay some attention to
books; but my first course of reading was, indeed, of
a very indifferent description, as I was obliged to listen to what was most convenient. However, I made
the best of what I heard, and in a short time, in conjunction with a boy of my own age who read to me,
I was master of the principal circumstances in Jack
the Giant Killer, Valentine and Orson, Robinson

Crusoe, and Gulliver's Travels. The subject of these formed my taste, was swallowed with avidity, and inspired me with a degree of enthusiasm which awakes even at the present day, on hearing a new and interesting work read. These, however, were soon laid aside for novels and romances, several hundred volumes of which I procured and got read in the course of three years; and, although there are few passages out of all I heard then which I think worth a place in my recollection now, yet, at that time, I was well acquainted with the most interesting characters and events contained in these works. My present dislike to this kind of reading I do not entertain without reason, for, first, a great deal of precious time is thereby lost that might be more usefully employed; secondly, the judgment is left without exercise, while the passions are inflamed; and thirdly, those who are much in the habit of novel reading, seldom have a taste for books of any other kind, and hence their judgments of men and things must differ as far from his who has seen the world, as most novels differ from real life. I am well aware that some of them are well written, and display ability in the author, have the circumstances well disposed, the characters ably delineated, and the interest preserved till the final close of the last scene, which generally proves impressive and affecting. But to what does all this tend? (Except in recording the customs and manners of the times which they represent,) only to mislead the imagination, to foster a morbid sensibility to fictitious woe, and a romantic admiration of ideal and unattainable perfection, without strengthening the judgment, cultivating active benevolence, or a just appreciation of real worth. In contrasting the characters of Tom Jones and Sir Charles Grandison, with those of the Duke of Sully and Lord Clarendon, we observe a striking difference between the real and fictitious personages; yet, the mere novel reader is neither improved nor amused in reading the lives of these illustrious characters, while the tear of sympathy steals down his cheek, as he pores over the imaginary sufferings of the heroes and heroines of romance. There are, I know, many novels to which the above observations do not apply, particularly some of modern date, which are very superior to those above mentioned; but still the best, even of these, present overcharged pictures of real life, and, in proportion as they are fascinating, they indispose the mind to more serious reading.

I now engaged with Mr Gordon, Editor of the Belfast News-Letter, to deliver the papers to subscribers on the days of publication. Half a dozen papers, and two shillings per week, were my wages in this service. The papers I lent to tradesmen at a halfpenny an hour, and when the time allotted to the first set of customers was expired, it afforded me an agreeable exercise to collect and distribute them to others. While in this employment, I had sometimes to go four or five miles into the country, but, having an accurate knowledge of the surrounding neighbourhood, and being well acquainted with every gentleman's seat in the vicinity of Belfast, however remotely situated from the public road, I was able to execute my business with exactness and despatch.

I hope the account of the following adventure will

be acceptable to my readers, as it will illustrate what I have said, respecting my perambulations through the town and neighbourhood where I was reared.

On a winter's evening, in 1797, as I stood in one of the principal streets, I was accosted by a person, who, in the southern accent, enquired its name. After I had imparted the desired information, he told me that he was a soldier, and belonged to a detachment of the Limerick Militia, which had marched into Belfast that day. "I went out," said he, "to look for the sergeant, to get the pay, and being a stranger in the town, I lost myself; I left my wife and my firelock in the lodging house, and I forgot the name both of the street and of the people that own the house. I have been wandering about these two or three hours, and nobody can tell me where they are." I enquired, if he had observed any particular building near the place where he left his wife. "I believe," replied he, "after turning one or two corners, I observed a church." I considered for a moment, in which of the streets in that quarter there was a lodging house, and recollected that a Mrs. Tawny kept a house of entertainment in William-street. I bade him follow me, and took good care to keep before him, that he should not discover that I was blind. At that time there were no houses on the S. W. side of William-street; and fronting the houses on the N. E., there was a deep ditch, which served as a receptacle for all the nuisances of the neighbourhood. As the night was very dark, and there were no lamps in that direction, his eyes were of no service to him whatever; consequently he resigned himself entirely to my guidance. We had to cross the puddle already mentioned, by six stepping stones; and though there was no danger whatever of being drowned, it was more than probable that, had the soldier got a dip, his plight, on coming out, would have been far different from that in which he appeared at parade. I groped with my staff for the first stepping stone, and getting on it, I took hold of his hand, and bade him put his foot where mine was, warning him at the same time, of the consequence of not balancing well. In this manner I conducted him from one stone to another, till I landed him safely on the opposite side, and was highly diverted to hear him observe, that my eyes were better than his. I brought him to Mrs. Tawny's, and left him standing at the door, while I went in to make the necessary enquiry. I soon learned that I had guessed right, for I found his wife almost in despair at his absence, but I bade her be of good cheer, for I had brought her husband to her; and so saying, I called him in. His wife was rejoiced to see him again, and saluted him by crying out, " Bless me, dear Barney, where have you been ? I thought you were lost !"—" Arrah, my dear, I couldn't find my way back," said he, " if it hadn't been for this decent man, that shewed me the house." " And more shame for you," said the landlady, " for you have your eye-sight, and yet you must be guided to your lodging by a blind man." On hearing this, they were both astonished, and began heartily to bless themselves. As their astonishment, however, subsided, the hospi-tality of their Irish hearts began to display itself; for, on discovering that I was only a mortal being, and

partook of the same nature and appetites as themselves, I was cordially pressed to stay and partake of
the fare, that Barney, in all his peregrinations through
the streets, had taken good care to bring safely to his
wife. I, however, declined the kind offer, and left them
to drink their tea themselves, and enjoy the happiness
that succeeds, when groundless fears and trivial disappointments have vanished away.

At this time the French Revolution gave a sudden
turn to the posture of affairs in Europe, and every
mail which arrived brought an account of some important change in the political state of that unhappy
country. All the powers on the Continent now armed
against France, and she, on her part, received them
with a firmness which reflected honour upon her arms.
The public mind at this period was agitated, and the
wisest politicians of the day were filled with alarm,
and dreaded the consequences which were likely to
result, from a revolution that threatened every government in Europe with a total overthrow. For my part,
I had little to lose as an individual, and the only
concern I felt was for the safety of my country ; politics therefore became my favourite study, and I soon
got acquainted with the passing news of the day.

A late writer, in speaking of memory, calls it " the
storehouse of the mind ;" but it has often been compared to a well-constructed arch, on which the more
weight is laid, the stronger it becomes. This I found
to be the case with mine, for the more I committed
to it, the more I found it was capable of receiving and
retaining. In what manner ideas of extrinsic objects,
and notions of certain relations, can be preserved in

the mind, it is impossible to determine; but we are sure that the thing is so, though the manner be unknown to us. As ideas and recollections are merely immaterial things, which can in no wise partake of the known properties of matter, so, the receptacle in which they are lodged, must be of a similar nature. That matter and spirit are united, we have no reason to doubt; for the pleasures of memory, in the moment of reflection, are evidently operative on the body, inasmuch as its motions and gestures are expressive of the inward feelings of the mind. As the memory, therefore, is more or less capacious, as the store of ideas laid up there is greater or less, and as they are pleasing or unpleasing in themselves, so the impressions derived from memory, are either powerful or weak either pleasing or painful. As my taste always inclined to literature, and the knowledge of things valuable in themselves, the remembrance of them is, consequently, a never failing source of amusement to me, whether I be found " in the void waste, or in the city full."

" Oh, Memory! how pure, how exquisite are thy pleasures!
" To thee, and to thy sister Hope, the bright handmaids who
" support us through the rude path of existence, how deeply
" are all men indebted!"

It was now, indeed, that I was able to appreciate the pleasures of memory in a superior degree, for I knew the names, stations, and Admirals, of almost all the ships in the navy, and was also acquainted with the number, facing, and name of every regiment in the army, according to the respective towns, cities, or shires from which they were raised. I served, of course, as an Army and Navy List for the poor in the neighbourhood, who had relations in either of these departments, and was capable of informing them of all the general news.

The following anecdote shews the powers of my memory at that period. Being invited by a friend to spend an evening at his house, I had scarcely sat down when three gentlemen entered; and the conversation turning on the news of the day, I was requested by my friend to repeat the names of as many of the ships of the British navy as I could recollect, telling me at the same time that he had a particular reason for making the request. I commenced, and my friend marked them down as I went along, until I had repeated 620, when he stopped me, saying I had gone far enough. The cause of the request was then explained. One of the gentlemen had wagered a supper that I could not mention 500; he, however, expressed himself much pleased at his loss, having been, as he acknowledged, highly entertained by the experiment.

Although, at this time, I had little relish for any other kind of reading but newspapers and novels, yet I was not wholly insensible to the charms of poetry. I amused myself with making verses at intervals, but I could never produce any thing in that way which pleased myself. My acquaintances, particularly the young people, gave me sufficient employment in composing epigrams, love songs, epistles and acrostics, in praise of their sweet-hearts. Many of those juvenile productions are still extant, and though miserable in themselves, continue to find admirers among the classes for whom they were composed.

The first of my productions which met the public eye, was " An Elegy on the death of an unfortunate Female." This poor maniac was known for more than twenty years in the neighbourhood of Belfast, by the appellation of Mad Mary, and was at last found dead in the ruins of an old house, where she had taken refuge during a stormy winter night. This little piece being much noticed, on account of the subject having excited a general interest, I was advised to collect my best productions, and give them to the public. Encouraged by the patronage of a few generous individuals, I set about the work, which in a few months made its appearance.

I will now, for the amusement of my readers, insert a few extracts from this little collection.

Ah ! you, who sport in pleasure's morn,
　Who ne'er have felt a pain,
Who never trod on trouble's thorn,
　Or heard affliction's plain ;

And you, whom Heav'n has doubly bless'd
　With light—Oh, gift divine !
And whom misfortunes never press'd
　With misery's sons to join :

Ah, did you know what others feel,
　Beneath the shafts of woe,
You'd kindly blunt the pointed steel
　That's aimed from sorrow's bow.

AN ADDRESS TO THE SUN.

Oh, glorious orb ! thy genial rays
Promote and renovate my lays ;
Though HE, who gave thee all thy charms,
Has folded me in darkness' arms.

But on that day when thou shalt shine
No more, in native beams divine;
When Erin's self, my muse's pride,
Shall be o'erwhelmed in ruin's tide;
And mankind summon'd from the tomb
To hear their everlasting doom;
The veil that now enshrouds my eyes
From viewing THEE and ambient skies,
Shall be withdrawn, while fulgent day
Shall o'er my eye-balls lambent play.

TO MEMORY.

COME MEMORY, and paint those scenes
  I knew when I was young,
When meadows bloomed, and vernal greens,
  By Nature's band were sung;

I mean those hours which I have known,
  Ere light from me withdrew—
When blossoms seemed just newly blown,
  And wet with sparkling dew.

Yet, ah! forbear, kind Memory cease
  The picture thus to scan!
Let all my feelings rest in peace,
  'Tis prudence' better plan;

For why should I on other days,
  With such reflections turn,
Since I'm deprived of vision's rays,
  Which sadly makes me mourn!

And when I backward turn my mind,
  I feel of sorrow's pain,
And weep for joys I left behind,
  On childhood's flowery plain;

Yet now, through intellectual eyes,
  Upon a happier shore,
And circled with eternal skies,
  Youth sweetly smiles once more.

Futurity displays the scene,
  Religion lends her aid,
And decks with flowers for ever green,
  And blooms that ne'er can fade.

Oh, happy time! when will it come,
  That I shall quit this sphere,
And find an everlasting home,
  With peace and friendship there?

Throughout this chequered life 'tis mine
  To feel affliction's rod,
But soon I'll overstep the line
  That keeps me from my God.

A DREAM.

Night o'er the sky her sable mantle spread,
And all around was hushed in sweet repose,
Nor silence suffered from intrusive noise;—
Save now and then, the Owl's unpleasing scream,
From yon old pile of ancient grandeur sent,
Broke in, obtrusive on the tranquil hours;
Reflection took my mind, and o'er my thoughts
Unnumbered visions flit with rapid speed;
I thought on man, and all his childless joys,
From rosy infancy to palsied age—
And oft the sigh of recollection stole
Then heaved my breast with sorrow's poignant throb;
For ah! I feel what some have never felt,
That is, to be in one continued night,
From January's sun, till dark December's eve;
And strange it is, when sleep commands to rest,
While gloomy darkness spreads her lurid veil,
That then by being blind, I suffer most!
O sight! what art thou? were my final words,
When sleep with leaden fingers sealed my eyes.—
Now free from care, and tumult's torturing din,
Young fancy led me from my humble cot;

And far through space, where suns unnumbered burn,
I with her took a grand excursive flight,
Then back again to Erin's hills of green,
I with her wandered; nor did night, nor gloom,
One step intrude to shade the prospects round.
I saw sweet Scarvagh, in her loveliest garb,
And all her trees in summer's dress were clad;
Her honoured mansion, seat of peace and love,
Gave rapture to my breast, for there I've found
True hospitality, which once did grace
The halls of Erin's chiefs of old ;—
But soon, alas! the hum of nightly bands,
And vagrants, strolling on in quest of sin,
Bore fancy from me with her golden train,
And once more left me in the folds of night.

VERSES ON THE RICHMOND NATIONAL INSTITU-TION FOR THE BLIND, IN IRELAND.

You from whose eyes the tender tear,
   Can gently drop for human woe,
Oh! pour your soft compassion here,
   And here your generous boon bestow.

Ah! you whom sympathy has blest,
   Whose hearts with pure devotion burn,
To you, of fortune's gifts possest,
   Those sightless orbs imploring turn.

For them the morning's rosy light,
   In vain the glowing east o'erspreads;
For them the empress of the night,
   In vain her silv'ry lustre sheds.

In vain the twilight shade descends,
   In magic softness, pure, serene,
In vain the star of evening blends
   Its dewy light to gild the scene.

O think what joys to you are giv'n,
   Which they must never hope to share,
To view the bright expanse of heaven,
   While sweet emotion speaks in prayer.

> Be yours, with liberal hand, to prove
>   The feelings of a grateful mind,
> Be yours, by acts of pious love,
>   To soothe the sorrows of the blind.
>
> Be yours, to speak the Saviour's name,
>   To hearts that catch the joyful sound,
> To kindle pure devotion's flame,
>   And shed immortal glory round.
>
> Thus when the veil of darkness spread,
>   In all the gloom of endless night,—
> " Let there be light," Jehovah said,
>   Creation heard, and all was light.

On the above passages the reader is left to comment as he thinks proper. Composed by one destitute of sight, of learning, and even of an intelligent friend who could correct my compositions, they must, of course, stand very low in the scale of merit. Still, however, they were of service to me, and I found the public rather disposed to pity, than to censure, an humble individual so far beneath the notice of the critic.

Lord Cornwallis, who succeeded Earl Camden in the vice royalty of Ireland, in making the tour of that kingdom in 1799, arrived at Belfast. This appearing a favourable opportunity, I was determined to petition his Excellency, in relation to the losses of my family in America. A petition was accordingly drawn up, stating my father's possessions in that country, his services in the army, and his death on his passage returning to Europe, as already related. This petition I put into the hands of the late George Joy, Esq., who kindly offered to present it, and bade me call on him next day ; I did so, but, to my utter

disappointment, I found that Mr. Joy, on dressing for
dinner the preceding evening, had unfortunately forgotten my petition, and had left it in the pocket of
the coat which he had worn in the morning.   Again
I was to feel the bitter pang of disappointment ; for,
on arriving at Annadale, I was informed that his
Excellency had, a few hours before, left that place
for Dublin.   This terminated the only hope I ever
had of obtaining an independence ; but, as there was
no use in repining, I endeavoured to submit to the
disappointment with resignation.

At this time I turned my attention to a new occu
pation, and fixed on that of an itinerant dealer ; for
this purpose I borrowed a few pounds from a friend,
with which I purchased a stock of such hardware articles as might suit the country people.

" Being at the bottom of fortune's wheel, every
new revolution might raise me, but could not possibly
depress me lower ;" and hence I commenced my peregrinations in the country.   While employed in this
way, I had an opportunity of meeting with a variety
of characters, and of mingling in different societies.
It is but justice here to remark, that among the peasantry of Ulster, I have met with many individuals
whose good nature, benevolent dispositions, and kind
hospitality, were not only an honour to their country,
but even to human nature.

While vending my hardware through the country,
I found the occupation ill-suited to my circumstances;
I was exposed to many inconveniences, and experienced much fatigue and distress, both of body and
mind.   The want of sight made it difficult for me to

steer my course aright, and I was often exposed both to hardships and danger. Many a time have I heard the thunder roll over my head, and felt the teeming rain drench me from head to foot, while I have unknowingly passed by a place of shelter, or stood like a statue, not knowing which way to turn though within a few paces of a house. Still, however, while reflecting on all these circumstances, and on the sympathy which I was sure to meet with after my sufferings, I have been often led to conclude that the balance was in my favour, when compared with many who enjoyed the use of every sense; there is no rose without its thorn, neither is there any state without its comforts. While travelling, I was in little danger from horses and carriages in motion, as the noise warned me of their approach ; hence, if I was injured, it was generally from something at rest. It may be imagined, however, that I was not much exposed to harm in the day-time, nor will it be supposed that any person could be so cruel as intentionally to injure a blind man ; yet I have suffered repeatedly from the intemperance of some, and the brutality of others ; and, had I trusted entirely to the good nature of the multitude, I might have been ridden down oftener than the humane mind would be willing to suppose.

In the early part of my life, I prided myself much on my activity as a pedestrian. I have frequently travelled through a part of the country with which I was totally unacquainted, at the rate of thirty miles in a day ; but this was only in case of emergency, for my usual rate was fifteen to twenty miles per day ; this, however, is too much for a person in my situa-

tion, for supposing a blind man sets out to travel
alone on foot, to a distance of twenty miles, he will
experience much more fatigue, and go over more
ground than one will do who has his sight, in a journey of twice that length. This is evident, from the
zig-zag manner in which he traverses the road, and
as Hammond says, in his description of the drunken
man staggering home, "from the serpentine manner
in which he goes, he makes as much of a mile as
possible." In the summer time, the blind man is subject to shock his whole frame, by trampling in the
cart ruts that are dried upon the road, and in the
winter, he travels through thick and thin; it is impossible for him to choose his steps, and at that season
of the year the water is collected into puddles, which
he cannot avoid; and hence, in walking to a distance,
he is sure to wet both his feet and legs, which is not
only disagreeable but frequently injurious to the health.
At one time he bruises his foot against a stone; at another he sprains his ankle; and frequently, when stepping out quickly, his foot comes in contact with something unexpectedly, by which he is thrown on his face.
Thus, in travelling on foot, he labours under various
disadvantages, unknown to those who are blest with
the sense of sight.

The above accidents, however, are not the only
misfortunes connected with the state of the blind; in
walking alone, he often wanders out of his direct way,
sometimes into fields, and sometimes into bye-
paths, so that the greater part of the day may be spent
before he can rectify his mistake. Often have I been
in this predicament myself, and frequently have I sat

a considerable part of the day, listening by the way-side for a passing foot, or the joyful sound of the human voice ; and sometimes I have been obliged in the evening, to retrace the ground I had gone over in the morning, and thus endured much fatigue of body and mind before I could regain the road from which I wandered. How different then is my situation from his who has his sight ? From the impediments which cause me so much pain he is happily exempt; while he pursues his journey he can trace the various beauties of the surrounding scenery ; the picturesque land-scape, the spreading oak, the flowing brook, the towering mountain that hides its blue summit in the clouds, the majestic ocean dashing on the 'shelly shore,' and the vast expansive arch of heaven, bespangled with innumerable stars, have all, for him, their respective beauties, and fail not to awaken pleasing and agreeable reflections ; but to the blind, these pleasures are unknown, the charms of nature are concealed under an impenetrable veil, and the God of light has placed between him and silent, but animated nature, an insuperable barrier.

> "While to the breezy upland led,
>   At noon, or blushing eve, or morn,
> He hears the red-breast o'er his head,
>   While round him breathes the scented thorn;
> But oh ! instead of Nature's face,
>   Hills, dales, and woods, and streams combined;
> Instead of tints, and forms, and grace,
>   Night's blackest mantle shrouds the blind."

A blind person always inclines to the hand in which his staff is carried, and this often has a tendency to lead him astray, when he travels on a road with which he is unacquainted. But were there no danger arising from this, still, from his situation, he is liable to imminent dangers on his way, from which nothing can preserve him but an all-directing providence; and this I have frequently experienced.

In a cold winter evening, as I travelled to Lisburn, I happened to wander from the direct road into a lane, which led immediately to the canal. Unconscious of the danger to which I was exposed, I was stepping on pretty freely, when my attention was suddenly arrested by a cry of " Stop ! Stop !" Of the first and second call I took no notice, as I judged some other person was addressed ; but at the third warning I stopped, when a woman came running up almost breathless, and asked me, where I was going ; I replied, "To Lisburn." " No," said she, "you are going directly to the canal, and three or four steps more would have plunged you into it." My heart glowed with thankfulness to the all-wise Disposer of events, and to the woman who was made the instrument of my preservation. She said, she happened to come to the door to throw out some slops, when she saw me posting on ; and thinking, from my manner of walking, that I was intoxicated, she became alarmed for my safety, as a person had been drowned in the very same place, not many days before.

About three miles from Strabane, at the little village of Clady, there is a bridge across the Finn. I had just passed along it on my way to Strabane, when a man enquired if I had been conducted over by any person; I replied in the negative. " It was a fortunate circumstance then, indeed," said he, " that you kept the left side, for the wall is broken down at the right side, just above the centre arch, and the river is there very rapid, and the bank on each side steep. Had you fallen in, you must have been inevitably lost."

The following instance of Providential preservation is still more singular than either of the preceding. From Ballymena, I was one day going out to the Rev. Robert Stewart's. At the end of the town the road divides, one branch leads to Ballymena, and the other to Broughshane. In the forks, an old well was opened for the purpose of sinking a pump. It being two o'clock in the day, the workmen were all at dinner, and I was groping about with my staff to ascertain the turn of the road, when a man bawled out to me, to stand still, and not move a single step. I did so, when he came forward and told me, that two steps more would have hurried me into a well eighty feet deep, and half full of water. He held me by the arm, and made me put forth my staff to feel and be convinced of my danger; when I found that I was actually not more than one yard from the edge, the blood ran cold in my veins; I was scarcely able to stand erect—

" And every limb, unstrung, with terror shook."

These are but a few of the numerous instances of hair-breadth escapes, which I have experienced in my peregrinations through life.

> When in the slippery paths of youth,
>   With heedless steps I ran,
> Thine arm, unseen, conveyed me safe,
>   And led me up to man.

In the year 1800, there was an institution established in Belfast, for the purpose of instructing those who were deprived of sight, in such employments as were suited to their unfortunate situation; it was styled, " The Asylum for the Blind." As it is of vast importance to the well-being of society, that all who have not independent fortunes should be enabled to support themselves by their own industry, for, which the blind are seldom qualified, owing to their unhappy state, and the want of a suitable education, this Asylum promised to be of the greatest utility. I was entered on the books of the Institution as an apprentice, and continued in it, until within a few months of its dissolution. When I left the Asylum, I proposed working on my own account, and having acquired a partial knowledge of the upholstery business I was soon employed. My friends exerted themselves on this occasion to promote my interest, and though there were several individuals who had learned the business in the same Asylum, and who could work better than I, yet I generally had the preference. Many of my friends went so far as even to contrive work for me, for which they had not immediate use, merely to keep me employed. Although my pecuniary circumstances were not much improved, yet, I now experienced a greater share of happiness than I had ever enjoyed before. I was in a situation that afforded me better opportunities of acquiring knowledge than I had ever possessed, previously to this time I also met with much friendship from many to whom I was but very little known ; and when it was understood that I was desirous of information, I generally received assistance in this way, even where I could not have expected it ; either the lady of the house in which I was employed, or one of the children, generally read to me while I was at work. Thus I improved my mind, while labouring for my support; time glided pleasantly away, no room being left for idle speculations or gloomy forebodings.

In 1803, a number of young men formed a Reading Society in Belfast, and, although they were all mechanics, yet some of them were also men of taste, and possessed considerable talents. Into this society I was admitted a member, at the same time that I was kindly exempted from the expense attending its regulations. One of the members was a man of the most extraordinary character I had ever known; and, therefore, I attached myself to him. To good-nature, he united an original genius, good taste, and great sensibility; and, had an early education been his lot, or had his mind been sufficiently expanded by study, he would have become an ornament to society; but he was totally devoid of ambition, and never had a wish to rise above the rank of an humble mechanic. This man proposed to read to me, if I would procure books; our stated time for this employment was from nine o'clock in the evening until one in the morning, in the winter season, and from seven until eleven, in the summer; when I was not particularly engaged, I frequently attended him at other intervals. At breakfast he had half an hour allotted to him, at dinner a whole hour, and every minute of this was filled up, for he generally read to me between every cup of tea. By this means, I committed to memory a vast collection of pieces, both in prose and verse, which I still retain, and which have been, until the present hour,

a never-failing source of amusement to me. The
more I heard read, the more my desire for knowledge
increased, while I learned, at the same time, that
" the more a man knows, he finds he knows the less."

So ardent and steady was my desire for knowledge
at that time, that I could never bear to be absent a
single night from my friend; and often, when walking
in the country, where I could have been comfortably
accommodated, I have travelled three or four miles,
in a severe winter night, to be at my post in time.
Pinched with cold, and drenched with rain, I have
many a time sat down and listened for several hours
together, to the writings of Plutarch, Rollin, or Clarendon. For seven or eight years we continued this
course of reading; but to give a catalogue of the authors we perused in that time, would be foreign to my
present purpose: suffice it to say, that every book in
the English language, which we could procure, was
read with avidity. Ancient and Modern History,
Poetry, Biography, Essays, Magazines, Voyages,
Travels, &c. were among our studies.

I continued, occasionally, to compose some pieces
of poetry consisting, principally, of songs, written on
the wit and good humour that prevailed in the club
of which I was a member, with a few prologues to
plays that were performed by the young men in the
neighbourhood, for charitable purposes. These I
collected together to prepare them for the press, but,
on examination, I found they had many faults, which
had at first escaped my notice; and though warmly
urged by my friends to give them to the public, yet
I was so well convinced they were destitute of merit,

that I committed them to the flames, with the first two acts of a play, called "The Irish Exile's Return."

The person to whom I had entrusted the management of my little domestic concerns, did not hesitate to take advantage of my ignorance of such affairs, as well as of my situation. Many of my friends felt for me, and strongly advised me to marry, as I should be more comfortable, and be out of the power of such unprincipled people. They said, that could I meet with a sober steady woman, who would be likely to make a good wife, the change would be advantageous to me in more respects than one. I objected to this proposal, on the ground of my inability to provide for a family; the precarious manner of earning my subsistence put such a change beyond my expectation—it was enough for me to suffer alone—I could not think of entailing misery upon others. This they could not deny, but they then reasoned in this way: no one required the kind assistance of an affectionate wife more than a blind man: that I had not one friend, one relative to look after me—what then would become of me in my old age? I should be helpless in the extreme. These, and many other arguments, were used, to induce me to assent to a measure which they thought would finally conduce to my happiness. Their anticipations have since been fully realized—I am happy. I had the pleasure of being known, for some time, to a young woman who lived in the neighbourhood; having met her occasionally at the house of a friend, whom I used to visit. Her plain sense and unassuming manners, recommended her to my notice, but what most endeared her to me was

her filial piety. Her aged mother and she lived together, loved and respected by all who knew them; and
without any other dependence than the work of her
own hands, she supported herself and parent.   I
thought that she, who was such an attentive and feeling daughter, must necessarily make an affectionate
wife, and in this opinion I was not disappointed.
Filial affection is so endearing a virtue, that whenever
we meet with an instance of it, whether in an exalted or
an humble station, the exhibition of it must be, to the
benevolent mind, a source of the highest gratification.
It is a duty which our gracious and kind Creator has
enjoined us to fulfil, commanding us in his holy word,
" to honour our father and mother," as an inducement
or motive to the performance of which, he has promised that our " days shall be long in the land ;" and
he who has promised this, is able and willing to
perform it.

I addressed a copy of verses to her, who had now
become the object of my affection, which were printed
in the first collection of my Poems. They had the
desired effect—they produced an impression, which
never has been, and I may venture to say, never
will be effaced. After the expiration of two years,
our correspondence happily terminated, and we were
married on the 27th of November, 1802. Though
she could boast of no high descent, no shewy accomplishments, nor of having brought me a fortune,
yet she was possessed of such qualities as every virtuous mind will admire;—she was sober, modest, and
unassuming ; and though her education was not according to the rules laid down by Mrs. Hamilton,

yet she understood, in her own way, the principles of domestic economy, prudence, and frugality. Well has the wise man described a virtuous woman, when he says —"Who can find a virtuous woman? for her price is far above rubies."

We have now lived thirty-six years together, happy in each other's society; and though we have had many trials in the course of that time, such as the loss of children, bad health, and distressed circumstances, a murmur has never escaped her lips. In our pilgrimage here below, these little crosses are necessary—they teach us to know ourselves. Were we to pass the little time, which is allotted to us in this world, without trials and afflictions, we should soon forget that we are dependent creatures; but a merciful Providence has wisely guarded us against this danger, by letting us feel our infirmites, and how little we can do for ourselves. We are assured in the word of God, that he never afflicts his creatures but for their good, and when these visitations are sanctified by his Holy Spirit, they then become profitable to us— they wean us from the world, and we become tired of its flimsy joys and imaginary pleasures; we learn from them, "that here we have no abiding city, but we seek one to come."

We have had eleven children, of whom four only are now alive; and, with the exception of the diseases common to children, those living are all healthy and stout. It is certainly one of the greatest blessings which parents can enjoy, to see a vigorous offspring rise around them, and to listen to their innocent prattle. How often have I been struck with the force and beauty of that passage in holy writ, where Jesus, in order to teach humility to his disciples, "called a little child unto him, and set him in the midst of them." To descend from the Divine Author of our religion to creatures like ourselves, we read in Cox's life of that pious reformer, Melancthon, that he was particularly fond of his children; and notwithstanding the multiplicity of his engagements, the discharge of which, in those perilous times, was attended with difficulties and danger, he would often descend from that lofty station where genius and public opinion had enthroned him, to the more endearing scenes of domestic retirement. A Frenchman one day found him holding a book in one hand, and with the other rocking his child's cradle. Upon his manifesting considerable surprise, Melancthon took occasion from this incident, to converse with his visitor on the duties of parents, and on the regard of Heaven for little children, in such a pious and affectionate manner, that his astonishment was quickly transformed into admiration.

The first of my literary acquaintances of great respectability, was John Lushington Reilly, Esq. of Scarvagh, to whose family I was warmly recommended, by a lady who introduced me as a lover and composer of poetry. In this gentleman's house I was employed for some time, and during my residence there, was not treated as a common workman, but was kindly entertained by Mr. and Mrs. Reilly, who had the goodness to read to me by turns, whilst I was at work ; and in their absence, a person was appointed to supply their place. Here was a fine library, where

I first met with Spenser's Fairy Queen. When I left home, I did not expect to remain at Scarvagh longer than three or four weeks at farthest, but such was the partiality of that worthy family for me, that I was detained there for nearly three months. On taking leave of my benefactors, Mr. Reilly observed, that I ought not to be tired of them, as they were not tired of me. To Mr. Reilly I addressed a few verses on his return from the army, which appeared in the second edition of my Poems. I had listened with much pleasure to the Treatise on Solitude, by that inimitable philosopher, Zimmerman; but, although I had learned from books to imagine the pleasures of solitude, yet I never had an opportunity of experiencing its enjoyments, until my residence, at that time, in the country. Some of our busy town's-people shudder at the idea of a country life, and conclude that the want of variety would render them miserable in retirement; but the happiness of such is derived from bustle and confusion—from sources unstable as the wind, and nature is to them destitute of charms. It was not so with me; the murmuring of the streams, the rustling of the leaves, the singing of the birds, the lowing of the cattle, and bleating of the lambs, each had for me its charms, and excited in my mind the most pleasing sensations. As nature is superior to art in all her operations, so are the pleasures derived from the one far superior to the pleasures derived from the other, and every man of experience will acknowledge, that independently of religion, there is not any thing which affords such delight to the contemplative mind, as the works of creation;

" By boundless love, and perfect wisdom formed,
    And ever rising with the rising mind."

From Scarvagh I went to Drumbanagher, the seat
of John Moore, Esq. where I was employed for some
time.   Mr. and Mrs. Moore were particularly attentive to me, and shewed me much kindness ; and after
spending some time in a few other gentlemen's houses,
I returned home.

The sense of sight is not the only one of which I
am deprived, for I never remember to have enjoyed
that of smell.   In my opinion, this sense can be more
easily dispensed with, than any of the other four.   I
remember a lady of my acquaintance, who possessed
this sense so exquisitely, that the least disagreeable
odour was so offensive, as to produce a severe head-
ache ; when she understood that I was destitute of
what she possessed in so extraordinary a degree, she
observed very justly, " it is well for you, for if you
have no pleasure from that source, you have no pain."
When spring unfolds itself in all its genial influ-
ences, it is, no doubt, pleasant to range through the
country, and inhale the fragrance arising from shrubs
and flowers; but, on coming into a large town or po-
pulous city, the circumstances are entirely changed,
and the effluvia arising from the narrow lanes and
alleys become exceedingly disagreeable.

The improvement of my mind, by the acquisition
of useful and substantial knowledge, now engrossed
my attention.   To attain this, I knew that books and
conversation were the only means, and therefore, I
carefully cultivated the friendship of such persons as
were distinguished by their taste and intelligence.   I

was very fortunate in getting acquainted with a number of individuals, whose literary acquirements and love of virtue, reflected honour on their names. In the society of such persons, I could not fail in acquiring much mental improvement, and their conversation, remarks, and advice were of great use to me.

It has been remarked by an elegant writer, that geography is the eye of history, the latter recording the time, and the former the place, in which any remarkable event has happened. To be acquainted with the names, situations, and boundaries of places, together with the transactions of other years, forms now an essential part of a good education. To the blind, in this respect, a large field is laid open, and if a good memory accompanies conversation, and to hearing history and geography read, they may lay up a store that will not fail, as a source of amusement, both to themselves and to others. In these two branches of knowledge I was very assiduous, and find, that to the present day, my memory is exceedingly tenacious of what I then learned. In relation to geography, I became acquainted with every place of note on the habitable globe, so that, on being examined by some who were either curious, or doubtful of my knowledge, my descriptions have been found to coincide with the best constructed maps. Respecting history, the reader will best judge of the power of my memory by the following relation.

To a few select friends who wished to prove my knowledge of English history, I repeated, to their entire satisfaction, an epitome of the history of Eng-

land, from the Norman conquest till the peace in
1783, including invasions, conspiracies, insurrections,
and revolutions; the names of all the Kings and
Queens, the year of their accession, the length of their
reigns, and the affinity each had to his predecessor,
together with the names and characters of all the
great statesmen, heroes, philosophers, and poets, who
flourished in the different reigns. In consequence of
this and similar rehearsals, I was termed, "The
Living Book," and "A Walking Encyclopædia;" to
others, my knowledge, in such circumstances, appeared
as a prodigy, but to myself it proved a source of consolation, and beguiled many a tedious hour.

The circle of my acquaintance was at this time
greatly enlarged, and I had the honour of ranking
among my friends some of the most distinguished
characters in this country. Among these was Dr.
Percy, Bishop of Dromore. This great man was the
last of that illustrious school of which Johnson, Goldsmith, and Burke, were members; his fine taste and
literary talents were accompanied by sweetness of
temper and a benevolent disposition. From the Rev.
H. Boyd, (a gentleman well known in the literary
world as the translator of the Italian Poet, Dante, and
author of some other original works of great merit,)
I received the most marked attention. His kindness
and that of his family, indeed, I cannot easily forget;
on several occasions he has rendered me very essential
services, and it yields me no small degree of pleasure
to reflect, that I still enjoy the friendship of a man
as eminently distinguished for his virtues as for his
talents.

There are few blind persons who are not blessed with strongly retentive memories, and added to this, their ear is open to all the variety of sweet sounds; but the sense of sight gives to the mind a more ample range, lays open the book of universal knowledge, which, to the blind, is covered over with an impenetrable veil. The art of Printing, which has diffused knowledge to an extent unknown even to the brightest ages of antiquity, sheds not its enlivening rays for their instruction and amusement. Ever dependent on the generosity of others, the streams of knowledge flow to them through narrow and irregular channels; but Providence, in all things just, depriving them of one perceptive power, seems to have bestowed additional vigour on those which remain. I have often experienced much difficulty in procuring readers, for it would have been unreasonable to expect persons to forego their pleasures, or quit their business, in order to gratify me; yet, some have done both, for my amusement. Men, however, vary in their taste with respect to books, as they do with regard to food; some readers can find no charms in poetry, others can find no interest in biography, and some have a particular aversion to books of a philosophical nature, and I was, therefore, necessitated to adopt the subject which best agreed with the taste of my readers. From these circumstances, I was generally obliged to listen to two or three different kinds of books in a day:—for instance, history before breakfast; natural philosophy during the day; poetry in the evening; and, by way of dessert, a few passages from some of our sentimental writers.

It appears that, as the attention of the blind is not diverted by objects presented to the sight, they are peculiarly fitted to attain perfection in whatever is conveyed to the mind by oral instruction. Some of the best poets and musicians that have ever appeared in the world, were men from whom the fair face of nature was shut out, who never saw the refulgent sun dart his rays through the opening clouds, tinging with rosy light the hills and plains, and gladdening all animated nature. How many thousand objects which give pleasure to the beholder present themselves on every side, but the rich variety of colours which decorates the ample field of nature, is displayed in vain before the blind, and to them this fair scene is shrouded in universal night. Perhaps the loss of sight has never been described in more pathetic language than by that master of sublimity, Milton, who in Paradise Lost, thus touchingly refers to his own melancholy condition ;—

————————————" Thus with the year

" Seasons return, but not to me returns,

" Day, or the sweet approach of Even or Morn," &c.

A friend, at this time, proposed to teach me English Grammar, and, in order to encourage me, he said it would only require three weeks or a month at most, and as soon as I had attained a knowledge of the English language, he proposed to teach me the French. But owing to the narrowness of my circumstances, I could not afford to devote to these studies the time which they would have required. I had a large family depending on me for support, for which I had no other means of procuring bread but by my own industry, and my poor wife having been long afflicted

with bad health, was unable to render me any assistance, and to add to this, I was often employed in the
country. Had I then turned my attention to these
studies, my children might have starved; and I was
therefore obliged to decline this friendly offer, of which
I was desirous to avail myself, as it might have been
of much future advantage to me. This was one of the
greatest sacrifices I ever made. It is true, I had a
few friends, who, had they been made acquainted
with these circumstances, would have been sorry to
let me lose such an opportunity. But I was too sensible
of their kindness, and was therefore unwilling to make
any farther claim upon their bounty.

The state of my affairs at this time wore rather an
unfavourable appearance. The profits arising from
my publications were very small;—they did little
more than satisfy the demands of the printer and
paper manufacturer. I wished above all things, to
select a subject on which I could employ my mind
more extensively than it had hitherto been engaged,
and having devoted much of my time to the study of
biography; I found, on acquaintance with this useful
branch of history, that there were many in all ages,
and in every country, who had laboured under the
same calamity with myself, and who had eminently
distinguished themselves by their attainments in literature and science. I thought, if these were collected
together, and moulded into a new form, it might not
only become an amusing, but an useful work, so far
as it would show what perseverance and industry could
do, in enabling us to overcome difficulties apparently
insurmountable. It concerned not me at what time

of life, or by what cause they lost their sight, provided that they distinguished themselves after they became blind. My chief object was to prove the energy of the human mind, under one of the greatest privations to which we are liable in this life. In contemplating the lives and characters of these illustrious individuals, who had devoted their time and applied their talents to promote the happiness of their fellow-creatures, we shall find, that they have been, considering their number, as usefully employed as any class of men, with whose works we are acquainted. Poets, the foremost in renown, have been incapable of the perception of external objects. The two finest poems in the world, the Iliad and Paradise Lost, are the immortal productions of the blind. The eyes of Homer and Milton rolled in vain, and found no dawn; yet in the forcible expression of the latter, were their minds " inly irradiated," and they have sung of things invisible to mortal sight. It has not been only in the different departments of literature that they have distinguished themselves, but also in the more extensive fields of science and of the arts, they have reaped honours which will transmit their names to the remotest posterity. It was partly with a view of rescuing my fellow-suffers from the neglect and obscurity in which many of them were enveloped, that I undertook the present work—an undertaking attended with immense labour and much research to one like me, which will readily be allowed, when it is considered I had often to depend on the good nature of strangers for such books as were necessary to my purpose, and even for readers and amanuenses. However, after wading through innumerable difficulties, which nature and fortune threw in my way, the work made its appearance in 1820, in one volume 12mo. containing nearly 400 pages, closely printed. The reception it met with from the public was gratifying to my feelings, and far surpassed any thing I could have expected.

A history of the blind, by a blind man, excited a good deal of curiosity among the reading portion of the public, and called forth the sympathy of several benevolent individuals in favour of its afflicted author. I will conclude my narrative by inserting the two following letters, which I hope my friends will be pleased with.

Keswick, June 30, 1834.

I have read Mr. James Wilson's account of his own life with much interest; it is indeed a narrative which may very properly accompany the lives of those persons who, being blind, have nevertheless rendered themselves remarkable by their attainments, and thereby shown how much may be performed by patient and ingenious industry under the most unfavourable and discouraging circumstances.

This testimony is given in the hope that it may be useful to him in his travels.

ROBERT SOUTHEY.

———

132, George-street, Edinburgh,
Monday, 10th July 1837.

*   *   *   *   *   *   *   *   *

Dear Sir,

I have read your " Life" with much interest, and I may add instruction, for it is always instructive to see that cheerfulness and contentment are the result of virtuous actions, and that generous and manly efforts in a good cause, though they may not always be crowned with what the world calls success, never fail, if duly persevered in, to secure that peace of mind which is, after all, the best kind of success, even in a worldly point of view. But in such a case as yours this perseverance requires no small faith in the principles upon which it rests.

I have not had time to read your larger work, which my children have carried off to the country, but I shall go through it with attention, and I have no doubt with advantage as well as amusement.

I return the copy of the " Life" which you were good enough to lend me, and remain,

    With sincerest good wishes,

        Your most obed. humble servant,

           BASIL HALL.

Thus far I have endeavoured to give some account of myself, but have been obliged to omit several particulars which might be interesting to the Reader. I commit this narrative to the indulgent kindness of my friends, and shall be highly gratified to have the approbation of those to whose generosity and disinterestedness I owe the most sincere gratitude, and with these feelings, I take my leave of my friends and the public for the present.

        JAMES WILSON.

Birmingham, September, 12, 1838.

LITERATURE

BLIND people have long assumed important roles as storytellers, preserving history, culture, and wisdom through oral traditions. Today, in societies where oral traditions still exist, the blind continue to be actively involved.

Wilson's mention of Homer (c. 850 B.C.) in all four editions, as well as the inclusion of his portrait in the second edition, indicates Homer's importance as a legendary literary figure. There is great debate among modern scholars over Homer's authenticity. Some deny that he existed or say that he was a composite of many poets, some of whom were blind. Wilson took the traditional view of his time and saw Homer as an extraordinary genius. Despite the debate, Homer is significant today not only as a major contributor to the world's classic literature but also as a representative of the countless blind people who have participated in oral traditions.

Wilson follows Homer with another literary legend—John Milton (1608-74), the epic poet and political pamphleteer. According to Ishbel Ross in her book *Journey into Light: The Story of the Education of the Blind* (1950), Milton lost his sight completely at age forty-four as a result of various eye conditions, possibly amaurius, glaucoma, myopia, detached retina, congenital diseases, or, according to his political enemies, judgment from heaven. After becoming blind he turned from political writings to poetry and often cited other famous blind people, including Timoleon of Corinth, Appius Claudius, Dandolo of Venice, General Ziska, Samson, and Homer.

Milton's famous work *Paradise Lost* (1667), often considered the greatest epic poem in the English language, was finished after he became blind. Milton composed *Paradise Regained* (1671) and *Samson Agonistes* (1671) in his later years, dictating them to his daughters. Soma Orlai Petrics painted a scene of Milton sitting in a chair dictating *Paradise Lost* to one of his daughters while the other two are seated by their father waiting to take their turn to write his words.

John Gower (1325–1402), whom Wilson calls one of the most ancient English poets, was a contemporary, friend, and possibly teacher of Chaucer's. He became blind in old age but remained a popular poet and sage. Today Gower is remembered more as an intellectual than as a poet. Michael Clancy, a contemporary of Jonathan Swift's, is mentioned only briefly by Wilson. According to Wilson, he became blind from a cold. Although Clancy turned his attention from medicine to dramatic poetry, there is no indication in any sources that he made a living from his literary works.

Anna Williams (1706–83) was a poet and one of the few women Wilson mentions. In 1730 she came from Wales to London with her father and worked as a seamstress. Williams became blind

at the age of thirty-four after developing cataracts. She maintained her interest in literature
after losing her sight, and in 1746 she published
an English translation of the French work *Life of
the Emperor Julian* by Le Bleterie. Her father introduced her to Samuel Johnson, who invited her
to be his wife's companion. After the death of
Mrs. Johnson in 1783, Williams continued to live
in Johnson's house. Bishop Percy, in his *Life of
Samuel Johnson, LL.D.* by Robert Anderson
(1815), suggests that Johnson's biographers have
not recognized Williams fully. "Her mind was so
well cultivated, and her conversation so agreeable, that she very much enlivened and diverted
his solitary hours."

It was not until the eighteenth and nineteenth
centuries, with the advent of embossed-letter systems and braille, that blind people were able to
read and write for themselves. The invention of
the typewriter and the computer have made it
possible for blind writers to convey their thoughts
in writing to sighted readers more easily.

Since Wilson's lifetime, many other notable
writers have suffered loss of vision. James Joyce
(1881–1941) was in pain for many years because
of iritis, glaucoma, and cataracts. The humorist
James Thurber (1894–1961) is said to have written some of his best works after losing most of
his sight. Jorge Luis Borges (1899–1986), a major figure in modern literature, continued to

write after becoming blind in later life because of a detached retina. Notable blind writers of recent years have included Helen Keller (1880–1968), Ved Mehta (1934–) and Deborah Kent Stein (1948–).

No longer limited to oral forms of literary expression or dictation to sighted people, a growing number of blind writers are writing their works using braille writers and typewriters, voice recording machines, and computers.

AN

ACCOUNT OF THE LIFE AND WRITINGS OF

HOMER.

"High on the first, the mighty HOMER shone;
"Eternal adamant composed his throne;
"Father of verse, in holy fillets drest,
"His silvery beard waved gently o'er his breast:
"Tho' blind, a boldness in his looks appears;
"In years he seemed, but not impaired by years."

THE Man, an account of whose life and writings
is given in these pages, was the most extraordinary
genius that any age or country has ever yet produced.
Whether we view him as a Poet, a Philosopher, or an
Historian, he excites our astonishment, and he claims
our admiration. Whoever has read his truly sublime
compositions will join with me in regretting that so
little is now known of his history; and we have to
lament, that the few particulars of his life which have
been handed down to us, are in such a mutilated and
imperfect state, that they can afford but little pleasure
to the admirers of ancient literature. As many of
his early biographers have substituted fiction for facts,
it is no easy task to unravel their irregular accounts,
and form a connected story. I have consulted the
best writers who mention him, and have endeavoured
to select such parts as tend to illustrate both the man

and his writings : but, alas, after all my enquiries,
how little have I been able to procure! The veil
of time is now thrown over both the author and the
scene which called forth the gigantic powers of his
mind.

> " And now by Time's deep plough-share harrow'd o'er,
> " The seat of sacred Troy is found no more :
> " No trace of all her glories now remains,
> " But corn and vines enrich her cultured plains—
> " Silver Scamander laves the verdant shore;
> " Scamander oft o'erflowed with hostile gore."

This venerable father of Epic Poetry, as he has
been justly called, flourished, according to some accounts, 340 years after the siege of Troy, and according to others, 907 years before the Christian era.
The place of his nativity is not known, but such was
the veneration the Greeks had for his memory, that
no less than seven illustrious cities contended for the
honour of his birth, as is well expressed in the following lines—"SMYRNA, CHIOS, COLOPHON, SALAMIS,
RHODOS, ARGOS, ATHENÆ, Orbis de Patria certat,
Homere, tua."

The opinion, however, which appears to have the
best foundation is, that he was born at Smyrna. We
have not on record any thing that is certain respecting the particulars of his birth ; but the following is
the only account that I have seen, which can be
relied upon. A man of Magnesia, named Mena-
lippus, went to settle at Cumæ, where he married the
daughter of a citizen called Homynes, and had by
her a daughter called Critheis. Her parents dying,

Critheis was left to the care of one Cleonus, her
father's friend, by whom she was seduced; this coming
to the knowledge of her guardian, he was anxious to
conceal it; and sent her to Smyrna, which was then
building. Critheis being near her time, went one
day to a festival, which the inhabitants were celebra-
ting on the banks of the river Meles,* where the pains
of labour coming upon her, she was delivered of the
immortal HOMER; whom, from that circumstance,
she called MELESIGENES. Critheis, having no other
means of subsistence, was forced to spin; but a man
named Phemius,† who taught literature and music
in Smyrna, having often seen Critheis, and being
pleased with her good housewifery and behaviour,
took her into his house to spin the wool which he received from his scholars for their schooling. In this
situation she behaved so modestly and agreeably that
Phemius married her, and adopted her son, in whom
he discovered early marks of an extraordinary genius,
enriched by an excellent natural disposition. After
the death of Phemius and Critheis, Homer succeeded
his father in his school; and was admired, not only
by the inhabitants of Smyrna, but also by strangers,
who resorted from all parts to that place of trade. A

---

* A river of Asia Minor, in Ionia, near Smyrna. The
Ancients supported this opinion of Homer's being born on its
banks, and said that he thence got the name of Melesigenes,
and his compositions, Melitoea Charta. They even say that he
composed his poems in a cave near the source of that river.

† A man introduced by Homer as a Musician among Pene-
lope's suitors. Some say he taught Homer, for which the
grateful Poet immortalized his name.

person called Mentes, who traded thither, being a man of learning and a lover of poetry, admired him so much, that he requested him to accompany him in his voyages. Homer, who had then begun his Iliad, thought it of great consequence to see the places he should have occasion to mention ; and therefore embraced this opportunity, and embarked with Mentes. During these voyages, he passed through all Greece, Asia Minor, and many other places, where he never failed carefully to note down all that he thought worthy of notice. He travelled into Egypt, whence he brought into Greece all the names of their gods, the chief ceremonies of their religion, and a more improved knowledge of the arts. He next visited Africa and Spain : returning thence, he touched at Ithaca, where he was seized with a complaint in his eyes. Mentes being desirous of returning to Leucas, his native country, left Homer well recommended to the care and protection of Mentor, one of the chief men of the island, who took great care of him. There Homer was informed of many things relating to Ulysses, which he afterwards made use of in composing his Odyssey. On his return to Ithaca, Mentes found Homer cured ; they embarked together, and after much time spent in visiting the coast of Peloponnesus, and the islands, they arrived at Colophon, where he was again seized with a disease in his eyes, which proved so severe, that it is said to have been the occasion of his blindness. This misfortune obliged him to return to Smyrna, where he finished his Iliad. Some time after, the bad state of his affairs forced him to visit Cumæ, where he hoped to have found

relief. Here his poems were highly applauded, and
he was received with great joy; but when he proposed
to immortalize their city, if they would allow him a
salary out of the public treasury, he was told there
would be no end of maintaining the "Homeroi, or
blind men," and it was from this he got the name of
Homer, or a blind man. On this being refused, he
left that city, uttering this imprecation, "May no
Poets ever be born in Cuma, to celebrate it by their
poems;" and came to Phocæa. He afterwards
wandered through several places, and arrived at
Chios, where he married, and composed his Odyssey.
Some time after, having added many verses to his
Poems, in praise of some cities of Greece, especially
Athens and Argos, he went to Samos, where be spent
the winter, singing at the houses of the great, with a
crowd of boys after him. From Samos, he went to
one of the Sporades, intending to prosecute his
voyage to Athens. Where he died, or where he was
buried, is altogether uncertain; however, the inhabitants of Cos, one of the Sporades, claimed that honor, which was also contended for by the Cyprians.

It has been doubted by some of Homer's Commentators, whether he was blind or not; but thus, the
ancients generally represented him, as appears from
all the portraits, busts, and medals which have been
preserved.

I have already observed that he had composed some
part of his Iliad before his sight began to fail him;
but that he laboured under this privation when he
comp,sed his Odyssey, has never been questioned.
In the eighth book of that poem, in the person of

Demodocus, he has described his own helpless situation in the most tender and pathetic language.

> " Dear to the Muse, who gave his days to flow
> " With mighty blessings, mix'd with mighty woe;
> " With clouds of darkness quenched his visual ray,
> " But gave him power to raise the lofty lay."

Neither the virtues nor the talents of Homer could procure him a single patron, in the country which at that time was the seat of literature and science! Shame to Greece, that suffered a man who reflected more honour upon her than all the warriors or statesmen she ever produced, thus to live in poverty, and die in obscurity! The only incontestable works which Homer has left behind him, are the Iliad and Odyssey; both of which, for masterly invention, grandeur of sentiment, nobleness of character, and richness of colouring, excel any thing of the kind, in that or any other language. Nothing is equal to the clearness and majesty of Homer's style, to the sublimity of his thoughts, to the strength and sweetness of his verses; or to that easy, natural simplicity of manner, which is the crowning ornament of composition; which gives lustre to every other beauty, and is justly called " the dress of Nature.'' All his images are striking, his descriptions lively and exact, the passions so well expressed, and nature so justly and finely painted, that he seems to give to every thing motion, life, and action. In a word, the more he is read by a person of taste, the more he is admired. Nor are his works to be esteemed merely as interesting poems, nor as the monuments of a sublime and varied genius; no, he was in general so accurate with respect to customs, that he seldom mentions persons or things, that we may not conclude to have been well known during the time in which he wrote. It is Pope's opinion, that his account of people, princes, and nations, is purely historical, founded on the real transactions of that age, and is by far the most valuable piece of history and geography extant, concerning the state of Greece in that early period of the world. His geographical divisions of that country were thought so exact, that we are told of many controversies, concerning the boundaries of Grecian cities, being determined by the authority of his poems. Alcibiades once gave a rhetorician a sound box on the ear for not having the writings of Homer in his school. Alexander the Great was so charmed with them, that he commonly placed them under his pillow beside his sword; he enclosed the Iliad in the most precious box of Darius, "in order," said he to his courtiers, "that the most perfect production of the human mind may be enclosed in the richest casket in the world;" and one day seeing the tomb of Achilles in Sigæum, "Fortunate hero," said he, "thou hast had a Homer to sing thy victories!"

Longinus, the most refined of critics, beautifully compares the Iliad to the mid-day, and the Odyssey to the setting sun; and observes, "that though the Iliad claims an uncontested superiority over the Odyssey, yet in the latter, the same force, the same sublimity and elegance prevail, though divested of their most powerful fire; and it still preserves its original splendour and majesty, though deprived of its meridian heat." Lycurgus, Solon, and the kings and princes of Greece set such a value on Homer's works, that they took the utmost pains in procuring correct editions of them, the most esteemed of which was that of Aristarchus.* Didymus† was the first who wrote notes on Homer, and Eustathius,‡ archbishop of Thessalonica in the twelfth century, is the most celebrated of his commentators. Homer composed several other works beside the Iliad and the Odyssey. There are ascribed to him the Battle of the Frogs and the Mice, thirty-two Hymns, and several other pieces, most of which are Epigrams; but the most probable opinion is, that there are none of Homer's works now extant, except the Iliad and the Odyssey. Pope has given us an elegant translation of the Iliad, adorned with all the harmony of poetic numbers; this inimitable poem is so much read and so generally admired, that I will not attempt to describe its many

---

* A celebrated grammarian of Samos, disciple of Aristophanes; he lived the greatest part of his life at Alexandria, and Ptolemy Philometer entrusted him with the education of his sons. He was famous for his critical powers, and revised Homer's poems with such severity, that ever after all severe critics were called Aristarchi: he wrote above eight hundred commentaries on different authors, much esteemed in his day. In his old age he became dropsical, upon which he starved himself to death in the seventy-second year of his age, B.C. 157.

† A Scholiast on Homer, surnamed Chalkenteras, flourished, B.C. 40.

‡ A Greek commentator on the works of Homer. It is to be lamented that the design of Alexander Politus, begun at Florence, in 1735, and published in the first five books of the Iliad, is not executed, as a Latin translation of these excellent commentaries is among the desiderata of the present day.

beauties: the Moonlight Scene, in the eighth book, I
here give as a specimen of Pope's translation:—

> " As when the moon, refulgent lamp of night!
> " O'er Heaven's clear azure spreads her sacred light;
> " When not a breath disturbs the deep serene,
> " And not a cloud o'ercasts the solemn scene:
> " Around her throne the vivid planets roll,
> " And stars unnumbered gild the glowing pole;
> " O'er the dark trees a yellower verdure shed,
> " And tipt with silver every mountain's head;
> " Then shine the vales, the rocks in prospect rise!
> " A flood of glory bursts from all the skies:
> " The conscious swains, rejoicing in the sight,
> " Eye the blue vault, and bless the useful light."

Madame Dacier translated both the Iliad and
Odyssey into French prose, of which there is an
English version by Broome.   Cowper has also trans-
lated the works of Homer into blank verse.

I here insert, for the information of my readers,
Cowper's translation of the above passage; and though
at first sight they may not be able to judge which is
the more literal, they will easily perceive which is
the more poetical.

> " As when around the clear bright Moon, the stars
> " Shine in full splendour, and the winds are hushed,
> " The groves, the mountain tops, the headland heights
> " Stand all apparent, not a vapour streaks
> " The boundless blue, but æther opened wide—
> " All glitters, and the shepherd's heart is cheered."

But those who wish to know the several editions of
Homer, and the writers who have employed themselves
on the works of that great poet, may consult Fabricius,
in the first volume of his Bibliotheca Græca.

AUTHORITIES.

WOOD's Essay on the Genius and Writings of HOMER.—
CUMBERLAND's Observer.—ENCYCLOPÆDIA BRITANNICA.—
LEMPRIERE's Classical Dictionary.

JOHN GOWER,

One of our most ancient English Poets, contemporary with Chaucer, and his intimate friend.

"But age has rusted what the Poet writ,
Worn out his language, and obscured his wit ;
In vain he jests in his unpolished strain,
And tries to make his readers laugh, in vain."

Of what family, or in what county this poet was born, is uncertain. He studied the law, and was sometime a member of the Society of Lincoln's Inn, where his acquaintance with Chaucer began. Some have asserted that he was a Judge, but this is by no means certain. In the first year of Henry the 4th, he became blind, a misfortune which he laments in one of his Latin Poems. He died in the year 1402, and was buried in the church of Saint Mary Overie ; which he had rebuilt, chiefly at his own expense, so that he must have lived in affluent circumstances. His tomb was magnificently and curiously ornamented and it still remains, but has been repaired in latter times. From the collar of S. S., round the neck o his effigies upon the tomb, it is conjectured that he had been knighted. As to his character as a man, it is impossible, at this distance of time, to say any thing with certainty. With regard to his poetical talents, he was certainly admired at the time when he wrote, though a modern reader may find it difficult to discover much harmony or genius in any of his compositions. He wrote first, *Speculum Meditantis*, in French, in ten books; there are two copies of this in the Bodleian Library. A work entitled *Vox Clamantis*, in Latin verse, in seven books, is also preserved in the Bodleian Library, and in that of All Souls; it is a chronicle of the insurrection of the Commons, in the reign of Richard the 2nd. The first edition of *Confessio Amantis*, was printed at Westminster, by Caxton, in 1493; and the second and third editions were printed in London, in the years 1532, and 1554. This book is a sort of practical system of morality, interspersed with a variety of moral tales. There are several historical tracts in M S., written by our author, which are to be found in different libraries; also some short poems printed in Chaucer's Works.

———

AUTHORITIES.
Encyclopædia Britannica.—Warton's History of English Poetry.

THE LIFE

OF

JOHN MILTON.

"But MILTON next, with high and haughty stalks,
" Unfettered in majestic numbers walks;
"No vulgar Hero can his Muse engage,
" Nor earth's wide scene confine his hallowed rage."

WITH the name of Milton, must ever be associated
in a British mind the highest sentiments of veneration.
He who makes the least pretension to liberal knowledge and taste, and who, notwithstanding, feels no
wish to learn the circumstances of the life of such a
writer, may justly be suspected of some dislike, not
only to the Muse, but to goodness itself, and to that
greatness of mind which procures distinguished honours.

"Paradise Lost," however, has established an imper-
ishable fame.   Human nature must suffer an awful
wreck, before that work can cease to interest the numerous thousands of its readers !   No wonder then,
that memoirs of the life of its Author have long
followed one another, with increasing success, till the
subject, through all its authorities, is now nearly ex-

hausted: the substance of the whole I shall endeavour faithfully and briefly to comprise in the following sketch.

This great Poet was descended from a respectable family of Milton, in Oxfordshire. His grandfather was a bigoted Papist, and disinherited his son for embracing the Protestant religion; upon which he came to London, and settled there as a scrivener; where the subject of this narrative was born, on the 9th of Dec. 1608. He received the first rudiments of his education from a private tutor, who was brought into the family for that purpose: from his father's house he went to St. Paul's School, and entered a student of Christ's College, Cambridge: during his residence there, he composed most of his Latin poems, in a style exquisitely imitative of the best models of antiquity. Milton is said to have been the first Englishman who wrote Latin verse with classical elegance. On leaving the university, after having taken out his degree of A.M., in 1632, he returned to his father, then residing at Horton, in Buckinghamshire, where he pursued his studies with unparalleled assiduity and success. They did not, however, so entirely absorb his attention, as not to afford him time to produce "The Mask of Comus," a work adorned with all the ornaments of diction, where allusions, images, and beautiful epithets embellished every period with lavish decoration: for though it is a drama too much in the epic style to please on the stage, yet, in whatever light it is viewed, whether as a series of lines, a masque, or a poem, it can be considered as inferior only to Paradise Lost. His

next production was Lycidas, a poem no less beautiful
of its kind, than the last; being a monody on the
death of his friend Edward King, son of Sir John
King, secretary for Ireland, and who was lost on his
passage to that country. Milton having now remained with his father about five years, obtained, on
the death of his mother, the liberty to travel, which
he so ardently desired; he left England in 1638;
first went to Paris, where he visited the celebrated
Grotius, and thence hastened into Italy, whose language and literature he studied with uncommon diligence. There he was received with marked attention
by the learned and great ; for, notwithstanding the
undissembled openness of his political and religious
opinions, he was introduced to a musical entertainment by Cardinal Barberini (afterwards Pope Urban
VIII.) in person, who waited for him at the door,
and led him by the hand into the assembly. From
Rome he went to Naples; where he was received with
no less respect by Manso, Marquis of Villa, who had
been before the patron of Tasso: after which, he
visited the rest of Italy, caressed and honoured by
every one conspicuous for high rank, or distinguished
abilities. Among the last was the great Galileo,
whom he did not omit to visit, although, at that time,
a prisoner in the Inquisition, for having taught the
annual and diurnal motions of the earth! After having
spent two years in his travels, which were designed to
extend to Sicily and Greece, he hastened home, on
hearing of the troubles in his native country, judging it criminal to remain indifferent, or to indulge
in amusements, while his countrymen were contending
for their liberties. On his return he took a house in

Aldersgate-street, where he superintended the education of his nephews; and also received other young
gentlemen to be boarded and instructed. In his 35th
year, he married Mary, the daughter of Richard
Powel, Esq. of Forrest-hill, Oxfordshire; but a separation, or rather a desertion on the wife's part, took
place a month after the ceremony; on her refus-
ing to return, in compliance with repeated requisi-
tions, he was so provoked, that he was induced to publish several treatises on the doctrine of divorce, and
also to pay his addresses to a young lady of great wit
and beauty. A reconciliation was the consequence,
for his wife, in an unexpected interview, throwing
herself at his feet, implored his forgiveness: impressed with this event, he is said to have conceived
the pathetic scene in Paradise Lost, in which Eve
addressed herself to Adam, for pardon and peace.

"————————————— Her lowly plight
Immoveable, till peace obtained from fault
Acknowledged and deplored, in Adam wrought
Commiseration; soon his heart relented
Towards her, his life so late and sole delight,
Now at his feet submissive in distress!
Creature so fair, his reconcilement seeking,
His counsel, whom she had displeased, his aid:
As one disarmed, his anger all he lost."

From this period to the restoration, our author
was so deeply engaged in the controversies of the
times, that he found no leisure for polite literature.
The Allegro and Penseroso, however, appeared in a
collection of Latin and English poems, published in
1645. These delightful pieces are, undoubtedly, the
two best descriptive poems that ever were written;

had he left no other monuments but Comus, Lycidas, and the Matchless Pair, yet they alone would be sufficient to render his name immortal. They were, however, little noticed on their publication, and remained nearly a century disregarded, or at least scarcely known ; while his polemical tracts, (now only in their titles remembered,) made their author's fortune, and spread his fame over Europe : of these, the most celebrated is his "Defensio Populi Angli-cani," or "Defence of the English People," in an-swer to Salmasius, professor of polite literature at Leyden, who was employed by Charles the II. when in exile, to write the "Defensio Regis," or " Defence of the King." Milton's piece wasso severe, and so much admired, that it is said to have killed his anta-gonist with vexation.* For this tract he was rewarded

---

* This celebrated controversy was of that magnitude, that all Europe took a part in the paper-war of these great men. Salmasius was a man of vast erudition, but no taste. His writings are learned, but sometimes ridiculous. The opening of his " Defensio Regis," provokes a laugh :—

" Englishmen, who toss the heads of Kings as so many tennis balls; who play with crowns as if they were bowls ; who look upon sceptres as so many crooks !" He reproaches Milton, as being but a puny piece of man; an homunculus; a dwarf deprived of the human figure; a bloodless being, com-posed of nothing but skin and bone ; a contemptible pedagogue, fit only to flog his boys; and sometimes, elevating his mind into a poetic frenzy, he applies to him the words of Virgil. 'Monstrum, horrendum, informe, ingens, cui lumen ademptum,' ' A monster, horrid, hideous, huge and blind.'

To this senseless declaration, our great Poet made a spirited reply, and concluded with these words : 'Even my eyes, blind as they are, are unblemished in their appearance: in this alone, and much against my inclination, I am a deceiver.'

with £1000, a sum twenty times greater than he made by all his poetical works put together! and was also promoted to be Latin Secretary to the Protector.   On the 2nd of May, 1652, his family was increased by the birth of his fourth child, Deborah; and the mother dying in child-bed, he was left with three orphan daughters, and in a state rapidly advancing to blindness.

The prediction of his physicians was now hastening to its fatal accomplishment; his sight naturally weak, and impaired by incessant study from the earliest period of his life, had for several years been sensibly declining: and when he engaged in his last great work, had discovered symptoms of approaching extinction.   In the course of that honourable labour he entirely lost the vision of one eye, and that of the other closing soon afterwards, he was resigned to total darkness.

The fortitude with which he supported himself, under this afflicting privation, isad mirably discovered in that Sonnet to his friend Cyriac Skinner, the grandson of the great Lord Coke, which I shall now transcribe.   I could never read it without paying to its author the profound homage of my respect.

> Cyriac, this three-years-day, these eyes, though clear,
> To outward view, of blemish, or of spot,
> Bereft of light, their seeing have forgot;
> Nor to their idle orbs doth sight appear
> Of sun, or moon, or star throughout the year!
> Or man, or woman,—Yet I argue not
> Against Heaven's hand, or will, nor bate a jot
> Of heart, or hope, but still bear up and steer
> Right onward.   What supports me, dost thou ask!

The conscience, friend, to have lost them, overplied
In Liberty's defence, my noble task,
Of which all Europe rings from side to side:
This thought might lead me through the world's vain
    mask,
Content, though blind, had I no other guide.

Of the completion of his misfortune, the date is
by no means accurately settled. All his biographers,
with the exception of Todd, place it in 1654; but
it unquestionably happened in some antecedent period, as appears by his letter to Phalaris, written in
the autumn of that year;*and we know, that when

---

* Known to you only by my writings, and widely separated
in our abodes, I was first honoured by your kind correspondence; and afterwards, when an unexpected occasion brought
you to London, with the same kindness you came to see me,
who could see nobody; one labouring under an affliction
which can entitle him to little observation, and may perhaps
expose him to much disregard. As, however, you entreat
me not to abandon all hopes of recovering my sight, and state
that you have a medical friend at Paris, (M. Thevenot,) particularly eminent as an oculist, whom you could consult upon
the subject, if I would transmit to you the causes and the
symptoms of my disease; that I may not seem to neglect any
means, perhaps divinely suggested, of relief, I will hasten to
comply with your requisition. It is now, I think, about ten
years since I first perceived my sight to grow weak and dim,
and at the same time my spleen and other viscera heavy and
flatulent. When I sat down to read, as usual in the morning,
my eyes gave me considerable pain, and refused their office
till fortified by moderate exercise of body. If I looked at a
candle it appeared surrounded with an iris. In a little time a
darkness, covering the left side of the left eye, (which was
partially clouded some years before the other,) intercepted tne

he was visited by his Athenian friends, at a time not
greatly posterior to the publication of his defence, he
was totally blind. Todd has noticed in Thurloe's
State Papers, a letter from the Hague, dated June 20,
1653, in which Milton is mentioned as blind. We
must conclude, therefore, that his total loss of sight
soon followed the publication of his answer to Salmasius, and happened early in 1652. He was forewarned

---

view of all things in that direction.   Objects also in front,
seemed to dwindle in size, whenever I closed my right eye.

This eye too, for three years gradually failing, a few months
previous to my total blindness, while I was perfectly stationary,
every thing seemed to swim backward and forward; and now,
thick vapours appear to settle on my forehead and temples,
which weigh down my eye-lids, with an oppressive sense of
drowsiness.

I ought not, however, to omit mentioning, that, before I
wholly lost my sight, as soon as I lay down in bed, and turned
on either side, brilliant flashes of light used to issue from my
closed eyes, and afterwards on the gradual failure of my powers
of vision, colours proportionally dim and faint seemed to rush
out with a degree of vehemence, and a kind of noise. These
have now faded into uniform blackness, such as ensues on the
extinction of a candle ; or blackness only varied, and inter-
mingled with dunnish grey. The constant darkness, however,
in which I live day and night, inclines more to a whitish than
to a blackish tinge; and the eye turning round, admits as
through a narrow chink, a very small portion of light. But
this though perhaps it may offer a small glimpse of hope to
the physician, does not prevent me from making up my mind
to my case, as one evidently beyond the hope of cure; and I
often reflect, that as many days of darkness, according to the
wise men, are allotted to us all, mine, (which by the favour of
the Deity, are divided between leisure and study,) are recre-
ated by the conversation and intercourse of my friends, and

by his physicians of the contingent calamity, and in the alternative of evils, preferred the loss of sight to the dereliction of his duty.

Milton, however, did not long remain a widower; he shortly after married Catharine, daughter of Captain Woodcock, of Hackney : she seems to have been the object of her husband's fondest affection: and like her predecessor, dying in child-bed, within a year after her marriage, she was lamented by him in a pleasing and pathetic Sonnet, which will be felt by every sensible bosom; it may not be irrelevant to remark, that the thought in the concluding line, which on a cursory view may be branded as a conceit, is strictly correct and just. In his dreams, a blind man may expatiate in the full blaze of the sun, and the morning, in which he awakes, unquestionably restores him to his darkness. The fault is in the expression alone—"I waked, she fled, and I replunged in night;" would perhaps be sufficiently unexceptionable.

> Methought I saw my late espoused saint,
> Brought to me, like Alcestis, from the grave,

---

far more agreeable than those deadly shades of which Solomon is speaking; but if, as it is written, " Man shall not live by bread alone, but by every word that proceedeth out of the mouth of God," why should not each of us likewise acquiesce in the reflection, that he derives the benefit of sight, not from his eyes alone, but from the guidance and providence of the same Supreme Being. Whilst He looks out and provides for as He does, and leads me about, as it were with His hand, through the paths of life, I willingly surrender my own faculty of vision, in conformity to his good pleasure, and with a heart as strong and steadfast as if I were a Lynceus, I bid you, my Phalaris, farewell.

Whom Jove's great son to her glad husband gave,
Rescued from death, by force, though pale and faint.
Mine as whom washed from spot of child-bed taint
Purification in the old law did save,
And such, as yet once more I trust to have
Full sight of her in heaven without restraint,
Came vested all in white, pure as her mind;
Her face was veil'd, yet to my fancied sight,
Love, sweetness, goodness, in her person shined
So clear, as in no face with more delight:
But Oh! as to embrace me she inclined—
I waked, she fled, and day brought back my night!

The daughter whom she bore him, soon followed
her to the tomb.   On the Restoration, he was obliged
to quit his house, together with his employment, and
to secrete himself in an obscure abode, in Bartholomew
Close: his friends had some difficulty to prevent him
from being excepted in the act of oblivion; to lull research and to gain time, they had recourse to the expedient of a mock funeral.   By the act of oblivion he
was at least freed from danger, but his polemical writings
were burnt by the common hangman.   From Bartholomew Close he removed to Jewry-street, and married
for his third wife, Elizabeth Minstur, daughter to a
gentleman in Cheshire.   He was now in his 52nd
year, blind, infirm, and comparatively poor, for he
had lost by the civil wars his paternal estate, and by
the Restoration his acquired property; but neither
his infirmities, nor the vicissitudes of fortune, could
depress the vigour of his mind, or prevent him from
executing a design he had long conceived, of writing
an heroic poem.   The great work of Paradise Lost,
was finished in 1665, at Chalfont, in Bucks, where
the author had taken refuge from the plague; and

published in 1667, when he returned to London. He
sold the copy to Samuel Simmons, for five pounds
in hand, and five pounds more when 1300 copies
should be sold; and the same sum on the publication of the second and third editions, for each edition. Of this agreement, Milton received £15, and
his widow afterwards sold her claims for £8. Such
was the first reception of a work, which constitutes
the glory and boast of English literature; a work
which, notwithstanding the severity of criticism, may
be ranked among the noblest efforts of human genius;
for though in variety of character and choice of
subject, it may yield to some, yet in grandeur and
sublimity, it is confessedly superior to all. The
measure of this divine poem is blank verse, between
which and rhyme there are endless disputes for pre-
eminence—but surely the essential qualities of poetry
can no more depend on either, than those of a man
on the fashion of his clothes. Dr. Johnson, who
could not endure blank verse, yet confesses, that " he
could not prevail on himself to wish that Milton had
been a rhymer." Paradise Lost is not, however, without faults; perfection in this life is unattainable.
The attempt of the author to give language and
sentiment to the Deity, is where he seems to have
failed most in the execution; but in such an attempt,
what mortal could have succeeded ? Other exceptions
it has endured in passing the fiery ordeal of Doctor
Johnson's criticism; yet, every reader capable of
relishing true poetry, will agree with him in concluding, that "this is not the greatest of heroic poems,
only because it is not the first."

Three years after the publication of Paradise Lost, he published "Sampson Agonistes" a tragedy in the purest style of the Greek Drama, and "Paradise Regained;" which he is said to have preferred to his great work, but in which preference he remains alone. Paradise Regained has suffered much in the comparison. It is said the following circumstance gave rise to this poem: Elwood, the Quaker, who had been introduced to him for the purpose of improving himself by the perusal of the classical writers, suggested the idea of such a work just before he came to Chalfont, and the Poet presented him with it on his return to London. Milton had indeed given him the perusal of Paradise Lost in manuscript, and he having read it, upon returning the copy, put this quaint interrogation,—"What hast thou to say to Paradise Found?" This simple, yet natural question, gave rise to Paradise Regained; a work as much obscured by the splendour of Paradise Lost, as the lustre of the morning star by the sun's meridian blaze; but if any other than Milton had been the author, it would have justly claimed and received universal praise. Our great Poet at last, worn out by the gout, paid the debt of nature on the 10th of November, 1674, in his 66th year, at his house in Bunhill-fields, and was buried in St. Giles's, Cripplegate; his funeral was splendidly and numerously attended. On the Restoration, Milton's friends were greatly alarmed for his safety, lest he should be proceeded against as a regicide; they therefore used all their influence to procure him a pardon, in which I am happy to say, they succeeded. The Government contented themselves with calling

him before the House, as may be seen by the following
extract from the journal of the House of Commons.*

Milton seems to have been saved principally by the
earnest and grateful interposition of Sir William
Davenant, who had been captured by the fleet of the
Commonwealth, on his passage from France to America, and had been ordered by the Parliament, in 1651,
on his trial before the High Court of Justice.   The
mediation of Milton; had essentially contributed to
snatch him from danger; and urged by that generous
benevolence which shone conspicuously in his character, he was now eager to requite, with a gift of equal
value, the benefit which he had received.   For the existence of Davenant's obligation to Milton, we have the
testimony of Wood, and for the subsequent part of the
story, so interesting in itself, and so honourable to
human nature, the evidence is directly to be traced
from Richardson to Pope, and from Pope to Betterton,
the immediate client and intimate of Davenant.

His nuncupative Will, which has lately been discovered in the Prerogative Registry, and published by
Mr. Warton, opens a glimpse into the interior of Milton's house, and shows him to have been both amiable

---

* *Saturday, 15th December*, 1660.—" Ordered, that Mr.
Milton, now in custody of the sergeant attending this house,
be forthwith released, paying his fees." A complaint made
that the sergeant at arms had demanded excessive fees for the
imprisonment of Mr. Milton, the house again

" Ordered,—that it be referred to a committee of privileges,
to examine this business, and to call Mr. Milton and the
sergeant before them, and to determine what is fit to be given
to the sergeant for his fees in this case."

and injured, in that private scene, in which alone he has generally been considered as liable to censure, or rather, perhaps not entitled to our affection. In this Will, and in the paper connected with it, we find the venerable father complaining of his "unkind children," for leaving and neglecting him, because he was blind; and we see him compelled, as it were, by their injurious conduct, to appeal against them, even to his servants. We are assured also, by the deposition on oath, of one of these servants, that his complaints were not extorted by slight wrongs, or uttered by capricious passion on slight provocation; that his children, (with the exception probably of Deborah, who, at the time immediately in question, was not more than nine years old,) would occasionally sell his books to the dunghill-women, as the witness calls them ; that they were capable of combining with the maid servant, and advising her to cheat her master and their father in her marketings; and that one of them, Mary, on being told that her father was to be married, replied, "that is no news, but if I could hear of his death, that were something."

Much has been said on the unequal flow of our Poet's genius ; and by some it has been represented as under the influence of particular seasons, while by others it has been regarded as the effect of immediate and positive inspiration. Phillips declares, that his uncle's poetic faculty was vivid only in the winter, and Toland assigns the spring as the season of its peculiar activity ; while Richardson, with a proper respect to the ardent character of the author's mind, expresses a doubt whether such a work could be suffered for any

considerable period to stand absolutely still.   Phillips,
to whom his relation was accustomed to shew the
poem in its progress, informs us that, not having seen
any verses for some time, on the approach of summer
he requested to know the cause of what appeared to
him to be extraordinary; and that he received as a
reply from the poet, that " his vein never flowed happily, but from the autumnal equinox till the vernal;
and that what he attempted at other times was never
to his satisfaction, though he courted his fancy ever
so much."   In opposition to this, and in support of
his own opinion, Toland adduces the information
given to him by a friend of Milton's, and the testimony of the bard himself, who, in his beautiful elegy,
" On the Arrival of Spring," speaks of that delightful
season, as renovating and invigorating his genius.
While the former part of this evidence cannot be
poised against that of the author's confidential friend
and nephew, the latter must be considered as too weak
and uncertain to be entitled to any great regard.
Mrs. Milton, who survived her husband, says that
he composed principally in the winter, and on his
waking in the morning, would make her write down
sometimes twenty or thirty verses.   On being asked
whether he did not frequently read Homer and Virgil,
she replied, "that he stole from nobody but the Muse
who inspired him."   To a lady who inquired who that
Muse was, she said, " it was God's grace, and the
Holy Spirit that visited him nightly."

A small monument, with his bust, was erected
not long since to his memory, in Westminster Abbey.
Milton, in stature, did not exceed the middle size,

but was formed with perfect symmetry, and was more-over, in his youth, eminently beautiful; of which many portraits yet to be seen, and the following epigram of the Marquis of Villa, are incontestable proofs.

" So perfect thou, in mind, in form, in face;
" Thou'rt not of English, but Angelic race."

In his habits, he was abstemious in his diet, and naturally disliked all strong liquors. In his youth he studied late, but afterwards reversed his hours. His amusements consisted in the conversation of his friends, and in music, in which he was a great proficient. After he became blind, he was assisted in his studies by his daughters, whom he taught to read Hebrew, Greek, and Latin, without their understanding any of them; and for transcribing, he employed any casual acquain-tance. His literature was great; he was a perfect master of Hebrew, Greek, Latin, Italian, French and Spanish. Of the English Poets, he preferred Spencer, Shakspeare, and Cowley. His deportment was erect, open, and affable; his conversation easy, cheerful, and instructive; his wit on all occasions at command, facetious, grave, or satirical, as the subject required; his judgment just and penetrating; his apprehension quick; his memory tenacious of what he read; his reading, only not so extensive as his genius, for that was universal. With so many accomplishments, not to have faults and misfortunes to be laid in the balance, with the fame and felicity of writing Paradise Lost, would have been too great a portion for humanity.

As Milton equalled Homer in his genius, so he equalled him in his misfortunes. Homer had reached the years of manhood before he lost his sight; so had Milton. Homer's great work was his Iliad; Milton's, his Paradise Lost. Homer's second great work was his Odyssey; Milton's, his Paradise Regained. The Odyssey is as much inferior to the Iliad, as Paradise Regained is to Paradise Lost. Homer had Zoïlus for an enemy, and Milton had Lauder. These two epic poets, like Saturn and Jupiter in the planetary system, shine bright stars of excellence, round which inferior orbs for ever move in dull succession. Homer and Milton have long held the first rank among poets; the vigour of their minds, the brilliancy of their imaginations, the flights of their genius like those of inspiration, extended to the very boundaries of time and space.

I will close these remarks with the following panegyric on Milton, by the author of "The Seasons."

> " Is not each great, each amiable muse
> " Of classic ages in thy Milton met?
> " A genius universal as his theme:
> " Astonishing as chaos, as the bloom
> " Of blowing Eden fair, as Heaven sublime."

AUTHORITIES.

SYMMON's Life of Milton.—JOHNSON's Lives of English Poets.—HAYLEY's Life of Milton.—ANDERSON's Lives of the Poets.—M'NICOLL's Life of Milton.

MISS ANNA WILLIAMS,

THE BLIND POETESS.

THIS lady came to London in 1730, when twenty-four years of age, with her father, a Welsh surgeon, who had given up his practice, under the impression that he had discovered a method of finding the longitude at sea, which would make his fortune. After many efforts, however, to obtain the patronage of Government for his scheme, having exhausted his resources, he was obliged to take refuge in the Charterhouse. His daughter, who had been liberally educated, and had at first mingled in all the gaieties of the metropolis, was now obliged to support both her father and herself, by working at her needle. After struggling in this way for a maintenance several years, she lost her sight by a cataract; her situation, it might be imagined, was now both helpless and hopeless in the extreme, but a strong mind enabled her to rise above her calamity. We are told, she not only continued the exercise of her needle, with as much activity and skill as ever, but, never suffering her spirits to droop, distinguished herself, as she had been used to do, by the neatness of her dress. She likewise preserved all her old attachment to literature, and, in the year 1746, after she had been six years blind, published a translation from the French, of Le Bleterie's "Life of the Emperor Julian." Her father having, some time after this, met with Dr. Johnson, told him his story, and, in mentioning his daughter, gave so interesting an account of her, that the Doctor expressed himself desirous of making her acquaintance, and eventually invited her to reside in his house, as a companion to his wife. Mrs Johnson died soon after, but Miss Williams continued to reside with the Doctor till her death. In 1752, an attempt was made to restore her sight by the operation of couching, but without success. About three years after, Garrick gave her a benefit at Drury Lane, which produced two hundred pounds. Miss Williams appeared again as an authoress in 1766; when she published a volume entitled, "Miscellanies in Prose and Verse," written partly by herself, and partly by several of her friends. She died in 1783, at the age of 77.

AUTHORITY.

The Library of Entertaining Knowledge, vol. 1st.

THE LIFE

OF

DR. CLANCY,

A DRAMATIC POET;

" His comic vein had every charm to please,
'Twas nature's dictate, charm'd with nature's ease."

WANT of sight, even in an animal, demands and excites our commiseration, but a rational creature afflicted with blindness, is one of the most deplorable objects that the feeling mind can possibly contemplate; for we possess not any faculty which affords so many resources of utility and entertainment as the power of vision, nor is there any loss or privation, which can be productive of calamities so multiform, so various, and so bitter, as the want of sight.

Michael Clancy, M.D. was born in the county of Clare, Ireland, and received part of his education at one of the colleges in Paris, which he, however, abruptly left before he had completed his studies; and in this early part of his life, he experienced many vicissitudes and hardships. In 1737, he was deprived of his sight by a severe cold, and was thus rendered incapable of following his profession as a physician. As the Doctor had, in his earlier days, paid his addresses to the Muses, he was advised, by some

friends, to try his success as an author ; and, supposing the theatre was open alike to all, his first attempt
was in the dramatic line.   Flushed with the hope of
immediate distinction, as well as with the expectation
of gain, he composed a comedy in a short time, and
thought, when he had wound up the plot, that all his
labour was at an end.   He found, however, to his
cost, that every avenue to the theatre, in those days,
as well as our own, was blocked up by a set of dramatic undertakers, who were ready, at any price, to
work by the pound, or by the yard : and that it was
as difficult to get a sight of the manager, as it would
be to get a sight of the Grand Lama.   He, however,
at last succeeded in bringing out his comedy, called
" The Sharper," which was acted five times at the
theatre, in Smock-alley, Dublin, and obtained for
him the notice of Dean Swift.   The Doctor, having
detailed a number of the difficulties he was doomed to
encounter, in his efforts to get the piece upon the
stage, relates the following circumstance, which is
given in his own words :—"On my return to Dublin,
I brought the play to Dr. Helsham, who was conscious of his insufficiency in matters so foreign to his
way of life ; I requested him, therefore, as he was very
familiar with Dean Swift, to put the comedy into his
hands, as I judged that his approbation, or dislike,
would at once determine the fate of the performance.
'Not I, indeed ;' said Dr. Helsham.   'Have you a
mind that I should go faster down his stairs than I
went up ? Shall I subject myself to be laughed at, or
perhaps ill treated ? Not I, indeed ; I do not care to
bring his tongue upon me.   Go to Dr. Grattan ; the

Dean will probably hear from him what he would not from me.' I went to Dr. Grattan, and solicited his assistance in the same way. 'Who, I?' said Dr. Grattan. 'Not I, by any means; What have I to do with plays? I know nothing of writing books; I should have a fine time of it were I to bring such a piece of stuff before the Dean, and have it thrown in my face, or be called a blockhead for my pains. I should be glad to serve you, but you must find somebody else to befriend you on this occasion. Dr. Grattan's brother, Minister of St. Andrew's, who happened to be present, was pleased to say, that he would find an opportunity of laying the book on the Dean's table, and, if it was good, he would be likely to enquire how it came there. This gentleman accordingly did so, and there it lay for some time, without the author's hearing one word about it. Swift, however, read it, and not knowing how the play came there, asked all his friends which of them had brought it; none of those to whom it was known would, however, venture to tell, as he had not declared his opinion of it. One day, as Dr. Helsham saw it on his table, he took it up to look at it, and asked the Dean what it was? The Dean smiled, and told him, it was a villain well painted, and that, whoever had written the piece, it conveyed a good moral. Dr. Helsham, who saw that he had nothing to fear, then told him the author's name, and what he knew of him. 'Tell him,' said the Dean, 'that in a few days I will pay him a visit.' He then went into his closet, and wrote the following letter, which Dr.

Helsham brought, together with a small packet.

'To Dr. Clancy.

' Sir,

' Some friend of mine lent me a comedy, which I was told was written by you. I read it carefully, and with much pleasure, on account both of the characters and the moral. I have no interest with the people of the playhouse, else I would gladly recommend it to them. I send you a small present, in such gold as will not give you trouble to change ; for I much pity your loss of sight, which, if it had pleased God to let you enjoy, your other talents might have been your honest support, and have eased you of your present confinement.

' I am, Sir, your well wishing Friend,

and humble Servant,

' JONATHAN SWIFT.

' Deanery House, Christmas-day, 1737.

'P.S. I know not who lent me the play ; if it came from you, I will send it back to-morrow.'

This letter and the packet were sealed with the head of Socrates. The packet contained five pounds, in small pieces of gold, of different kinds, of which the largest did not exceed five shillings. A little time after," says Dr. Clancy, " I sent him a parcel of tickets ; he kept but one, which he said he had paid for ; and afterwards sent me two four pound pieces for more." Thus ends the correspondence between the Dean and our author.

From this period, his life seems to have been

passed amid all the inconveniences that result from confined circumstances. He however, obtained from George II. a pension of £40. a year during life; and, in the year 1746, he received a sum of money for performing the part of Tiresias, the blind prophet in Œdipus, which was acted for his benefit at Drury-lane Theatre. He afterwards settled at Kilkenny, at the Latin school there. He was the author of three dramatic pieces, and also of a Latin Poem, called " Templum Veneris, sive Amorum Rhapsodiæ." By the following fragment found among the papers of Mrs. Pilkington, it would seem that poor Clancy was cursed with a termagant wife :

> Hapless Clancy ! grieve no more,
> Socrates was plagu'd before;
> Though o'ercast, thy visual ray
> Meets no more the light of day,
> Yet ev'n here is comfort had,
> Good prevailing over bad.
> Now thou canst no more behold
> The grim aspect of thy scold;
> Oh ! what raptures wouldst thou find,
> Wert thou deaf as well as blind.

AUTHORITIES.

Mrs. Pilkington's Memoirs, vol. 2, p. 151.—Swift's Miscellaneous Works.

MUSIC AND ART

Music

THROUGHOUT history blind people have frequently pursued careers as artists and musicians. On the tomb of Nakht in ancient Egypt (1400 B.C.), a blind harpist is shown entertaining at a party. In addition to blind performers, there have been blind music teachers and blind composers. It is recorded that Confucius had a blind music teacher as well as another blind man, Shih K'uang, who played for him and interpreted the philosopher's thoughts through music.

Wilson's discussion of blind musicians extends only to those who received recognition or remuneration for their work, but countless blind street musicians have also displayed their talent in cities around the world.

The man whom Wilson names "Henry, the Minstrel" or "Blind Harry" also appears in Ishbel Ross's *Journey into Light: The Story of the Education of the Blind* (1950). There he is termed the best-known blind minstrel of the Middle Ages, and Ross credits him with composing the saga of William Wallace of Scotland. Ross puts Harry's date of birth at 1361.

Franciscus Salinas (1512–90), a musician at the University of Salamanca, Spain, became abbot of St. Pauciate della Rocca Salegna, according to Ross. His career was largely church related, and he lived in Rome as well as in Spain. Other writers to relate the story of Salinas are Berthold

Lowenfeld in *The Changing Status of the Blind: From Separation to Integration* (1975), Alexander Mell in *Encyklopädisches Handbuch des Blindenwesens* (1900, in German), and Heinrich Scholler in *Enzyklopädie des Blinden- und Sehbehindertenwesens* (1993, also in German).

Caspar Crumbhorn (1542–1621), spelled "Krumbhorn" by Ross, Mell, and Scholler, was a well-known German composer and a skillful player of the violin, flute, and organ. He was organist at the Church of St. Peter and St. Paul in Ligniz, where he also served as the director of the musical academy.

Turlagh Carolan (1670–1738), also spelled "Turlough" and "O'Carolan," was an important Irish harpist and composer who is often referred to as "The Last of the Great Irish Bards." He is studied by modern folklorists, and recordings of his music are available in stores and libraries. *Carolan: The Life and Times of an Irish Harper,* a two-volume illustrated work by Donal O'Sullivan, was published in 1958 and republished in 1983.

The famous composer George Frederick Handel (1685–1759), whom Wilson discusses in the third and fourth editions, was blind during the last six years of his life. According to Francis Collingwood in *The New Beacon* (March 1959), Handel was diagnosed with a retinal condition caused by diabetes or a kidney problem just as he started his oratorio *Jephtha*. He struggled with pain and failing vision during the completion of the work, finally losing his sight altogether. He continued to compose and conduct to great acclaim until his death.

John Stanley (1713?–86) became famous largely because of his association with Handel. Blind from childhood, Stanley was a skilled musician, playing the organ and other instruments. He helped conduct performances of Handel's oratorios both before and after Handel's death.

Wilson refers to Joseph Strong (1732–98) as a mechanic and musician, while George Clarke, in *The Life and Sketches of Curious and Odd Characters* (1833), calls him only a mechanic. Although Strong enjoyed performing music professionally, for his livelihood he relied on his ability to construct musical instruments, especially organs, and on weaving.

Like Strong, William Talbot (1781–?) combined a musical career with the construction of useful objects. He made miniature windmills and sailing ships of considerable intricacy as a child and later constructed an organ and made adjustments to the Irish pipes. He is also discussed by John Kitto in *The Lost Senses* (1845).

Theresa Paradis (1759–1824) is one of the most interesting musicians featured in Wilson's *Biography;* her story appears in the works of several other chroniclers of the blind. Interpretations of

Paradis's life differ somewhat, but all agree that she was charming, talented, and popular. Empress Maria Theresa of Austria arranged for her to receive musical training and gave her an annual allowance. Paradis traveled with her mother and performed in major European cities. Paradis's blindness may have been psychological in origin, caused by a severe scare as a child. Anton Mesmer treated her with "magnetism" and, according to Ross, seemed to have restored her sight. But she was not immediately able to process the new sensory input, so she lost concentration and her music suffered. Ross indicates that the medical profession became upset over the attention Mesmer was receiving and denied the "cure," telling her parents that if she regained her sight, Paradis would lose part of her appeal to audiences. According to Ross, her parents asked Mesmer to stop treatment and send Paradis home, but she refused to go. The ensuing commotion so upset her that she lost what sight she had regained and in the end Mesmer was forced to discontinue treatment. Paradis, protesting, went home and remained blind.

Paradis eventually developed ways to make music accessible to the blind, with raised lines to indicate a music staff and words spelled out with pin pricks. She has been compared to Helen Keller in her efforts to make these and other devices available to blind children. She believed that mass education of blind people was possible and is credited with influencing Valentin Haüy, who founded the first school for the blind in Paris in 1784, and Johann Wilhelm Klein, who established one in Vienna in 1804.

It was these schools that first fully trained large numbers of blind people in music, including piano tuning. Francis Campbell (1832–1914), a blind educator of the blind, made music a genuine profession for the blind through his insistence that a job placement program be a part of blind students' education. Soon after he developed braille, Louis Braille adapted it for musical notation. Many blind people earn a living as music and voice teachers, instrumentalists, organists, and piano tuners.

Art

WILSON'S *Biography* includes only one artist, John Gonelli (1602–64), also called "The Blind Sculptor." He studied in Florence under Pietro Tacca and created a number of works before losing his sight as a result of ill treatment during the 1630 siege of Mantua. Researchers differ on the credibility of works attributed to Gonelli and the extent of his artistic achievement after he became blind.

Artists who have developed vision problems are not uncommon. Patrick Trevor-Roper, in his book *The World Through Blunted Sight* (1970), mentions several of them. He points out that the British painter J. M. W. Turner developed cataracts late in life, and he argues that Cézanne and Renoir were myopic, "like many other Impressionists."

In the contemporary world, many blind and visually impaired artists work in painting, sculpture, drawing, photography, and ceramics. Some artists become blind or visually impaired later in life and continue to work, and some take up art in school or rehabilitation programs for the adult blind. Their works can often be seen in shows presented by agencies and organizations relating to blind persons and in galleries featuring blind artists.

HENRY, THE MINSTREL,

COMMONLY CALLED "BLIND HARRY."

"What time in God, and freedom's holy cause,
Wallace and Bruce opposed a tyrant's laws.

HENRY, the Minstrel, commonly called "Blind
Harry," was an antient Scottish author, distinguished
by no particular sir-name, but well known as the
composer of an historical poem, reciting the achievements of Sir William Wallace. This poem, continued for several centuries to be in great repute, but
afterwards sunk into neglect, until very lately, that it
has been released from its obscurity, by a very neat
and correct edition published at Perth, under the
inspection and patronage of the Earl of Buchan.
It is difficult to ascertain the precise time in which
this poet lived, or when he wrote his history, as the
two authors who mention him, speak somewhat differ-
ently. Dempster, who wrote in the beginning of the
sixteenth century, says, that he lived in the year
1361; but Major, who was born in the year 1446,
says, that he composed his book during the time of
his infancy, which we must suppose to have been a
few years posterior to 1446; for if it had been composed that very year, the circumstance would pro-

bably have been mentioned. As little can we suppose from Mr. Dempster's words, that Harry was
born in 1361 ; for though he says, that he lived in
that year, we must naturally imagine, rather, that
he was come to the years of maturity, or began to
distinguish himself in the world, than that he was
only born at that time. The author of the Dissertation on his life, prefixed to the new edition of the
poem, endeavours to reconcile matters in the following manner. " It is not, indeed, impossible that he
might be born in or about that year, (1361.) In
the time of Major's infancy, he might be about 83
years of age—in that case, it may be supposed that
it was the work of his old age, to collect and put in
order the detached pieces of his history of Wallace,
which he had probably composed in those parts of
the country where the incidents were said to have
happened."

We are entirely ignorant of the family, from which
Harry was descended ; though, from his writings, we
should be led to suppose that he had received a liberal
education. In these, he discovers some knowledge
in divinity, classical history, and astronomy, as well
as of the languages. In one place, he boasts of his
celibacy, which seems to indicate his having engaged
himself in some of the religious orders of that age.
From what Major says further of him, we may suppose his profession to have been that of a travelling
bard ; though it does not appear that he was skilled
in music, or had any other profession than that just
mentioned. His being blind from his birth, indeed,
makes this not improbable; though, even this cir-

cumstance is not inconsistent with the supposition of
his being a religious mendicant.   " The particulars,
(says Major) which he heard related by the vulgar,
he wrote in the vulgar verse, in which he excelled.
By reciting his histories before princes and great men,
he gained his food and raiment, of which he was
worthy."   It is thus probable that he would be a
frequent visitor at the Scottish court; and would be
made welcome by those great families, who would
boast of any alliance with the hero himself, or took
pleasure in hearing his exploits, or those of his companions.

With regard to the authenticity of his histories,
Major informs us only, that " he does not believe
every thing he finds in such writings ;" but from other
testimonies, it appears, that he consulted the very best
authorities which could at that time he had.   Though,
according to the most early account of Harry, it appears to have been at least 56 years after the death of
Wallace, that Harry was born; yet, he is said to
have consulted with several of the descendants of
those who had been the companions of that hero,
while he achieved his most celebrated exploits, and
who were still capable of ascertaining the veracity of
what he published.   The principal of these were
Wallace of Craigie, and Liddie of that Ilk ; who, he
says, persuaded him to omit in his history, a circumstance which he ought to have inserted.   Besides
these, he consulted with the principal people of the
kingdom ; and he utterly disclaims the idea of having
adhered entirely to any un-written tradition, or having
been promised any reward for what he wrote.

His chief authority, according to his own account, was a Latin history of the exploits of Sir William, written partly by John Blair, and partly by Thomas Gray, who had been the companions of the hero himself. Harry's account of these two authors is to the following purpose. " They became acquainted with Wallace, when the latter was only about six-teen years of age, and at that time a student in the school of Dundee ; and their acquaintance continued till his death, which happened in his 29th year. John Blair went from the schools in Scotland, to Paris, where he studied for some time, and received Priest's orders. He returned to Scotland in 1296, where he joined William Wallace, who was bravely defending the liberties of his country. Thomas Gray, who was a parson of Libberton, joined Wallace, at the same time. They were men of great wisdom and integrity, zealous for the freedom of Scotland, and were present with Wallace, and assistants to him, in most of his military enterprises. They were also his spiritual counsellors, and administered to him godly comfort. The history written by these two clergymen was attested by William Sinclair Bishop of Dunkeld, who had himself been witness to many of Wallace's actions. The Bishop, (if he had lived longer) was to have sent these books to Rome, for the purpose of obtaining the sanction of the Pope's authority."

The book which Harry thus appeals to, as his principal authority, is now lost, so that we have no opportunity of comparing it with what he has written. The character given by Dempster of Harry, however, is more favourable, than that by Major. He tells us

that " he was blind from his birth; a man of singular
and happy genius, he was indeed another Homer. He
did great honour to his native country, and raised it
above what was common to it in his age. He wrote
in the vernacular verse, an elaborate and grand work,
in ten books, of the deeds of William Wallace."   In
this account there is a mistake, for the poem contains
eleven or twelve books ; but Dempster, who wrote in
a foreign country, and had not a printed copy of
Harry's works by him when he wrote his eulogium,
is excusable in a mistake of this kind.

With regard to his poetical merit, it must undoubtedly rank very far below that of Homer; whom
indeed, he scarcely resembles in any other respect
than that he went about as Homer is said to have
done, reciting the exploits of the heroes of his
country, and that he was blind.   In this last circumstance, however, he was still worse off than Homer; for
Harry was born blind, but Homer became blind after
he was advanced in years.   The reader will be able to
judge how far Harry is entitled to a comparison with
Homer, from the poem I refer to. (See the end of this
article.) It is a description of the last mournful interview between Wallace and his wife, which bears
some resemblance to the parting of Hector and
Andromache, in the Iliad of Homer.   Hence, Harry,
even supposing his genius to have been equal to that
of Homer, must have lain under great disadvantages,
and these are very evident in his works.   The descriptive parts are evidently deficient.   However, I
think the following description of a winter-day, from
the Earl of Buchan's version, has some claim to poetic
merit.

" Cold Winter now his hoary aspect shews,
Frost-bound the glebe, whilst Boreas fiercely blows;
Sweeping the snow along the rising hills,
Which every glen and slanting hollow fills:
Cold grew the beams of the far distant sun,
And day was finish'd ere 'twas well begun—
Long, dark, and hateful, was the gloomy night,
Uncomfortable to each banished wight,
Who durst not trust a roof to hide his head,
But sculks from hill to hill with cautious dread."

This passage is followed by another of equal merit.

————————————Valiant Wallace stood,
In shining arms, few were his men, but good;
Not one to seven—now past their power to fly,
Resolved to cut their way, or bravely die :
The hardy chief unsheathed his conquering sword,
Besought the aid of heaven, then gave the word :
Fiercely he met his bold attacking foes,
And quick as light'ning dealt his fatal blows;
With horrid din the tempered edges clash,
On coats of steel whence hasty sparkles flash ;
But massy armour and defensive shield,
Must to the nervous arm of Wallace yield,
Like a swoln current rushing from a hill,
Which does with wreck the lower vallies fill :
Thus, through the martial press he made a lane,
Who durst oppose—no sooner did, than slain :
Forty of which, unfortunately bold,
With gaping wounds upon the earth lay cold ;
Thrice five there fell of Scotsmen, brave and true,
For great the loss, when good men were so few !

The allusions are taken principally from the way in which nature affects those senses, of which he was possessed. Thus speaking of the month of March,

he calls it the month of right digestion, from the
supposed fermentation then begun in the earth. Of
April, he says that the earth is then able, or has obtained the power of producing its different vegetables;
and of this productive power, he appears to have been
more sensible, than of the effects which commonly
strike us most sensibly. " By the working of nature,"
(says he) "the fields are again clothed, and the
woods acquire their worthy weed of green. May
brings along with it great celestial gladness. The
heavenly hues appear upon the tender green." In
another place he describes the deity of some river,
whom he calls, Nymphæus, "building his bower
with oil and balm, filled with sweet odours." By
reason of these disadvantages, he seldom makes use
of similes, with which Homer abounds so much;
and few miraculous interpositions are to be found in
his poems; though, the prophecies of Thomas Ler-
mont, commonly called the Rhymer; and a prophetic
dream of Wallace himself, are introduced, as well as
the ghost of Faudon, a traitor, who had joined Wallace, and whom the latter, in a fit of passion, killed.
The circumstances were these; Wallace, with a few
brave followers, was pursued from St. John's town,
by the English, who had sent out their blood-hounds
to scour the country in quest of the flying patriots.

They at last reached Gaskall, where they determined to stop for the night; after partaking of some
refreshment, their attention is awakened by the sound
of a horn. Wallace sends one of his men to inquire
into the cause of the alarm, but he not returning, he
sends another upon the same errand, his lengthened

absence increases the agitation of Wallace's mind, and he dispatches all his followers successively in search of their fellows.

The same inextinguishable thirst of blood, which Homer ascribes to his hero, Achilles, is ascribed to Wallace; though, in all probability, the mind of Wallace was too much enlightened to admit of such sentiments. A vast degree of courage and personal strength is ascribed to him, by means of which, the exploits of the whole army are in effect transferred to a single person. As long as he is invested with the command, the Scots are victorious and irresistible; when deprived of it, they are enslaved and undone. Among the many lively descriptions which we meet with in this poem, of Wallace's heroism, and *amor patriæ*, the battle of Biggar affords one of the happiest examples of the kind.

After struggling for some time against an inveterate and powerful faction; disdaining to feign submission, he is taken by treachery, and dies a martyr to the freedom of his country. The poem, on the whole, is valuable, on account of our being able to trace, by its means, the progress which the English language had made at that time in Scotland; the manners of the Scots in that age, as the *green* colour of their dress, which at that time, was the taste of the inhabitants of Scotland, &c. With regard to the authenticity of his relations, it is impossible to suppose any other thing, than that they are partly true, and partly false. The general thread of the story, may, undoubtedly be looked upon to be genuine, though embellished with poetical fictions and exaggerations; and

his constant appeals to the book already mentioned,
though it is now lost, must be looked upon as a strong
testimony in his favour: for we cannot suppose that
at the time he lived, when we may say that the
transactions which he relates, were recent, he would
have had the confidence to appeal to a book which
had not been generally known to have an existence—
and its being now lost can never be any argument
against it, when we consider the difficulty there was
of preserving books before the invention of printing;
the confusions in which Scotland was frequently involved, and that the exploits of Wallace, who must
be supposed to have been a kind of rival to the great
Bruce, could not be so agreeable to the court as
those of the more successful hero; and therefore the
history of them might be suffered to fall into oblivion,
though written in elegant Latin, while a most ridiculous poem in that language, on the battle of Ban-
nockburn, has been preserved to this day.

THE PARTING OF WALLACE AND HIS WIFE.

'Twas now the time when all to rest repair,
And weary wretches laid aside each care,
When with fond arms the fair Fidelia prest,
Her panting hero to her snowy breast;
With grief she found the rising tears bedew
His manly face, and heard the sighs he drew:
With frequent sobs, her heaving bosom rose,
And caught the dear infection of his woes.
On her pale cheeks does livid paleness rise,
And sorrow speaks in silence from her eyes!
Then with a groan, thus he, " long I've supprest
The struggling passion in my labouring breast,

But now all sad restraints at last give way—
Fierce sorrow bids me speak, and I obey;
Behold our native country drowned in tears,
Around, one general face of woe appears:
In vain, we're blest with kind indulgent skies,
And suns in vain with genial ardour rise.
In vain, a yellow harvest crowns the plain,
And nodding boughs their golden load sustain.—
The peasant comfortless repining stands,
And sees his harvest reaped by others' hands.
See the fierce soldier rages o'er the land,
The flames wide spreading from the hostile hand;
Those shining spires which lately pierc'd the sky, ⎞
Now equal with the ground in ruins lie— ⎬
Oh! dire and curst effects of slavery! ⎠
Yet, once I nobly durst assert her right,
Bold in her cause, and dauntless in each fight;
But now the useless sword is laid aside,
And my once faithful helm long been untried:
But now the tyrant's power we dare restrain,
And liberty shall rear her head again—
With fell revenge another war prepare;
Bend the long unstrung bow, and launch the rusty spear.
But various cares solicitate my breast,
Invade my heart, and rob my soul of rest;
While to my drooping mind's prophetic eyes,
A thousand griefs in fatal prospect rise;—
Methinks I view the cruel raging foes
End that dear life to finish all my woes.
Methinks I see that sacred blood now spilt,
To fill up Hesilrig's black scene of guilt;
And now to save thee from the coming blow,
And shield thee from the malice of the foe,
I have prepared, of youth a chosen band,
Ready to march where'er thou shalt command.
Some well built tower, a hospitable seat,
Shall prove from war's alarms, a safe retreat;
There, nor the battle's voice shall wound thine ear,

Nor the fierce spoiler, black with guilt appear—
There may thy constant prayers bless my sword,
And waft thy kindest wishes to thy lord;
Till circling time bring back the happy day,
When Scotland shall be free from English sway;
Till her extended plains be called her own,
And yet a Scottish king ascend a Scottish throne."
He said, and ceas'd, nor groan'd, but deep supprest,
Each rising passion, in his manly breast;
But fiercer grief, her tender heart assailed,
She wept, and the frail woman all at once prevail'd.
" And wilt thou then," she said, " and wilt thou go, ⎫
Where thunders call thee, and where battle's glow, ⎬
And leave me here exposed to every foe? ⎭
See Hesilrig with lustful rage appears,
Derides my passion, and insults my fears—
With hasty steps he comes to be possessed,
Or stab his poinard in my hated breast;
In vain, with piteous shrieks I fill the air, ⎫
And stung with sorrow my bare bosom tear, ⎬
When he that should revenge me is not near. ⎭
Hast thou forgotten how his ruthless sword,
In my dear brother's blood has deep been gored?—
Fired with bright glory's charms both met the foe,
And sunk beneath the mighty warrior's blow;
'Tis true that fighting for their country's right,
They glorious died, nor recreant left the fight.
But say, in vain, is all this flow of tears,
Fantastic passion, a weak woman's fears;
No Hesilrig untainted with my kindred's stain,
No friends destroyed, and no brother's slain;
Yet, with her Wallace, let his consort go,
Join with his ills sad partnership of woe!
Or if propitious heaven shall deign to smile,
With faithful love reward my hero's toil.
What though, my tender nerves refuse to bend,
The twanging yew, and the fleet dart to send;
Round thy distinguished tent, yet will I stay,
And wait impatient, the decisive day,

When freedom on thy helm shall crested stand,
Nor fortune linger with her doubtful hand.
But canst thou, thou wilt say, endure alarms,
Hear war's rough voice and the hoarse sound of arms,
When the big drum and sprightly pipe prepare,
In dreadful harmony to speak the war?
Then shall thy breast with trembling heaving rise,
And female sorrow gather in thine eyes:
But let the war's rude shock assault my ears—
The woman, Wallace, shall throw off her fears.
On this weak breast shall love new force impress,
Nor let that doubt repel my happiness.
But whither can I go, or where retreat,
From following vengeance and impending fate?
Even should I go where dreary caves forlorn;
Horrid with night exclude the joyous morn,
And lonely hermits never cease to mourn;
Yet would keen Hesilrig find out the place,
And in my ruin finish all my race;
What tho' the bounding vessel waft me o'er,
To lands remote, and some far distant shore;
What tho' extended tracts of land and sea,
Divide the war, and my dear Lord from me;
The wife of Wallace can't be long concealed,
But soon by babbling fame shall stand revealed;
Then take me with thee whate'er chance betide,
Firm to thy cause, and honest I'll abide:
Nor let me mourn alone, when I am left,
Of thee, and every joy with thee bereft!
She said, and wept, nor yet his sorrows rise,
But awful grief sits decent in his eyes:
"Cease, cease!" he cried, "nor urge a vain relief,
Nor by thy ling'ring doubts increase my grief.
Now if kind heaven shall bless my enterprise,
Nor fate look on me with her envious eyes;
In flowing ease shall end her hated strife,
And joy conduct us to the verge of life;

But if just heaven shall otherwise ordain,
'Tis heav'n that wills it, why should we complain ?"
Thus while the faithful pair their grief exprest,
And sooth'd the passions in each other's breast ;
The beauteous morn disclosed its early ray,
And the grey east shone with the future day.
The hero rose, and with becoming art,
Feigns a false joy, at the same time his heart
Was filled with grief which touched each tender part :
Then to the fields he went with sorrow fraught,
While thousand woes surcharg'd each rising thought ;
With patriot groans he fills the morning air,
And spreading both his hands to heavén, this was his prayer—
Hear me, kind heaven ! if still my feet have trod,
In virtuous paths, nor devious from my God :
Since first with floods of tears and constant prayer,
My weeping parents gave me to thy care :
When round my head the guardian angels flew,
And conscious heaven approved my little vow ;
That if propitious fate increased my span,
And lengthened tender child-hood out to man ;
My country's foes should always feel my might,
Nor my sword sparkle in another's fight;
Thence soon commenced my woes and hateful strife,
With war embroiled my tender years of life—
Oft has the soldier, under my command,
From slavery base redeemed his native land ;
But now oppressed with foes we droop again,
And panting liberty forsakes the reign ;—
Yet, bold in virtue's cause, we nobly dare,
To raise the sleeping embers of the war :
No impious itch of empire fires our mind,
Nor are our hearts to these base thoughts inclined :
But our fierce breasts glow with a holy rage,
Thine are the fields we fight and thine the war we wage :
But if alas ! some unforeseen offence,
Lies latent in the book of providence,

For which the trembling Scots shall shameful fly,
And leave the field to the fierce enemy ;
Then let me die, preventing all my foes,
And close these eyes, nor see my country's woes.

AUTHORITIES.

Encyclopædia Britannica, vol. 18, Edinburgh, 1797—
BLIND HARRY's Life of Wallace, a poem, Perth edition,—
WARTON's History of English Poetry, vol. the 1st—MISS
PORTER's Scottish Chiefs, vol. the 1st.

THE LIFE

OF

FRANCISCUS SALINAS,

A CELEBRATED MUSICIAN OF THE UNIVERSITY OF SALAMANCA.

> "From what blest spring did he derive his art
> To soothe our cares, and thus command the heart?
> He did but think, and music did arise,
> Dilating joy, as light o'erspreads the skies.
> From an immortal source, like that it came;
> But *light* we know—*this* wonder wants a name!
> What art thou? From what causes dost thou spring?
> O music! thou divine mysterious thing!"

Franciscus Salinas, the son of the quæstor or treasurer of Burgos, was born about the year 1513. Although, from the day of his birth, he laboured under the misfortune of an incurable blindness, he was the author of one of the most valuable books on music now extant in any language. He began very early to devote himself to the study of music, and during his youth, nearly the whole of his time was employed in singing and playing on the organ. While he was a boy, a young female, who was about to take the veil, happened to come to the place where he resided. She expressed a desire of learning to play on the organ, and for that purpose became an inmate in his father's house, and was taught music by Salinas, while he, in return, received from her instruction in Latin.

His parents afterwards sent him to Salamanca, where, for some years, he assiduously applied himself to the study of the Greek language ; and also to the study of philosophy, and the arts. The narrowness of his circumstances, however, soon compelled him to leave the university, after which he was taken into the king's palace, where he was patronized by Petrus Sarmentus, Archbishop of Compostella. When the Archbishop was made a Cardinal, Salinas accompanied him to Rome, where he spent thirty years in studying the works of Boetius, and the writings of the ancient Greek harmonicians. He afterwards returned to Spain, hoping to spend the remainder of his days in his native country ; but at the end of three years, he was recalled into Italy, and afterwards invited to Salamanca, as professor of music, on a liberal salary. He was an excellent composer for the organ and other instruments, and was much esteemed by persons of rank, particularly by Pope Paul the Fourth, through whose favour he was created Abbot of St. Pauciato de la Rocca Salegna, in the kingdom of Naples. He died in the month of February, 1590, at the advanced age of seventy-seven years.

He wrote a treatise, "*De Musicâ*," which is divided into seven books. In the *first*, he treats only of the different methods of calculating the ratios of sound. In the eighth and ninth chapters of the *second* book

he contends, against the musicians of his time, that
the diatessaron, or fourth, is a concordant interval;
the diatone and semidiatone he ranks among the consonances. The author then proceeds to explain how
the lesser intervals are produced. In the nineteenth
chapter of the second book, is contained the description of an instrument, invented by Salinas, for de-
monstrating the ratios of the consonances, and also of
the lesser intervals. In the *third* book, he treats of
the genera of the ancients, with so much learning and
sagacity, that Dr. Pepusch has declared that the true
enharmonic, which for many ages had been supposed
lost, was in this work accurately determined. Salinas, in another part of his work, shews the method
of constructing what he calls, "the type of the diato-
nic." He next treats of the temperament of the organ
and other instruments, and makes some interesting
observations on the powers of the human voice; he
then speaks of the lute and the viol, and of the tem-
peraments best adapted to each. In the tenth chapter of the *fourth* book there is a diagram, representing,
in a collateral view, the tetrachords of the ancients
conjoined with the hexachords of Guido, shewing how
the latter spring out of the former; the ancient division of the genera into the species is afterwards noticed. In a subsequent chapter, he exposes the errors
of Aristoxenus, in a manner very different both from
Ptolemy and Boetius. The last subject treated of by
him, is, the Rhythmus of the ancients; and he enters into a copious dissertation on the various kinds of
metre used by the Greek, the Roman, and the Spanish poets.

Of this work it may be sufficient to say, that a greater degree of credit is due to it, than to almost any other production of modern writers, of the same kind. The author was a practical, as well as a theoretical, musician; and, throughout the whole of his book, he manifests a disposition, the farthest removed that can possibly be imagined, from that credulity which betrayed Glareanus and others into error. This disposition led him to enquire accurately and minutely into the doctrines of the Greek writers; and, from the confidence with which he sometimes blames them, we are led into the persuasion that the truth was on his side.

AUTHORITIES:

SIR JOHN HAWKINS's History of Music, vol. 4.—DR. BURNEY's History of Music, vol. 3.—Musical Biography.

CASPAR CRUMBHORN,

———————

" Music hath charms to soothe the savage breast,
Rend the rough rocks, and bend the knotted oak."

———————

If we look back to former periods, we shall find
illustrious and abundant proofs, how amply nature
has capacitated the blind to excel, both in the scientific and practical departments of music.   In the sixteenth century, when the progress in musical science
was rapid and conspicuous in almost every country in
Europe, flourished CASPAR CRUMBHORN, who was
blind from the third year of his age ; yet he composed
several pieces of music in parts, with so much success,
and performed, both upon the flute and violin, so
exquisitely, that he was distinguished by the favour
of Augustus, elector of Saxony.   But, preferring his
native Silesia to every other country, he returned
thither, and was appointed organist of the church of
St. Peter and St. Paul, in the city of Lignitz, and
likewise had the chief direction of the Musical College, in that place.   He died there on the 11th of
June, 1621.

The writer of the article "Blind" in the Encyclopædia Britannica, speaking of this musician, and of
the blind in general, makes the following remark ;
which, though it may be considered somewhat severe,
is not altogether out of place.

"To these individuals might be added Martini Pesenti, of Venice, a composer of vocal and instrumental music, of almost all kinds, though blind from his nativity; with other examples equally worthy of public attention. But if vulgar prejudice is capable of blushing at its own contemptible character, or of yielding to conviction, those already quoted are more than sufficient to show the musical jugglers of our times, who are generally as absolute strangers to learning and taste, as to virtue, that their art is no monopoly, with which those who see are alone invested, by the irreversible decree of Heaven."

AUTHORITIES.

SIR JOHN HAWKINS's History of Music, vol. 4—DR. BURNEY's History of Music, vol. 3.

JOHN GONELLI,

THE BLIND SCULPTOR.

"From theme to theme my wandering muse retire,
And the dumb shew of breathing rocks admire!
Where the smooth chisel all its force has shewn,
And softened into flesh the rugged stone."

The following anecdote respecting JOHN GONELLI, surnamed the Blind of Cambassi, from the place of his birth in Tuscany, is taken from the article Blind, in the Edinburgh Encyclopædia. "He was a scholar of Pietro Iacca, and discovered genius, but lost his sight at the age of twenty. The statue of Cosmo, 1st grand Duke of Tuscany, was performed by him after he became blind, and he had equal success in various other works of the same nature.

He died at Rome under the Pontificate of Urban the VIII. We read also of a celebrated blind sculptor, who took the likeness of the Duke of Bracciano, in a dark cellar, by means of moulding the face with wax; and made a marble statue of King Charles the 1st of England, with great elegance and justness."

AUTHORITY.

Edinburgh Encyclopædia.

THE LIFE

OF

TURLAGH CAROLAN,

THE CELEBRATED

IRISH POET AND MUSICIAN.

" Then happy bard ! awake thy fire—
Awake the heart-string of thy lyre:—
Invoke thy muse. Thy muse appears;
But robed in sorrow, bathed in tears.
No blithesome tale, alas ! she tells ;—
No glories of the ' hall of shells : '
No joy she whispers to the lays—
No note of love, no note of praise."

CAROLAN was one of the last, and most celebrated
of the Irish Bards, whose compositions have been as
much admired for their extraordinary variety, as for
their exquisite melody ; he is said to have composed
upwards of four hundred pieces. This account, however, is perhaps exaggerated, but be this as it may, the
Irish national music has been greatly enriched by his
productions : but it was not only in the composition
of music that he distinguished himself; his poetry is
also fine, for he wrote according to nature, and to use
the language of an ingenious author, " His composi-

tions are like the dreams of joys that are past, pleasant and mournful to the soul." I am sorry to say
that we know but little of the history of this extraordinary genius. It appears that he spent his life as an
itinerant musician, and was made welcome at the
houses of the great; and there, with the tales of other
days, enlivened the convivial hours. It reflects no
great credit on the times in which Carolan lived, that
he was suffered to live in poverty, and die in obscurity; but it has too frequently been the lot of great
geniuses to meet with neglect while living, and when
dead to be lamented, and admired; as if mankind
knew not their value until they were gone, and posterity were willing to compensate for the injuries
they had experienced through life, by erecting to their
memories splendid monuments. A trifle bestowed on
them while living, and starving in an empty garret,
would have rendered them more essential service than
all the sums lavished on the decorations of Westminster
Abbey, to which they are insensible.

This celebrated poet and musician, was born in
the year 1670, in the village of Nobber, in the county
of Westmeath, on the lands of Carolan's town, which
were wrested from his ancestors by the family of the
Nugents, on their arrival in that kingdom. His father
was a poor farmer, the humble proprietor of a few
acres, which yielded him a scanty subsistence. Of his
mother, nothing is known. The cabin, in which our
bard was born, is still pointed out to the inquisitive
traveller. As it is in a ruinous state, it must soon
become a prey to all-devouring time; yet the spot on
which it stands may perhaps be visited at a future

day, with as much true devotion, by the lovers of
national music, as are Stratford and Binfield, by the
admirers of Shakespeare and Pope.

The small-pox deprived him of his sight, at so early
a period of his life, that he retained no recollection of
colours. Thus was " knowledge at one entrance quite
shut out," before he had taken even a cursory view of
nature. From this misfortune he felt no uneasiness;
" my eyes," he used to say, " are transplanted to my
ears." His musical talents were soon discovered, and
his friends determined to cultivate them. About the
age of twelve, a proper master was engaged to instruct
him in the practice of the harp; but though fond of
that instrument, he never struck it with a master's
hand. Genius and diligence are seldom united, and
it is practice alone which can perfect us in any art.
Yet his harp was rarely unstrung, but in general he
used it only to assist himself in composition; his fingers wandered through the strings in quest of melody.
When young Carolan became enamoured of Miss
Bridget Cruise, of Cruisetown, in the county of Longford, his harp now, like the lute of Anacreon, would
only sound of love. Though this lady did not give
him her hand, yet it is supposed she did not deny
him her heart, or perhaps, as a brother poet says:—

" Like Phœbus thus acquiring unsought praise,
" He snatched at love, and filled his arms with bays."

The song which bears her name is considered his
master-piece, it came warm from his heart while his
genius was in full vigour. A very extraordinary instance of the effects of Carolan's passion for this lady

is related by Mr. O'Connor.   He went once on a pilgrimage to St. Patrick's Purgatory, a cave in an island
in Loughderg, in the county of Donegall.   On his
return to shore, he met several pilgrims waiting the
arrival of the boat that conveyed him.   In assisting
some of these devout travellers to get on board, he
chanced to take a lady's hand, and instantly exclaimed,
" by the head of my gossip, this is the hand of Bridget
Cruise."   His sense of feeling had not deceived him.
It was the hand of her whom he had once adored.   " I
had this anecdote from his own mouth," says the person by whom it is recorded, " and in terms which
gave me a strong impression of the emotions which
he felt on meeting the object of his early affections.
Carolan at this time was about the middle of his
earthly career."

Our bard solaced himself for the loss of Miss Cruise
in the arms of Mary Maguire, a young lady of good
family in the county of Fermanagh.   Miss Maguire
proved a proud and extravagant dame; but she was
the wife of his choice; he loved her tenderly, and
lived harmoniously with her.   It is probable that on
his marriage, he fixed his residence on a small farm
near Moss-hill, in the county of Leitrim.   Here he
built a neat little house, where he gave every friend a
kind and hearty welcome.   Hospitality consumed the
produce of his little farm; he ate, drank, and was
merry, and improvidently left to-morrow to provide
for itself.   This sometimes occasioned embarrassments
in his domestic affairs, but he had no friend to remind
him, that nothing can supply the want of prudence,
and that negligence and irregularity, long continued,

will make knowledge and wit ridiculous, and genius contemptible.

At what period of his life Carolan became an itinerant musician, is not known, nor is it consistently told whether he was urged to this change in his manner of living by want, or induced by his fondness for music. By some of his biographers it has been imputed to an early disappointment in love: however this may be, he continued during the remainder of his life, to travel through the country in this character, mounted on a good horse, attended by a domestic on another, who carried his harp. Wherever he went, the gates of the nobility and gentry were thrown open to him; he was received with respect, and a distinguished place assigned him at the table.

On his return from one of those excursions, he was asked by one of his friends whether he had visited Colonel Archdall? "No," replied the bard emphatically, "but I visited a prince;" thus intimating the hospitable reception this gentleman had given him. But he had not more reason to extol the hospitality of Colonel Archdall, than that of Mr. Jones of Moneyglass, in the county of Antrim; nor was he deficient in gratitude for the civilities he received during his stay in that mansion: he has enshrined his hospitable character in one of his best Planxties. Of this, the air alone is now to be had; the words are forgotten since the well known English version, written by Arthur Dawson, Esq., admirably adapted to the original air of Carolan. It is in every body's hand, and therefore needless to be quoted here.

It was during his peregrinations that Carolan composed all those airs, which are still the delight of his countrymen. He thought the tribute of a song due to every house in which he was entertained, and he never failed to pay it, choosing for his subject either the head of the family, or one of the loveliest of its branches.

The subject of one of his favourite and most admired compositions, was a sister of a Mr. Nugent. She lived with one of her sisters, near Bellangar, in the county of Roscommon, at the time she inspired the bard, and he endeavoured to do justice to her merits, in the song now well known by the name of Gracey Nugent. As it may gratify some of my readers, I shall here insert a translation.

Song.—GRACEY NUGENT.

With delight I will sing of the maid,
  Who, in beauty and wit doth excel;
My Gracey the fairest shall lead,
  And from beauties shall bear off the bell.

Beside her, by day and by night,
  No care and no sorrow I'll know;
But I'll think on her form with delight,
  And her ringlets that beauteously flow.

Her neck to the swan's I'll compare,
  Her face to the brightness of day;
And is he not blest who shall share
  In the beauties her bosom display.

'Tis thus the fair maid I commend,
  Whose words are than music more sweet;

No bliss can on woman attend,
  But with thee dearest Gracey we meet.

Your beauties should still be my song,
  But my glass I devote now to thee ;
May the health that I wish thee, be long,
  And if sick, be it love-sick for me.

The following incident gave birth to the piece called
Carolan's Devotion. A Miss Fetherston, of the county
of Longford, on her way to church, in Granard, one
Sunday accidentally met with the bard, when the following conversation, as related by a friend of both
parties, took place :—

MISS FETHERSTON.—Your servant, Mr. Carolan.

CAROLAN.—I thank you. Who speaks to me ?

MISS F.—It is I, sir, one Miss Fetherston.

CAR.—I have heard of you, madam : a young lady
of great beauty and much wit. The loss of one sense
prevents me from beholding your beauty, and I believe
it is a happy circumstance for me, as it has made
many captives. But your wit, madam, I dread it.

MISS F.—Had I wit, Mr. Carolan, this is not a
day for displaying any ; it should give place to the
duty of prayer. I apprehend that in complying with
this duty, you go one way and I go another. I wish
I could prevail on you to quit your way for mine.

CAR.—Should I go your way, madam, I dread you
yourself would be the chief object of my devotion.

MISS F.—And what if I should go your way,
Carolan ?

CAR.—I have already declared the sense of my danger in being near you. I well know that the power

which some men have of making female converts to their religion, can have no effect in regard to you, madam. Your own inherent powers would conquer every thing. In a church, or in a mass-house, you would draw all the devotion to yourself; and so madam, in my own defence I must now take my flight.

Miss F.—Hold, Carolan, we must not part so abruptly; as I have been long charmed with your compositions in music, I could wish to see you in our house, and that your visit would be as speedy as possible.

Car.—Could you, madam, suspend the music of your wit, I should obey your commands cheerfully.

Miss F.—Away with your mockery of wit and danger. In listening to your notes, the danger will be on my side. Come speedily, however.

Car.—To please you, madam, is the utmost I can expect; and on the terms I proposed, I will wait on you.

Miss F.—You will assuredly be welcome; but pray for me where you are going.

Car.—Could I withdraw my devotion from your-self, I would obey; but I will make the best effort I can. Adieu.

The event justified his fears; instead of praying for Miss Fetherston, he neglected his religious duties to compose a song on her. In it he complains with more gallantry, than piety, that the mass is no longer his devotion, but that now his devotion is she. The air of this song is reckoned among one of the best of his musical compositions.

It is remarkable that in his gayest mood, and even

when his genius was the most inspired, he never could compose a Planxty for a Miss Brett, in the county of Sligo, whose father's house he frequented, and where he always met with a reception due to his taste and endowments. One day, after an unsuccessful attempt to compose something in a sprightly strain for this lady, he threw aside his harp in a mixture of rage and grief, and addressing himself in Irish to her mother : "madam," said he, " I have often, from my great respect to your family, attempted a Planxty in order to celebrate your daughter's perfections, but to no purpose. Some evil genius hovers over me. There is not a string in my harp that does not vibrate a melancholy sound, when I set about this task. I fear she is not doomed to remain long amongst us ; " may be," added he, emphatically, " she will not survive twelve months." The event verified his melancholy prediction. The truth of this anecdote has been attested by several of the family.

From a neglect in his education, Carolan at an early period of life, contracted a fondness for spirituous liquors, which in after life he relinquished; but inordinate gratifications carry their punishment with them, nor was Carolan exempt from this general imposition : his physicians assured him that unless he corrected this habit, a scurvy, which was the consequence of his intemperance, would soon put an end to his mortal career. He obeyed, though with reluctance, and seriously resolved upon never again tasting the forbidden cup.

The fame of Carolan as a musician having reached the ears of an eminent Italian music master, in Dublin, he put his abilities to a severe test, the result of which convinced him how well founded had been the report of his musical talents. The method he made use of was as follows:—He singled out an elegant piece of music in the Italian stile; but here, and there, he either altered or mutilated the piece, in in such a manner, however, that no one but a real judge could detect the alterations.

Carolan bestowed the deepest attention on the performer while he was playing it, not knowing it was intended as a trial of his skill; and that the critical moment was now at hand, which was to determine his reputation for ever. He declared it to be an excellent piece of music; but, to the astonishmant of all present, said very humourously in his own language, " here and there, it limps and stumbles."

He was requested to rectify the errors, which he accordingly did. In this state the piece was sent from Connaught to Dublin, and the Italian no sooner saw the amendment, than he pronounced Carolan to be a true musical genius.

Another anecdote of the kind is also recorded of him. In the beginning of the 18th century, Lord Mayo brought from Dublin a celebrated Italian performer, to spend some time with him at his seat in the country. Carolan, who at that time was on a visit at his Lordship's, found himself greatly neglected, and complained of it one day in the presence of the foreigner. " When you play in as masterly a manner as he does," replied his Lordship, " you shall not be overlooked." Carolan wagered with the musician, who is said to have been the famous Geminiani, that though he was a total stranger to Italian music; yet, he would follow him in any piece he played, and that he himself would play a voluntary, in which the Italian could not follow him. The proposal was acceded to, and Carolan was victorious.

But Carolan's muse was not always employed in extolling the great, in praising beauty, or in heightening the mirth of a convivial hour; it was sometimes devoted to the services of his God. He has frequently assisted with his voice and his harp, at the elevation of the host; and has composed several pieces of church music, which are deemed excellent. " On Easter day," says a person who resided all his life in that part of the country, "I heard him play a piece of his sacred music at mass;" he called it " Gloria in Excelsis," and he sung that hymn in Irish. While he played at the Lord's prayer he stopped, and after the priest ended it he sung again, and played a piece which he denominated the "Resurrection."

The enthusiasm of his devotion affected the whole congregation. This enthusiasm was very much increased by an idea he had conceived, that he was inspired during the composition of these devotional pieces.

The period was now approaching when Carolan's feelings were to receive a violent shock. In the year 1733, the wife of his bosom was torn from him by the hand of death. This melancholy event threw a gloom over his mind, that was never after entirely dissipated. As soon as the transports of his grief had a little subsided, he composed a Monody to her memory, now known by the name of Mary Maguire, of which I subjoin a translation.

MONODY

ON THE DEATH OF MARY MAGUIRE.

Were mine the choice of intellectual fame,
    Of skilful song and eloquence divine,
Painting's sweet power, philosophy's pure flame,
    And Homer's lyre, and Ossian's harp were mine,
The splendid arts of Erin, Greece and Rome,
    In Mary lost would lose their wonted grace—
All would I give to snatch her from the tomb,
    Again to fold her in my fond embrace.

Desponding, sick, exhausted with my grief,
    Awhile the founts of sorrow cease to flow—
In vain I rest, and sleep brings no relief—
    Cheerless, companionless, I wake to woe!
Nor birth nor beauty shall again allure,
    Nor fortune win me to another bride;
Alone I'll wander, and alone endure,
    Till death restore me to my dear one's side.

Once every thought and every scene was gay,
    Friends, mirth, and music, all my soul employ'd;
Now doomed to mourn my last sad years away;
    My life a solitude, my heart a void—
Alas, the change! to change again no more,
    For every comfort is with Mary fled,
And ceaseless anguish shall her loss deplore,
    Till age and sorrow join me with the dead.

Adieu! each gift of Nature and of Art,
    That erst adorned me in life's earliest prime,
The cloudless temper and the social heart—
    The soul ethereal, and the flight sublime;
Thy loss, my Mary chased them from my breast!
    Thy sweetness cheers, thy judgment aids no more;
The Muse deserts a heart with grief opprest—
    And lost is every joy that charmed before.

Carolan did not long continue in this vale of sorrow after the death of his beloved wife. While on a visit at the house of Mrs. Mc Dermott, of Alderford in the County of Roscommon, he died in March 1738, in the 68th year of his age. He was interred in the parish church of Kilronan, in the diocese of Ardagh; but no memorial exists of the spot in which he was laid. His grave was, and perhaps is, still known to a few of his admirers, and some of the neighbouring peasants; and his skull was long distinguished from those of others, which were promiscuously scattered through the church-yard, by a perforation in the forehead, through which a small piece of ribbon is drawn.

He had seven children by his wife—six daughters and one son. His son, who had studied music, went to London, where he taught the Irish harp; before his departure, he published in the year 1747, a collection of his father's music, omitting, through mercenary motives, some of his best pieces. It was republished in Dublin, by John Lee, in 1780.

It is much to be wished that a complete collection of the musical compositions of this interesting character, had been given to the public. Many, it is to be feared, are now irrecoverably lost. Many others are in danger of experiencing the same fate, unless preserved by the *National Spirit.* To this wish might also be added another, of having a more complete and authentic history of his life, than can at present be collected from the imperfect and sometimes contradictory accounts, that have been handed down,

mostly by oral tradition. I shall here subjoin a character of the bard, from the pen of Mr. O'Connor.

" Very few have I known who had a more vigorous
mind, but a mind undisciplined, through the defect,
or rather the absence of cultivation. Absolutely the
child of nature, he was governed by the indulgencies,
and at times, by the caprices of that mother. His
imagination, ever on the wing, was eccentric in its
Poetic flight ; yet, as far as that faculty can be employed in the harmonic art, it was steady and collected
In the variety of his musical numbers, he knew how
to make a selection, and was seldom content with me-
diocrity—so happy, so elevated was he in some of
his compositions, that be excited the wonder, and
obtained the approbation of a great master who never
saw him; I mean Geminiani.

" He outstripped his predecessors in the three species of composition used among the Irish ; but he
never omitted giving due praise to several of his
countrymen, who before excelled him in his art. The
Italian compositions he preferred to all others ; Vi-
valdi charmed him ; and with Corelli he was enraptured. He spoke elegantly in his maternal language ;
but advanced in years before he learned English, he
delivered himself but indifferently in that language,
and yet he did not like to be corrected in his sole-
cisms.

" Constitutionally pious, he never omitted daily
prayer, and fondly imagined himself inspired, when
he composed some pieces of church music. This idea
contributed to his devotion and thanksgiving; and,
in this respect, his enthusiasm was harmless, and

perhaps useful. Gay by nature, and cheerful from habit, he was a pleasing member of society; and his habits, and his morality, procured him esteem and friends every where."

Carolan seems to have been born to render the termination of his Order memorable and brilliant. If we reflect on the disadvantages under which he laboured; born blind, with slender opportunities of acquiring ideas; the inhabitant of a country desolated by a civil war; the flames of which had scarcely subsided, and add to this, his own propensity to idleness, we cannot but be astonished at the prodigious powers of his mind. He has occasionally tried almost every style in music;—the elegiac, the festive, the amorous, and sacred; and has so much excelled in each, that we scarcely know to which of them his genius is best adapted. His first composition was amorous and plaintive—called, "Bridget Cruise,' addressed to a lady, to whom he was tenderly attached without the hope of success. He is said to have dedicated fifteen pieces to her—the first was originally imperfect, or the copy procured of it so corrupt, that a Bass could not be adapted to it.

His last tune was inscribed to his physician, Dr. Stafford. He composed the Fairy Queen, Rose Dillon, and other of his serious pieces, early in life; but after having established a reputation, and addicted himself too much to festive company, he dedicated his time to the composition of his Planxties, which required no labour or assiduity. We may form some idea of the fertility of his genius, from this circumstance, that one harper who attended the Belfast meeting, and who had never seen him, or was taught directly by any person who had an opportunity of copying from him, had acquired upwards of an hundred of his tunes, which he said constituted but a very inconsiderable part of the real number.

As Carolan never taught any itinerant pupils, except his own son, (who had no musical genius) and as we have never heard that any of his pieces were committed to writing, until several years after his death, when young Carolan, under the patronage of Dr. Delany, edited a small volume, we need not wonder if nine tenths of the whole be irreparably lost.

In Carolan's Concerto, and in his Madame Cole, the practitioner will perceive evident imitations of Corelli, in which the exuberant fancy of that admired composer, is happily copied. As an additional proof of his poetic talents, I give the following song, translated by Miss Brooke.

SONG—MABLE KELLY.
(BY CAROLAN.)

To thee harmonious powers belong,
That add to verse the charms of song ;
Soft melody with numbers join,
And make the poet half divine.

As when the softly blushing rose,
Close by some neighbouring lily grows ;
Such is the glow thy cheeks diffuse,
And such their bright and blended hues !

The timid lustre of thine eye,
With nature's purest tints can vie;

With the sweet blue-bell's azure gem,
That droops upon its modest stem !

The poets of Ierni's plains,
To thee devote their choicest strains ;
And oft their harps for thee are strung,
And oft thy matchless charms are sung.

Since the famed Fair of antient days,
Whom bards and worlds conspired to praise ;
Not one like thee has since appeared,
Like thee, to every heart endeared.

How blest the bard, O lovely maid !
To find thee in thy charms arrayed !—
Thy pearly teeth, thy flowing hair,
Thy neck, beyond the cygnet, fair.

Even he whose hapless eyes no ray
Admit from beauty's cheering day;
Yet, though he cannot see the light,
He feels it warm, and knows it bright.

In beauty, talents, taste refined,
And all the graces of the mind,
In all, unmatched thy charms remain,
Nor meet a rival on the plain.

Carolan, says " Mr. Ritson, seems from the description we have of him, to be a genuine representative of the antient bards."

Miss Brooke, in speaking of his descriptive poetry,
makes the following remark : " It is generally believed that Carolan, (as his biographer tells us) remembered no impression of colours ; but I cannot
acquiesce in this opinion ; I think it must have been
formed without sufficient grounds, for how was it possible that his description could be thus glowing, with-

out the clearest recollection, and the most animated ideas of every beauty that sight can convey to the mind.

> " Even he, whose hapless eyes no ray
> Admit from beauty's cheering day ;
> Yet, though he cannot see the light,
> He feels it warm, and knows it bright."

Every reader of taste or feeling, she proceeds to observe, must surely be struck with the beauty of this passage. Can any thing be more elegant, or more pathetic, than the manner in which Carolan alludes to his want of sight ! but indeed, his little pieces abound in all the riches of natural genius.

I have, in another part of this essay, given Mr. Walker's translation of the beautiful song of Gracey Nugent. I shall here, for the amusement of my readers, subjoin a literal translation of the same, by the ingenious Miss Brooke, to whom the Irish nation is much indebted, for her elegant translations of original Irish poetry.

GRACEY NUGENT.
A LITERAL TRANSLATION BY MISS BROOKE.

" I will sing with rapture of the blossom of whiteness, Gracey, the young and beautiful woman, who bore away the palm of excellence in sweet manners and accomplishments, from all the fair ones of the provinces.

Whoever enjoys her constant society, no apprehension of any ill can assail him. The queen of soft and winning mind, and manners, with her fair branching tresses flowing in ringlets.

Her side like alabaster, and her neck like the swan, and her countenance like the sun in summer ; how blest is it for him, who is promised, as riches, to be united to her, the branch of fair curling tendrils.

Sweet and pleasant is your lovely conversation; bright and sparkling your blue eyes! and every day do I hear all tongues declare your praises, and how gracefully your bright tresses wave down your neck.

I say to the maid of youthful mildness, that her voice and her converse are sweeter than the songs of birds! there is no delight or charm that imagination can conceive, but what is ever attendant on Gracey.

Her teeth arranged in beautiful order, and her locks flowing in soft waving curls! but though it delights me to sing of thy charms, I must quit my theme; with a sincere heart I fill to thy health."

Though Carolan died universally lamented, he would have died unsung, had not the humble muse of M'Cabe poured a few elegiac strains over his cold remains. This faithful friend composed the following short elegy on his death, which is evidently the effusion of unfeigned grief, unadorned with meretricious ornaments; it is the picture of a mind torn with anguish; with which I shall conclude his memoirs.

ELEGY ON THE DEATH OF CAROLAN.

I came with friendship's face to glad my heart,
But sad and sorrowful my steps depart;
In my friend's stead, a spot of earth is shown,
And on his grave my woe-struck eyes are thrown !
No more to their distracted sight remained,
But the cold clay that all they loved contained ;—
And there his last and narrow bed was made,
And the drear tomb-stone for its covering laid.
Alas! for this my aged heart is wrung,
Grief choaks my voice, and trembles on my tongue ;
Lonely and desolate I mourn the dead,
The friend with whom my every comfort fled !
There is no anguish can with this compare ;
No pains, diseases, suffering, or despair

Like that I feel, while such a loss I mourn,
My heart's companion from its fondness torn!
Oh! insupportable, distracting grief,
Woe that through life, can never hope relief.
Sweet singing harp, thy melody is o'er.
Sweet friendship's voice, I hear thy sound no more;
My bliss—my wealth of poetry is fled,
And every joy, with him I loved is dead :—
Alas! what wonder, (while my heart drops blood
Upon the woes that drain its vital flood)—
If maddening grief no longer can be borne,
And frenzy fill the breast with anguish torn.

AUTHORITIES.

WALKER'S Historical Memoirs of the Irish bards. vol. 2.—
MISS BROOKE's Relics of Irish Poetry, Dublin edition, 1802,
4to—Introduction to Bunting's Irish Music, Belfast 1807—
Belfast Magazine, vol. 3.

SOME PARTICULARS of the LAST YEARS

OF THE

LIFE OF HANDEL.

" While in more lengthen'd notes and slow,
"The deep, majestic, solemn organs blow."

In the beginning of the year 1751, Handel was alarmed by an affection in his eyes, which, upon consulting the surgeon, he was told was a cataract. From that moment, his usual flow of spirits forsook him, and scarcely left him patience during that crisis of his disorder in which he might hope for relief. He had been prepared to expect a total privation of sight, but was led to entertain hopes that it might only prove temporary, and that, by an operation, it might be restored; when, therefore, a total loss of sight had taken place, he submitted to an operation, which was performed by Mr. Samuel Sharp, of Guy's Hospital. The repeated attempts that were made to relieve him, were, however, fruitless; and he was at length told, that for the remainder of his days, a relief from pain in his visual organs, was all that could be hoped for. In this forlorn and dejected state, reflecting on his inability any longer to conduct his own oratorios, he called to his aid Mr. Smith, the son of his faithful copyist and friend, and, with his assistance, they continued to be performed, until the Lent season in

which he died. They were got up, with no other
omission in his own performance, than the accom-
paniment on the harpsichord ; the rich flow of his
fancy ever supplying him with subjects for extempore
voluntaries on the organ, and his hand still retaining
the power of executing whatever his invention suggested. It was a most affecting spectacle, to see the
venerable musician, whose genius had so long charmed
the ear of a discerning audience, led to the front of
the stage, in order to make an obeisance of acknow-
ledgment to the enraptured multitude. When Smith
played the organ, during the first year of Handel's
blindness, the oratorio of " Sampson" was performed,
and Beard sang, with great feeling—

> " Total eclipse ! No sun, no moon;
> All dark amidst the blaze of noon!"

The recollection that Handel had set these words to
music, with the view of the blind composer, then
sitting by the organ, affected the audience so forcibly,
that many persons present were moved even to tears.

The loss of his sight, and the prospect of his approaching dissolution, made a great change in the
temper and general behaviour of Handel. He was a
man of blameless morals, and, throughout his whole
life had manifested a deep sense of the importance of
religion ; in conversation, he would frequently speak
of the pleasure that he had experienced in setting the
words of the Sacred Scriptures to music, and how
much some of the sublime passages in the Psalms had
contributed to his comfort and satisfaction : but now,
when he found himself drawing near the close of his

mortal state, these sentiments were improved into solid and rational piety, accompanied by a calm and undisturbed mind. Towards the beginning of the year 1758, he found himself fast declining; and the general debility which had seized him, was rendered still more alarming by an almost total loss of appetite. When the latter symptom appeared, he considered his recovery as entirely hopeless; and, resigning himself into the hands of his Creator, he expired on the 14th of April, 1759, in the 76th year of his age.

AUTHORITY.
Musical Biography, vol. 2.

THE LIFE

OF

DENIS HAMPSON,

THE BLIND BARD OF MAGILLIGAN.

"The rolls of fame I will not now explore,
 Nor need I here describe in learned lay,
How forth the minstrel fared in days of yore,
 Right glad of heart, though homely in array,
 His waving beard and locks all hoary grey ;
While from his bending shoulders decent hung
 His harp, the sole companion of his way ;
 Which to the whistling wind responsive rung
And ever, as he went, some merry lay he sung."

THE following account of the blind bard of Magilligan was taken from his own lips, July 3, 1805, by the Rev. Mr. Sampson, at the request of Miss Owenson, now Lady Morgan.

" Denis Hampson, or the man with two heads, is a native of Derry ; his father, Bryan Darrogher Hampson, held the whole town-land of Tyrcrevan, and his mother's relations were in possession of the Wood-town, (both considerable farms in Magilligan.) He lost his sight at the age of three years, by the small-pox ; at twelve he began to learn the harp, under Bridget O'Cahan, ' for,' as he said, ' in those old times, women as well as men were taught the

Irish harp, in the best families, and every old Irish family had harps in plenty.' His next teacher was John C. Garragher, a blind travelling harper, whom he followed to Buncranagh, where his master used to play to Colonel Vaughan; he had afterwards Laughlin Hanning and Pat Connor in succession, as masters. All these were from Connaught, which was, as he added, 'the best part of the kingdom for music and harpers.'

"At eighteen years of age he began to play for himself, and was taken into the house of Counsellor Canning, at Garvagh, for half a year; his host, with Squire Gage and Doctor Bacon, bought, and presented him with, a harp. He travelled nine or ten years through Ireland and Scotland, and tells some facetious stories of gentlemen in both countries; among others, that, in passing near to the residence of Sir J. Campbell, at Aghanbrack, he learned that this gentleman had spent a great deal, and was living on an allowance of so much per week. Hampson, through delicacy, would not call, but some of the domestics were sent after him; on coming into the castle, Sir James asked him why he had not called, adding, 'sir, there never was a harper but yourself that passed the door of my father's house;' to which Hampson answered, that he had heard in the neighbourhood that his honour was not often at home, with which delicate evasion Sir James was satisfied. He added, that this was the highest-bred and stateliest man he ever knew; if he were putting on a new pair of gloves, and one of them dropped on the floor, (though ever so clean,) he would order his servant to bring him ano-

ther pair. He says that, in that time he never met
but one laird that had a harp, and that was a very
small one, played on formerly by the laird's father,
and that when he tuned it with new strings, the laird
and his lady were both so pleased with his music, that
they invited him back in these words ; ' Hampson, as
soon as you think this child of ours (a boy of three
years of age,) is fit to learn on his grandfather's harp,
come back to teach him, and you shall not repent it;'
but this, however, he never accomplished.

"He told me a story of the laird of Stone, with a
great deal of comic relish. When he was playing at
the house, a message came that a large party of gentlemen were coming to grouse, and would spend some
days with the laird ; the lady, being in great distress,
turned to her husband, saying, ' what shall we do,
my dear, for so many, in the way of beds?' ' Give
yourself no vexation,' replied the laird; ' give us
enough to eat, and I will supply the rest, and as to
beds, believe me, every man shall find one for himself,'
meaning that his guests would fall under the table.

In this second trip to Scotland, in the year 1745,
being at Edinburgh, when Charles the Pretender was
there, he was called into the great hall to play ; at first
he was alone, but afterwards four other fiddlers joined.
The tune called for was, ' The king shall enjoy his
own again.' He sung here part of the words following;

> ' I hope to see the day
> When the Whigs shall run away,
> And the king shall enjoy his own again.'

"I asked him if he heard the Pretender speak; he
replied, 'I only heard him ask, 'Is Sylvan there?'

on which some one answered, 'he is not here, please your Royal Highness, but he shall be sent for.' He meant to say Sullivan, continued Hampson, 'but that was the way he called the name.' Hampson, who was then above fifty years old, was brought into the Pretender's presence by Colonel Kelly, of Roscommon, and Sir Thomas Sheridan. He says that Capt. M'Donnel, when in Ireland, came to see him, and that he told the Captain, that Charley's cockade was in his father's house.

"He played in many Irish houses; among others, those of Lord De Courcy, Mr. Fortescue, Sir P. Bellew, and Squire Roche; also in the great towns of Dublin, Cork, &c. respecting all which he interspersed pleasant anecdotes, with surprising gaiety and correctness. As to correctness, he mentioned many anecdotes of my grand-father and grand-aunt, at whose houses he used to be frequently; in fact, in this identical harper, whom you sent me to survey, I recognized an acquaintance, who, as soon as he found me out, seemed exhilarated at having an old friend of what he called, 'the old stock,' in his poor cabin. He even mentioned many anecdotes of my own boyhood, which, though by me long forgotten, were accurately true; these things shew his surprising power of recollection, at the age of a hundred and eight years. Since I saw him last, which was in 1787, the wen on the back of his head is greatly increased; it is now hanging over his neck and shoulders, nearly as large as his head, from which circumstance he derives his appellative, 'the man with two heads.' General Hart, who is an admirer of music, sent a limner lately to take a drawing of him, which cannot fail to be interesting, if it were only for the venerable expression of his meagre, blind countenance, and the symmetry of his tall, thin, but not debilitated, person. I found him lying on his back in bed, near the fire of his cabin; his family being employed in the usual way. His harp was under the bed-clothes, by which his face was covered also. When he heard my name, he started up, (being already dressed,) and seemed rejoiced to hear the sound of my voice, which, he said, he began to recollect. He asked for my children, whom I brought to see him, and he felt them over and over; then, with tones of great affection, he blessed God that he had *seen* four generations of the name, and ended by giving the children his blessing, He then tuned his old time-beaten harp, his solace and bedfellow, and played with astonishing justness, and good taste. The tunes which he played were his favourites; and he, with an elegance of manner, said at the same time, 'I remember you have a fondness for music, and the tunes you used to ask for I have not forgotten;' these were Coolin, the Dawning of the Day, Ellen Aroon, Ceandubhdilis, &c. These, except the third, were the first tunes which, according to regulation, he played at the famous meeting of harpers at Belfast, under the patronage of some amateurs of Irish music. Mr. Bunting, the celebrated musician of that town, was at Hampson's, the year before, noting his tunes, and his manner of playing, which is in the best old style. He said, with the honest feeling of self-love, 'when I played the old tunes, not another of the harpers would play after me.'

He came to Magilligan many years ago, and at an advanced age married a woman of Innishowen, whom he found living in the house of a friend. ' I can't tell,' quoth Hampson, 'what it was that buckled us together; she being lame and I blind.' By this wife he had one daughter, married to a cooper, who has several children, and maintains them all, though Hampson (in this alone seeming to dote,) says, that his son-in-law is a spendthrift, and that he himself maintains them; the family humour his whim, and the old man is quieted. He is pleased when they tell him, as he thinks is the case, that people of character for musical taste, send letters to invite him; and he, though incapable now of leaving the house, is planning expeditions never to be attempted, much less realized. These are the only traces of mental debility, and as to his body, he has no inconvenience but that arising from a chronic disorder. His habits have ever been sober ; his favourite drink, once beer, now milk and water, and his diet chiefly potatoes. I asked him to teach my daughter, but he declined ; adding, that it was too hard for a young girl, but nothing would give him greater pleasure, if he thought it could be done.

"Lord Bristol, when lodging at the bathing house of Mount Salut, near Magilligan, gave three guineas, and ground rent free, towards the house where Hampson now lives ; and at the house-warming, his Lordship, with his Lady and family, came, and the children danced to his harp. The Bishop also gave three crowns to the family, and in the dear year, his Lordship called at the door in his coach and six, and gave them a guinea to buy meal.

" The following lines are sculptured on the old harp, the sides and front of which are of white sally, the back of fir, patched with copper and iron plates.

' In the time of Noah I was green,
After his flood I have not been seen,
Until seventeen hundred and two. I was found,
By Corman Kelly under ground ;
He raised me up to that degree ;
Queen of music they call me.'

" His daughter, now attending him, is only thirty-three years old.

"I have now given you an account of my visit, and even thank you, (though my fingers are tired,) for the pleasure you procured to me by this interesting com-mission.   Ever yours,

G. V. SAMPSON."

Hampson died at the advanced age of a hundred and ten years. A few hours before his death, he tuned his harp, that it might be in readiness to enter-tain some company who were expected to pass that way shortly after ; however, he felt the approach of death, and calling his family around him, he resigned his breath without a struggle, retaining his faculties in a considerable measure, until the last moment of his existence.

The foregoing account of Hampson does not men-tion whether he had been married more than once, but this seems probable, from the age of his daughter attending him at the time it was written, who, if thirty three years old then, must have been born when he was seventy-five.

LINES ON HAMPSON'S DEATH,

Which appeared in the Belfast Magazine, January, 1808.

"The fame of the brave shall no longer be sounded,
　The last of our bards now sleeps cold in the grave;
Magilligan's rocks, where his lays have resounded,
　Frown dark at the ocean and spurn at the wave.

For Hampson, no more shall thy soul-touching finger
　Steal sweet o'er the strings, and wild melody pour;
No more near thy hut shall the villagers linger,
　While strains from thy harp warble soft round the shore.

No more thy harp swells with enraptured emotion,
　Thy wild gleams of fancy for ever are fled;
No longer thy minstrelsy charms the rude ocean
　That rolls near the green turf that pillows thy head.

Yet vigour and youth with bright visions had fired thee,
　And rose buds of health have blown bright on thy cheek,
The songs of the sweet bards of Erin inspired thee,
　And urged thee to wander, bright laurels to seek.

Yes, oft hast thou sung of our kings crowned with glory
　Or sighing, repeated the lovers' fond lay;
And oft hast thou sung of the bards famed in story,
　Whose wild notes of rapture have long passed away.

Thy grave shall be screened from the blast and the billow,
　Around it a fence shall posterity raise;
Erin's children shall wet with tears thy cold pillow,
　Her youth shall lament thee and carol thy praise."

AUTHORITIES.

Lady Morgan's wild Irish Girl, vol. 3—Belfast Magazine.

THE LIFE

OF

JOHN STANLEY, B.M.

"For music's voice the icy bosom warms,
Strings the lax nerve, and fires the weak to arms."

THE English, it is said, have no national music;
but yet, they are by no means unacquainted with the
principles of that delightful science. Many of our
composers, as well as performers, have been men of
acknowledged talents; and their compositions would
bear comparison with some of the productions of the
first masters, of either the German or Italian schools.
John Stanley, whose life we are next to consider, was
a prodigy in his day: as a composer, few could equal
him, and as a performer, he had perhaps no superior.
Such was the opinion of two most distinguished
foreigners, at that time in England, (Handel and
Gazzini,) men, whose distinguished musical genius
well qualified them to judge of the merits of Mr.
Stanley's performances.

John Stanley was born in 1713. At two years of
age, he totally lost his sight, by falling on a marble
hearth, with a china basin in his hand. At the age
of seven he first began to learn music, as an art that

was likely to amuse him; but without his friends supposing it possible for him, circumstanced as he was, to make it his profession. His first master was Reading, a scholar of Dr. Blow's, and organist of Hackney; but his father, finding that he had not only received great pleasure in music, but had made a rapid progress, placed him with Dr. Green, under whom he studied with great diligence, and a success that was astonishing.* At eleven years of age, he obtained the

---

* The influence of music is still more generally to be observed than that of poetry. Music, almost without exception, appears to be the favourite amusement of the blind. There is no other employment, religious contemplation excepted, that seems so well adapted to soothe the soul, and dissipate the melancholy ideas which, it may naturally be expected, will sometimes pervade the minds of those who are utterly bereft of sight; this, together with the beneficial influence that results from the practice of this delightful art, by quickening and perfecting the sense of hearing, is a matter that deserves the most serious attention. The celebrated professor just now mentioned, excelled in performing on the flute, in his youth; and the refinement of his ear has been very justly attributed to his early attention to music. It is not, therefore, surprising, that so many blind people have distinguished themselves in this science. Stanley and Parry were deprived of their sight in early infancy; yet both these gentlemen have displayed extraordinary proofs of their abilities, not only as composers and performers of music, but likewise in matters that, at a first view, we might be apt to consider, as peculiar to those who are fully possessed of the faculty of vision. Their separate reputations, as musicians, are sufficiently known and acknowledged. The style of Stanley is truly his own, and his execution on the organ equal, if not superior, to any of his contemporary performers on that grand instrument;

place of organist of All-Hallow's, Bread-street; and
in 1726, at the age of thirteen, was elected organist
of St. Andrew's, Holborn, in preference to a great
number of candidates. In 1734, the Benchers of the
Honorable Society of the Inner Temple, elected him
one of their organists. The two latter places he retained till the time of his death. Few professors have
spent a more active life, in every branch of their art,
than this extraordinary musician; having been not
only a most neat, pleasing, and accurate performer,
but a natural and agreeable composer, and an intelligent teacher. He was the conductor and soul of the
concerts in the City, at the Swan and Castle, as long
as they existed. Upon the death of Handel, he and
Mr. Smith undertook to superintend the performance
of the oratorios during Lent; and after Mr. Smith
retired, he carried them on, in conjunction with Mr.
Lindley, till within two years of his death, which took
place on the 19th of May, in 1786. His remains
were interred on the evening of the 27th, the following Sunday, in the new burial ground of St. Andrew's.
Instead of the usual voluntary, a solemn dirge, and
after service, "*I know that my Redeemer livèth*," were,
with great propriety, given upon that organ at which
Mr. Stanley had for so many years presided. This
ingenious and worthy professor, whose blindness ex-

---

and Parry may be revered as the British bard of modern times.
The halls of the Cambrian chief resound with the melodious
vibration of his harp, and he has united the refinements of
taste and elegance, to the rude, but expressive modulation of
antiquity.

cited the pity,* and his performance, the admiration of the public for so many years, was long lamented by his surviving friends; for they lost in him, exclusive of his musical talents, a most intelligent and agreeable companion, who contributed to the pleasures of society, as much by his conversation in private, as by his professional merit in public. He was succeeded in his office, as master of the King's Band, by Sir William Parsons.

Besides various compositions for the organ, he was the author of two oratorios; *Jephtha,* which was writ-

* Amongst the various calamities to which the human species are subjected, there are none that excite compassion, or call forth our benevolent aid, more powerfully than blindness. The blind man, in all ages and countries, has ever been allowed an indisputable claim on the good offices of his fellow creatures; his necessities have generally been supplied, with sacred care, and his genius, if it approached to excellence, has been respected with a degree of reverence, superior to what is usually bestowed on such as are possessed of the faculty of sight. We not only find our gratitude for superior advantages warmed and elevated to piety and devotion, but are likewise conscious of an involuntary impulse, that urges us to exert our endeavours to assist such as are unfortunately deprived of this noble faculty, whenever they are presented to our notice. And here, again, we have every motive to inspire us with admiration of the providential wisdom and benevolence, displayed by the divine author of our existence; for, notwithstanding the great and comprehensive powers of sight, there is little of the actual knowledge acquired by this sense, that may not, by attentive and patient perseverance, be communicated to the man who has been doomed to darkness from his birth.

ten in 1757, and *Zimri*, which was performed at
Covent Garden, during the first season of Mr. Stanley's management of the oratorios there. He likewise
composed the music to an *Ode*, performed at Drury
Lane, in the year 1760, and intended at the same
time, both as an elegy on the death of King George
the Second, and as a compliment to his successor.
He also set to music a dramatic pastoral, entitled
Arcadia, or the Shepherd's Wedding, which was performed at the same theatre, in the ensuing year, immediately after the marriage of George the Third and
Queen Charlotte.

In proof of his masterly management of the organ,
it is well known, that when, at the performance of one
of Handel's Te Deums, he found the organ was half a
note too sharp for the other instruments, he, without
the least premeditation, transposed the whole piece ;
and this, with as much facility and address as any
person could have done, possessed of sight. This was
the more remarkable, since the key into which it was
transposed, (that of C sharp major,) from having *seven
sharps* in the clef, is so exceedingly difficult that it is
never made use of. It is probable, that there was not
then in the kingdom one performer beside himself who
would have attempted it, even though he had previously taken the trouble of writing out the whole of the
part.

This gentleman had two very favourite violins, one
of them made by the famous Stanier, which he always used in concert, and the other a Cremona, on
which he played his solos. These instruments were
esteemed to be as excellent as any in England, but

unfortunately they were both burnt, by a fire which happened at the Swan Tavern, in Cornhill.

The following additional particulars of this great man's life, were given to the public a few years after his death, by Dr. Alcock, a gentleman, on whose veracity the reader may place implicit confidence. He had been a pupil of Stanley's, and speaks of his scientific knowledge in the most exalted terms, adding, that most of the musicians contrived to get acquainted with him, as they found their advantage in it. " It was common, just as the service of St. Andrew's Church, or the Temple, was ended, to see 40 or 50 organists at the altar, waiting to hear his last voluntary ; and even Handel himself, I have frequently seen at both of those places. In short, it must be confessed, that his extempore voluntaries were inimitable, and his taste in composition wonderful. I was his apprentice, and I remember, the first year I went to him, his occasionally playing, (for his amusement only,) at billiards, mississipie, shuffle-board, and skittles, at which games he constantly beat his competitors. To avoid prolixity, I shall only mention his shewing me the way, both on horseback and on foot, through the private streets in Westminster, the intricate passages of the city, and the adjacent villages, places at which I had never been before. I remember also his playing very correctly, all Corelli's and Geminiani's twelve solos, on the violin. He had so correct an ear, that he never forgot the voice of any person he had once heard speak, and I myself have divers times been a witness of this. In April, 1779, as he and I were going to Pall Mall, to the late Dr. Boyce's auction, a gentleman met us who had been in Jamaica twenty years, and in a feigned voice, said, 'How do you do Mr. Stanley?' when he, after pausing a little, said, 'God bless me, Mr. Smith, how long have you been in England?' If twenty people were seated at a table near him, he would address them all in regular order, without their situations being previously announced to him. Riding on horseback was one of his favourite exercises; and towards the conclusion of his life, when he lived at Epping Forest, and wished to give his friends an airing, he would often take them the pleasantest road, and point out the most agreeable prospects. He played at whist with great readiness and judgment; each card was marked at the corner with the point of a needle, but the marks were so delicately fine, as scarcely to be seen by any person, not previously apprised of them. His *hand* was generally the first arranged, and it was not uncommon for him to complain to the party, that they were tedious in sorting their cards. He could also tell the precise time by a watch; the number of persons in a room upon his entering it, and direct his voice to each in particular, even to strangers, after they had once spoken; he would also miss any one absent, and tell who that person was. In a word, his conceptions of youth, beauty, symmetry, and shape, were, in a person of his condition, truly wonderful attainments. So delicate and correct was his ear, that he was able to accompany any lesson with thorough bass, though he had never heard it before; thus anticipating the harmony before the chords were sounded, and accompanying it in a manner suitable to its nature."

AUTHORITIES.

Dr. Alcock's Memoirs.—Eccentric Mirror, vol. 2nd.—Rees' Encyclopædia.   Musical Biography, vol. 2nd.

THE LIFE

OF

JOSEPH STRONG,

THE BLIND MECHANIC AND MUSICIAN OF CARLISLE.

" While in more lengthen'd notes and slow,
The deep and solemn organs blow."

THE propensity of persons who have had the misfortune to be denied the blessing of sight, to cultivate the science of music, is well known to every one of the least observation.   With this propensity is often combined, an extraordinary genius for mechanics ; and few have possessed both in a greater degree, than the individual whose history I am now about to present to my readers.

Joseph Strong was born in 1732, at Cummersdale, a village about two miles from Carlisle, where his father had a small estate.   He lost his sight by the small pox, when he was about four years of age.   He very early discovered a genius for music, and a mechanical talent likewise ; and, while yet a mere child, he made himself a kind of fiddle, of two or three pieces of wood. When a little older, his father bought him what is called a kit,* and placed him under a master at Carlisle, to be instructed in the use of that instrument. He afterwards made a bell harp, and soon learnt to play upon it. He then proceeded to a flute, and a hautboy, and after this his great ambition was to build an organ. The disposition of the keys he learnt from the spinet, but he was at a loss how to construct the other parts of an organ, and was very desirous of examining that in the cathedral. The following circumstance affords a striking instance of his ingenuity and perseverance, by means of which he contrived to manufacture every thing he thought worth possessing. At the age of fifteen, he one afternoon concealed himself in the cathedral of Carlisle, during the time of divine service, and when the congregation had retired, and the gates were shut, he proceeded to the organ loft, and examined every part of the instrument. He was thus occupied till about midnight, when, having satisfied himself respecting the general construction, he began to try the tone of the different stops, and the proportion they bore to each other. This experiment, however, could not be concluded so silently as the business which had before engaged his attention ; the neighbourhood was alarmed, and various were the conjectures as to the cause of the nocturnal music, but at length some persons mustered courage

---

* A kit is a small fiddle, which is put into the hands of children of eight or ten years old, on which they take their first lessons in music.

sufficient to go and see what was the matter, and
Joseph was found playing the organ. The next day
he was sent for by the dean, who, after reprimanding
him for the method he had taken to gratify his curiosity, gave him permission to play whenever he pleased.
He now set about building his first organ, and at
length completed it, though not altogether to his satisfaction.

Not long after, he went to London on foot, with
his mother for his guide. By means of Dr. Brown, he
was introduced to Mr. Stanley, who received him
with great kindness, and offered to teach him music,
if he would stay with him, but he could not bear the
thought of entirely leaving his native country. In
London, also, he became acquainted with an organ
builder, who gave him some instructions in his art, by
the help of which he built a second organ, after his
return home, much more complete than the former ;
after that he constructed a third still more perfect, and
sold it to a gentleman in the Isle of Man.

The next piece of mechanism which he produced
was a weaver's loom, in which he succeeded so well,
that he made weaving his principal employment ever
after. His loom differed from those in common use,
and had several contrivances, which it is not necessary
to notice here. Whenever a thread broke, either in the
weft or the woof, he could discover it almost instantly,
and set it right again, as expeditiously as any other
weaver. He not only could weave plain cloth, but
plush, damask, &c. the latter, however, he only did by
way of amusement, the former he applied to as a trade,
by which he was enabled to support himself and family
respectably.

He was accustomed to go about the city with no other guide than a stick, and to frequent several places in the country, where he had many fields to pass through, stiles to go over, and ditches to cross upon narrow planks; which he did without ever losing his way, or meeting with any accident. Till within a few months of his death, he was a constant attendant at the cathedral, but not being able to accompany the choir in chanting the psalms, he composed several hymns adapted to the music, which he substituted as an act of private devotion, during the performance of that part of the public service. It is not known whether these effusions were preserved, which certainly possessed some interest on account of the motive by which they were dictated; and for obtaining which, he afforded ample opportunity, as they generally constituted a portion of his musical performances before strangers, and were, indeed, that part in which he seemed to take the greatest pleasure. Mr. Strong was married at the age of twenty-five, and had several children. He died at Carlisle, in March, 1798, in his sixty-sixth year.

AUTHORITIES.

Dr. Alcock's Memoirs.—Eccentric Mirror, vol. 2nd.—Rees' Encyclopædia.

THERESA PARADIS,

MADEMOISELLE THERESA PARADIS, equally distinguished by her talents and misfortunes, was the
daughter of M. Paradis, Conseilleur Aulique in the
imperial service of Austria. At the age of two years
and eight months, she was suddenly blinded during
the night, as it should seem, by excessive fear : for
there being a dreadful outcry in her father's house of
fire ! thieves ! murder ! he quitted the child and her
mother in the utmost trepidation, calling out for his
sword and fire-arms ; which so terrified the infant, as
instantly and totally to deprive her of sight.

At seven years of age, she began to listen with
great attention to the music she heard in the church,
which induced her parents to have her taught to play
on the piano-forte, and soon after to sing. In three
or four years' time, she was able to accompany herself
on the organ, in the *Stabat Mater* of Pergolesi, of
which she sung a part at St. Augustine's church, in
the presence of the Empress Queen, who was so
touched with her performance and misfortune, that
she settled a pension on her for life. After learning
music from several masters at Vienna, she was placed
under the care of Kozeluch, an eminent musician,

who composed many admirable lessons and concertos, on purpose for her use, which she played with the utmost neatness and expression.

At the age of eighteen, she was placed under the celebrated empyric Dr. Mesmer, who undertook to cure every species of disease by " animal magnetism." He called her disorder a perfect *gutta serena*, and pretended, after she had been placed in his house as a boarder for several months, that she was perfectly cured, yet refused to let her parents take her away or visit her. At length, by the advice of Dr. Ingenhouze, the Barons Stoerck and Wenzell, and Professor Barth the celebrated anatomist, and by the assistance of the magistrates, she was withdrawn from his hands by force, when it was found that she could see no more than when she was first admitted as Mesmer's patient. He had, however, the diabolical malignity to assert that she could see very well, and only pretended blindness, to preserve the pension granted to her by the Empress Queen, in consequence of her loss of sight; and, after the death of her imperial patroness, this cruel assertion was made an excuse for withdrawing the pension.

In the year 1780, Mademoiselle Paradis quitted Vienna, in order to travel, accompanied by her mother, who treated her with extreme tenderness, and bore a very amiable and interesting character. After visiting the principal courts and cities of Germany, where her talents and misfortunes procured her great attention and patronage, she arrived at Paris early in the summer, and remained there five or six months; receiving every mark of approbation and regard in

that capital also, both for her musical abilities and
her amiable disposition. When she arrived in England, about a month or six weeks afterwards, she
brought letters from persons of the first rank, to her
Majesty Queen Charlotte, the Imperial Minister,
and other individuals of high rank, as well as to the
principal musical professors in London.   Messrs.
Cramer, Abel, Solomon, and other eminent German
musicians interested themselves very much in her welfare, not only as being a country-woman bereaved of
sight, but also as an admirable performer.   She went
to Windsor to present her letters to the Queen, and
had the honour of playing there to their Majesties,
who were extremely pleased with her performance,
and treated her with that condescension and kindness,
which all who were so happy as to be admitted to the
presence of their Majesties, in moments of domestic
privacy, experienced, even when less entitled to it by
merit and misfortunes than Mademoiselle Paradis.
She afterwards performed before his Royal Highness
the Prince of Wales, at a grand concert at Carlton-
house, to the entire satisfaction and wonder of all who
heard her; she also had a benefit night, which was
extremely well attended.

AUTHORITY.
European Magazine, 1781.

Mr. FRANCIS LINLEY,

THOUGH blind from his birth, became a most excellent performer on the organ. Nor were his abilities confined merely to the science of music, as he was a charming companion and acute reasoner, and well acquainted with the works of the most eminent authors, ancient and modern. Having completed his musical studies under Dr. Miller, of Doncaster, he went to London, and was the successful candidate, among seventeen competitors, for the place of organist of Pentonville Chapel, Clerkenwell. He was soon after married to a blind lady of large fortune; but, having subsequently sustained great losses by the treachery of a friend, he made a voyage to America, where his performances and compositions soon brought him into notice. He died, shortly after his return to England, at his mother's house at Doncaster, on September 13th, 1800, at the age of twenty-nine. Being a freemason, by his own request he was attended to the grave by the master and brethren of St. George's lodge, in that town.

WILLIAM TALBOT,

THE CELEBRATED PERFORMER ON THE IMPROVED IRISH PIPES.

" Erin from her green throne surveys
  The progress of her tuneful son;
Exulting as the minstrel plays,
  At the applause his pipes have won.

Then grieve not for the loss that shades
  Fair nature's landscape from your view—
The genius, that no gloom invades,
  She gave in recompense to you."

It is humiliating to the pride of man to trace the helplessness of his nature, but gratifying to consider the goodness of providence in the provision it makes for his wants and infirmities. In no situation, perhaps, is this better exemplified, than in the case of those who, condemned to perpetual darkness, are left to grapple with the difficulties of life, and to make their way through its mazy windings, under a privation, which, of all others, is the most appalling. The subject of the present memoir is of this class. He was born near Roscrea, in the county of Tipperary, in the year 1781, and lost his sight in the small-pox, when only four years of age; about that time, Talbot's mother being in a delicate state of health, was advised to remove to a situation more suited to her constitution, near the sea coast; and soon after, the family settled in the village of Tramore, within six miles

of Waterford. There young Talbot soon discovered considerable mechanical taste, in the construction of miniature wind and water-mills, and in the
fitting up of small ships and boats, with every rope
and appendage as exactly formed, as those found in
vessels on a larger scale. Being an only child, he
was much indulged by his parents, who afforded him
a greater facility in cultivating his favourite pursuits;
and it is not a little remarkable, that at the several
periods of the year, when boys amuse themselves with
kites, tops, hoops, marbles, bows and arrows, this
youthful adventurer was observed to be one of the
most expert at those juvenile recreations ; he has been
known to gain the ring at castle-top, and to hit the
mark with an arrow at thirty yards distance, when
others, who were considered adepts, and blessed with
the advantages of sight, found themselves far outstripped in this respect, by his adroitness and ingenuity.

At the age of thirteen, his performance on the Irish
pipes obtained him considerable celebrity, particularly
in country-dance playing ; and such was the fascina-
tion of his music, that no violin would be employed
for that purpose, when he could be procured; his
habits in this respect had been so confirmed, and his
practice so extensive, that he has been known to continue playing a tune at a ball although fast asleep,
and was only roused from his slumbers, by the reiter-
ated calls of the party, for a change in the air. While
travelling through the country in this way, he went,
on one occasion with a few companions to a ball,
about six miles distant, to amuse himself, and to hear
a piper who had been engaged for the night. During

the evening this man was continually boasting of his
pipes, and of his own judgment, taste, and execution.
Talbot, who had listened to his vaunts in silence, at
length proposed, by way of quietus, to get a man who
would produce better music out of an old stocking.
Bets were immediately made, judges appointed, and
the hour having arrived for the decision, Talbot actually drew from an old stocking, a set of small pipes,
on which, he himself commenced playing, to the utter
astonishment and confusion of his competitor, and to
the conviction of his audience, of his entire superiority.
At his leisure hours he frequently amused himself in
fishing, at which he was generally very successful, as
well as in playing cards and dominos, when occasion
afforded him an opportunity of exercising his ingenuity in that way. Sometimes in his rambles
through the country, he would indulge himself and
his friends with a laugh at the expence of some blind
companion, whom he would purposely lead out of the
way, and there leave him, until the entreaties of the
bewildered person would bring him again to his relief

About the seventeenth year of his age, he got accidentally acquainted with a captain in the navy, for
whom he had formed such a friendship, that he was
induced to go with him to sea, where he continued
about four years, during which he was in various parts
of the world, and received much civility, attention,
and kindness, from the inhabitants of the respective
ports at which he touched.

Mr. Talbot had become so accustomed to the ship,
that, he has been often seen going from rope to rope
to the mast head, with all the agility and skill of an

experienced seaman. However, he grew tired of this kind of life, as it possessed too little variety, and became again a landsman in 1803. At this period he formed a matrimonial connexion with a young woman, for whom he had long cherished an ardent attachment, and for their mutual support had recourse to the exercise of his musical talents. He shortly after settled with his wife in Limerick, where he met with much encouragement, and commenced there, his first attempt at building an organ. In this, although having no person to give him any instruction, he succeeded surprisingly. From Limerick, after a residence of nearly three years, he removed to Cork. Here he purchased an organ for the purpose of making himself better acquainted with its mechanism; his perfect knowledge in which, was soon evinced, by the ingenious and melodious organs which he afterwards constructed. Mr. Talbot's acquaintance with this branch of mechanical music, first led him to conceive the application of a deeper scale to the Irish pipes and by that means he has now brought the instrument to a state of perfection hitherto unparalleled in the annals of music. He has enabled it to descend a whole additional octave on the musical scale, even to G, on the first line in the bass; this instrument being at first only four notes under concert pitch. Independent of this, he has increased its power of forming and combining harmonious sounds, by various additional keys, and by other very elegant and original improvements. Of his execution on the pipes, the Irish nation have had long experience, and it must be admitted, that his taste, if equalled, has seldom been surpassed, in the performance of almost all those favourite airs which have given such deserved celebrity to our native bards.

In the city of Dublin, where he resided for many years, he was sought after, and his performance much admired, as was evident by the numerous resort of company to the houses where he played. While there, from the nature of his profession, he was often kept to a late hour in the evening, yet such was his knowledge of the city, that he would return alone to his own house, which was situate outside the grand canal, without making the least mistake; and has often been known, during these solitary perambulations, to serve as a guide and a guardian to many an unfortunate votary of the social board.

During his residence in Dublin, he was induced at one time to go with some friends on a boating party of pleasure in the bay; the day, however, becoming tempestuous, they were driven to sea, and obliged to take shelter in the Isle of Man. Here his music, had he not been previously engaged, might have proved of much advantage to him, as a young woman at the inn where he stopped, was so captivated by it, that she proposed him her hand in marriage, with a mass of wealth, which she had been for some years accumulating. This treasure, by way of temptation, she discovered to him as a great secret, which consisted of a large barrel of Isle of Man penny-pieces. This offer, however, he was obliged respectfully to reject, to the great mortification of the fair damsel.

The writer of this article has known Mr. Talbot

for some time, and thinks it but justice to his character to state, that he has much merit, in supporting himself and a large family, so respectably as he does, on the income derived alone from his musical abilities, The loss of sight, and want of the comforts depending upon it, although it may be deplored, seem not to be felt as a calamity by Mr. Talbot; for, notwithstanding that the great book of nature is for ever closed to him, he appears perfectly resigned to the will of providence, full of contentment and cheerfulness, and possesses at all times that independence of feeling, which renders life supportable under every misfortune.

AUTHORITIES.

Belfast Commercial Chronicle—Belfast News-letter.

MR. JOHN AXE,

WAS organist of Whiston, near Rotherham : although blind from his birth, his abilities were of a very surprising kind, having a correct and superior knowledge, particularly of mechanics, music, &c. of which his works will remain a lasting memorial—such as the chimes in the borough church of Hedon, in Holderness, and his improvements on a great number of organs and other musical instruments. He died 1823, at Sprotborough, Yorkshire, in the thirty-eighth year of his age.

WILLIAM CLEMENTSHAW,

WAS blind from his youth, and was organist of the parish church of Wakefield, in Yorkshire, which situation he held for upwards of forty years. He died in 1822, and was buried in the above church, and, at his own request, the following epitaph, which was composed by himself, was inscribed on his tomb-stone;

> Now like an organ robbed of pipes and breath,
> Its keys and stops all useless made by death ;
> Though mute and motionless, in ruins laid,
> Yet, when rebuilt by more than mortal aid,
> This instrument, new voic'd and tun'd, shall raise
> To God, its builder, hymns of endless praise.

MR. JAMES WATSON,

THE INVENTOR OF A METHOD OF PLAYING ON THE VIOLIN AND VIOLONCELLO AT THE SAME TIME.

THIS individual invented a method by which he can play upon these two instruments at once, with the greatest facility and correctness. He plays on the violin in the usual manner, and on the violoncello by means of his feet. His right foot goes into a sort of shoe at the end of the bow, and in consequence of his right thigh being supported by a spring attached to the chair on which he sits, he has the whole command of the foot, without suffering any fatigue. By means of his left foot, he acts upon a set of levers, by which he shortens the strings with great facility.

Mr. Watson has frequently played thirteen and fourteen hours in one day, without any extraordinary fatigue.

AUTHORITY.
Edinburgh Philosophical Journal, vol. 3.

EDUCATION

For centuries blind people have excelled in the field of education. Blind scholars first appeared in the ancient civilizations of the Middle and Far East, where blindness was common because of diseases such as trachoma and ophthalmia. Blind people are depicted in early paintings in the tombs of the ancient Egyptians and in the literature of later times. Didymus of Alexandria (313–98), a Greek grammarian, is mentioned by Richard French in *From Homer to Helen Keller* (1932) as the first recorded instance of the education of a blind person. Didymus is thought to have become blind at the age of four or five, although the causes are uncertain. According to Berthold Lowenfeld, in his 1975 book, *The Changing Status of the Blind: From Separation to Integration,* Didymus acquired a knowledge of written language using wooden letters that he formed into words and sentences. His most notable quality was his outstanding memory. While studying at the famous University of Alexandria, he employed readers to read the prodigious amount of literature available to him. He then became a professor at the university and tutored many men who later became famous. Perhaps his best-known pupil was St. Jerome.

Nicholas Saunderson (1682–1739) is recognized as one of history's foremost blind educators. He became blind at the age of one as a result of smallpox, a disease that until recently was a major cause of blindness in many countries. Wilson, Lowenfeld, and others, including Ishbel Ross in the book *Journey into Light: The Story of the Education of the Blind* (1950) and Alexander Mell in the *Encyklopädisches Handbuch des Blindenwesens* (1900), mention his achievements, especially his mathematical abilities. At the age of eighteen he was tutored in geometry and algebra. During this time he devised a ciphering board made up of blunt pins with different-sized heads that he was able to distinguish by touch. This system was a forerunner of the tactile mathematic equipment used today by the blind. The French essayist and encyclopedist Denis Diderot devoted much of his 1749 *Essay on Blindness* to Saunderson, who is remembered most as a mathematician and lecturer in Newtonian philosophy at Cambridge University. Francis Cardwell in *The New Beacon* (December 25, 1961) mentions that he was also an accomplished flute player.

Leonard Euler (1707–83) was another notable mathematician and remarkable blind scholar. Euler grew up in Switzerland at the same time that Saunderson was at the height of his career. Ross notes that Euler lost the sight of one eye at age twenty-eight and the other as he turned fifty-nine. His ability to continue functioning as a mathematician demonstrates that loss of sight did not deter him from his work. Ross states that he adopted the attitude of Democritus: "I gained more in faculty and methods than I lost by any diminution of sight." He worked as a professor of mathematics in the Royal Academy of St. Petersburg and in 1741 was appointed director of the Royal Academy in Berlin by Frederick II, king of Prussia. Mathematics was not his only field of study; over the years he studied the problem of vibrating chords, motion of fluids, and the general theory of light.

Another interesting figure in the ranks of notable blind people is Edward Rushton (1755–1814). Although he is not commonly remembered as an educator, his talents as a poet, writer, and humanitarian merit his inclusion in Wilson's *Biography*. Wilson finds that, "It is peculiarly pleasing to observe how many individuals in the middle and lower ranks of life without the advantages of education, have raised themselves to a distinguished place in society, by the cultivation of their literary talents; among those was Edward Rushton of Liverpool." In all four editions he includes extracts from Rushton's letter on slavery to General Washington. Rushton lost his sight at the age of nineteen through ophthalmia contracted while a sailor on a slaver bound for Dominica. He later regained it in 1807 following an operation. After becoming blind, Rushton did not have an easy life, although in time he did progress from a life of poverty to that of a successful bookseller.

Among his many concerns was the welfare of the blind, which inspired him to help found the Liverpool School for the Indigent Blind in 1791. His biographer, Mary G. Thomas, says that today, "He is gratefully honoured by all concerned with the welfare of the blind as a man who, in an age when the blind were normally regarded only as objects of pity, was among the first to see, and to show in his own person, that they could take their place in normal society, and that education and training were their right."

John Gough (1757–1825), a mathematician, was a contemporary of Rushton's. Gough became blind at the age of three because of smallpox. Lowenfeld mentions that he acquired a classical education as well as a thorough knowledge of zoology. Later on, he turned to what was then called experimental philosophy and mathematics. He became eminent as a teacher of mathematics. In his earlier work as a botanist and zoologist, he made use of his highly developed nonvisual senses. Wilson gives a list of thirty-six essays that Gough wrote and communicated to the Manchester Philosophical Society.

David McBeath (1792–1834) was a teacher of the blind in the Asylum for the Blind in Edinburgh. According to Wilson he devised a board for the study of music, arithmetic, algebra, and other branches of mathematics. He also mentions that McBeath developed a "string alphabet," which was little more than three feet long. Any blind person could learn it in an hour. An example of this used in the Glasgow Institute for the Blind in the early nineteenth century is in the Museum on the Education of the Blind at the Perkins School for the Blind in Boston. Ross mentions that in 1831 a Boston physician, Dr. Samuel Gridley Howe (1801–76), first director of the Perkins School for the Blind, met McBeath, and he explained his string alphabet. On returning to the United States, Howe brought with him John Pringle, a blind teacher from the Asylum for the Blind in Edinburgh, to teach mechanical subjects when Howe opened his new school in Boston in July 1832.

Nelson, the blind professor, is one of the few Americans Wilson mentions. Nelson (no first name or dates known) became totally blind after suffering eye problems at about the age of twenty. He went on to become a classics professor at Rutgers College in New Jersey. He distinguished himself by being an excellent teacher. Wilson relates that he entered the hall being followed, rather than directed, by the youth who attended him.

Thomas Holland (1760–1829), of Manchester, known as the blind teacher, lost his sight at the age of eighteen. He became a teacher of music in his mother's school and later a teacher in one of the most distinguished women's schools in

Manchester. Wilson recounts that what most distinguished Holland was his power to cultivate the attention and understanding of his pupils.

Since the founding of schools for the blind beginning in 1784, many blind people have become teachers. Their numbers greatly increased with the advent of the braille system, which gave them the advantage of not just reading books (using the original embossed-letter systems), but also being able to write their own notes and materials. Louis Braille (1800–1852), inventor of the braille system, was himself a teacher and taught in a school for blind students in Paris.

In recent years, the development of technology such as audio recordings, computers with both speech and braille output, and access to databases has made it possible for more blind mathematicians to teach on all levels in regular schools and universities. Blind and visually impaired researchers and professors use the information highway to gain access to information that until now has been difficult to obtain without the assistance of sighted people. No longer does lack of vision exclude blind instructors from full participation in the teaching profession.

DIDYMUS, OF ALEXANDRIA,

Didymus is known to us only as a theological writer, but we are informed by St. Jerome, who was his pupil, that, although he lost his sight at five years of age, he distinguished himself in the school of Alexandria by his proficiency, not merely in grammar, rhetoric, logic, music, and arithmetic, but also in the remaining two of the seven departments then conceived to constitute the whole field of human learning, geometry and astronomy ; sciences of which, remarks the narrator, it is scarcely conceivable how any knowledge could be obtained without the assistance of the eyes. Didymus, like Saunderson, pursued his studies by employing persons to read to him. One of his disciples, Palladius, remarks, that blindness, which is to others so terrible a misfortune, was the greatest of blessings to Didymus ; inasmuch as, by removing from him all objects that would have distracted his attention, it left his faculties at much greater liberty for the study of the sciences, than he would otherwise have enjoyed. He, himself, however, does not seem to have been altogether of this opinion, since we find it recorded, that when St. Anthony, (who, attracted by the report of his wonderful learning and sanctity, had come from the desert to pay him a visit,) put to him the question, "Are you grieved that you are blind?"—although it was repeated several times, Didymus could not be prevailed upon to return any other answer than that he certainly was; greatly to the mortification of the Saint, who was astonished that a wise man should lament the loss of a faculty, which we only possess, as he chose to express it, in common with the gnats and ants. The learned and pious Joseph Milner, in speaking of Didymus as a Christian philosopher, makes the following remarks: " as far as appears, he continued always sound, and I hope, humble and holy, in Christian doctrine; his treatise on the Holy Spirit, of which, only the Latin translation by Jerome has come down to us, is perhaps the best the Christian world ever saw on the subject, and, whatever has been said since that time in defence of the divinity and personality of the Holy Ghost, seems, in substance, to be found in that book. He was particularly attached to the study of the Scriptures, and was chosen as a proper person to fill the chair, in the famous divinity school at Alexandria. His high reputation drew a great number of scholars to him, among the principal of whom were Jerome, Rufinus, Palladius, and Isidore. He read lectures with wonderful facility, answered, upon the spot, all questions and difficulties relating to the Holy Scriptures, and refuted the objections which cavillers raised against the orthodox faith. Didymus was the author of a great number of works, the titles of which Jerome has preserved, in his catalogue of Ecclesiastical Writers;

his commentaries upon the Scriptures, which were very large, are lost. He died in 398, aged eighty-five years."

AUTHORITIES.

Milner's Church History, vol. 2nd.—The Library of Entertaining Knowledge, vol.. 1.

WILLIAM JAMIESON,

THE BLIND PROFESSOR OF HISTORY, IN THE UNIVERSITY OF GLASGOW.

Very little is known of the history of William Jamieson. It appears, from the few facts we have been able to collect from contemporary writers, that he was a native of Renfrewshire, in Scotland, and blind from his infancy. Crawford, in his history of this county, mentions a number of its distinguished natives, and, among the rest, the subject of this memoir, of whom he writes ; " near the house of Barochan, and within that barony, was born the learned Mr. William Jamieson, preacher of the gospel, and also professor of History, in the University of Glasgow, who was a miracle of learning, considering he was deprived of the sense of sight from his birth, and his works afford sufficient proof of his being a very able scholar."

Woodrow, in his history of the church of Scotland, in speaking of the martyrdom of that christian patriot, the Earl of Argyle, pays a very handsome compliment to the learning and talents of professor Jamieson. We give the passage as we find it.

" Let me conclude with observing that the Earl was so full of composure, and the thoughts of his death were so easy to him, that the day before his execution, he wrote some very pleasing and affecting lines, as his own epitaph. This epitaph, of the Earl's own composing, was turned into Latin elegiacs, by the

reverend and learned Mr. William Jamieson, preacher
of the gospel, and History Lecturer in the University
of Glasgow, my dearest and much honoured friend;
and they have so much of the spirit of the original
lines in them that I have likewise added them, with
two lines of his own, which fell from him when translating them, as a just debt he owed to this great man.
Though they were written in the days of his youth
a little after the Earl's death, I am persuaded he needs
not be ashamed of them in his advanced years, and
after he hath favoured the world, and defended the interests of religion, and the church of Scotland, by his
learned and valuable performances.

Watts, in his " Bibliotheca Britannica," thus refers
to him; " several books are mentioned as written by
him, all on the subject of the Episcopal controversy.
He carried on a controversy also with Mr. Robert Cal-
der, an Episcopal curate, who wrote with great bitterness and some talent."

That most excellent Divine, the Rev. Matthew
Henry, makes mention of our blind professor. At
the time he wrote, the more wealthy of the English
dissenters sent their children, particularly those that
were intended for the ministry, to some one of the
Scotch Universities for their education; among these
was the Rev. Dr. Benzon, the intimate friend of Mr.
H., from whose writings the following passage is taken.
"In June 1695, Dr. B. went to the college of Glasgow.
Among the learned men of that University, Mr.
Jamieson, History Professor there, did correspond
with him. That wonderful man is quite blind, and
has been so from his birth; and yet, as appears by

the learned works he has published, he is a most accomplished scholar, and very ready and exact in his quotations of authors."

Extracts from the Minutes of the " Senatus Academicus" of the University of Glasgow. " May 30, 1692. The Faculty this day taking into consideration the condition of Mr. William Jamieson, who though born blind, yet having been educated at this university, hath attained to great learning, and particularly is well skilled in history, both civil and ecclesiastical ; and having no estate to subsist upon, the Faculty considering that he may be useful in these sciences they have thought fit to allow to the said Mr. William Jamieson, two hundred marks Scots per annum, for two years, commencing from the first of April last ; the said Mr. W. J. employing himself according to his capacity, at the discretion of the Faculty."

" December 29, 1692. The Faculty determined that Mr. William Jamieson have a public lecture in civil history, once a week, on the Thursdays, at three of the clock in the afternoon, in the Common Hall."

We conclude this article with the following extract, from the preface of a work entitled, "The defence of the Church of Scotland," printed in 1713.

" I therefore earnestly wish, that the pastors of the Kirk of Scotland would spend more time in explaining this controversy, especially in their catechetical discourses, and confirm from Scripture the Presbyterian principles, and confute the adversaries. This I earnestly wish were done in a grave way and clear style, for it certainly would be of great use, especially to the common people. It would also be of great advantage to give from the pulpit now and then, calmly and plainly, a deduction of God's mercies unto this land, by delivering us from spiritual Babylon, Rome. We find in Scripture, that the prophets and godly Jews did spend much time in relating historically the deliverance that God gave to Israel, from the Egyptians and other enemies, and I am persuaded that in this our Pastors ought to imitate them; it would do much to carry down the sense of God's mercies from fathers to children, and from generation to generation."

" In the third place, I earnestly desire my readers, that they be earnest in prayer, and wait closely on God, that they have not only a form of godliness but also that they may know and feel the power of it. Knowledge is but cold and barren though a man would reason never so strongly, without charity or the love of God shed abroad in the heart ; the greatest measure of knowledge alone, will never make a man to take the spoiling of his goods with joy, or not to love his life unto the death. At a word, knowledge without godly warmth, only puffs up, and doeth little in the day of adversity; and zeal without knowledge, is ready to drive a man to error, but not to establish him in the truth."

AUTHORITIES.

Crawford's History of Renfrewshire, page 102.—Woodrow's History of the Church of Scotland, vol. 4, page 307.—Watts's Bibliotheca Britannica, Page 760, of quarto edition of Matthew Henry's Miscellaneous Writings, printed for Bagster, London.

THE LIFE

OF

NICHOLAS SAUNDERSON,

L.L.D. F.R.S.

And Professor of Mathematics in the University of Cambridge.

" Here Nature opens all her secret springs,
And heaven-born Science plumes her eagle wings."

THERE is no department of human knowledge, in which the blind have not distinguished themselves; many of them have attained the highest academical honours that their own, or foreign Universities, could confer upon them. It is certainly a spectacle highly gratifying to the benevolent mind, to contemplate such men, eliciting light from darkness; and to learn by what progressive steps they have been enabled to make their way through life, in despite of the most discouraging obstacles, with no other guide but industry and genius, even to the very summit of science. Dr. Saunderson, the subject of the present essay, was a striking proof of the justness of the above remarks.

This great man was born at Thurlston, in Yorkshire, in 1682. When he was but 12 months old he lost not only his eye sight, but even his very eyeballs, by the small pox, so that he could retain no more ideas of vision, than if he had been born blind. At an early age, however, being of very promising abilities, he was sent to the free school at Pennistone ; and there laid the foundation of that knowledge of the Greek and Latin languages, which he afterwards improved so far by his own application to the Classic Authors, as to hear the works of Euclid, Archimedes, and Diophantes, read in the original Greek.

Having acquired a grammatical education, his father, who was in the excise, instructed him in the common rules of arithmetic ; and here it was that his excellent mathematical genius first appeared. He very soon became able to work the common questions; to make very long calculations by the strength of memory ; and to form new rules for himself, for the better resolving of such questions as are often proposed to learners as trials of skill. At the age of 18, our author was introduced to Richard West, Esq. of Underbank, who, being a great lover of mathematics, and observing Saunderson's uncommon capacity, took the trouble of instructing him in the principles of algebra and geometry, and gave him every encouragement in his power to the prosecution of these studies. Soon after this, he became acquainted also with Dr. Nettleton, who took the same pains with him ; and it was to these two gentlemen that Saunderson owed his first instruction in mathematical science. They furnished him with books, and often read and explained them to him ; but he soon surpassed his masters, and became fitter to teach, than to learn from them. He was now sent to a private academy at Attercliffe, near Sheffield, where logic and metaphysics were chiefly taught; but these sciences not suiting his turn of mind, he soon left the academy. He lived for some time in the country without any instructor, but such was the vigour of his own mind that few instructions were necessary; he only required books and a reader. His father, besides the place he had in the excise, possessed also a small property; but being burdened with a numerous family, and finding a difficulty in supporting him, his friends began to think of providing both for his education and maintenance; and having remarked his clear and perspicuous manner of communicating his ideas, suggested the propriety of his attending the University of Cambridge, as a teacher of mathematics, to which his own inclination strongly led him. Accordingly he went to Cambridge in 1707, being then 25 years of age, accompanied by Joshua Dunn, Fellow Commoner of Christ's College. His fame in a short time filled the University, and though he was not acknowledged a member of the College, yet he was treated with great attention and respect; he was allowed a chamber, and had free access to the library. Mr. Whiston was at that time professor of mathematics; and as he read lectures in the way that Saunderson intended, it was to be expected that he would view his project as an invasion of his office. But being a good natured man, and a lover of learning, instead of meditating any opposition, the plan was no sooner mentioned to him, than he freely gave his consent in behalf of so uncommon a genius. While thus employed in explaining the principles of the Newtonian Philosophy, he became acquainted with its illustrious author. He was also known to Halley, Cotes, Dr. Moore, and many other eminent mathematicians.

Upon the removal of Mr. Whiston from his professorship, Saunderson's merit was thought so much superior to that of any other competitor, that an extraordinary step was taken in his favour, to qualify him as the statutes require. The heads of the University applied to their Chancellor, the Duke of Somerset, who procured the Royal Mandate to confer on him the degree of A.M; in consequence of which, he was elected Lucasian professor of mathematics in Nov. 1711, Sir Isaac Newton interesting himself much on the occasion. His inauguration speech was composed in classical Latin, and in the style of Cicero, with whose works he had been much conversant. From this time he applied himself closely to the reading of lectures, and gave up his whole time to his pupils. He continued to reside among the gentlemen of Christ's College, till the year 1723, when he took a house in Cambridge. He shortly afterwards married the daughter of the Rev. Mr. Dickens, Rector of Boxworth, in Cambridgeshire, by whom he had a son and a daughter. When George the II. in 1728, visited the University, he requested to see Professor Saunderson. In compliance with this desire, he waited on his Majesty in the Senate House, and was then by the King's command created Doctor of Laws. He was admitted a member of the Royal Society, in 1736.

Dr. Saunderson was naturally of a vigorous and healthy constitution; but having confined himself to a sedentary life, he at length became scorbutic; in the spring of 1739, he complained of a numbness in his limbs, which ended in a mortification in his foot, and unfortunately his blood was so vitiated by the scurvy, that assistance from medicine was not to be expected. When informed that his death was approaching, he remained for a short time calm and silent; but he soon recovered his former vivacity, and conversed with his accustomed ease. He died on the 19th April, 1739, aged 57 years, and was buried at his own request in the chancel of Boxworth.

Dr. Reid, who was an intimate friend of Saunderson, in speaking of his scientific acquirements, observes, "One who never saw the light, may be learned and knowing in every science, even in optics; and may make discoveries in every branch of philosophy. He may understand as much as another man, not only of the order, distances, and motions of the heavenly bodies, but of the nature of light, and of the laws of the reflection and refraction of its rays. He may understand distinctly how those laws produce the phenomena of the rainbow, the prism, the camera obscura, the magic lantern, and all the powers of the microscope and telescope. This is a fact sufficiently attested by experience."

" Dr. Saunderson understood the projection of the sphere, and the common rules of perspective, and if he did, he must have understood all that I have mentioned. If there were any doubt of Dr. Saunderson's understanding these things, I could mention having heard him say in conversation, that he found great difficulty in understanding Dr. Halley's demonstration of that proposition,—that the angles made by the circles of the sphere, are equal to the angles made by their representatives in the stereographic projection. 'But,' said he, 'when I laid aside that demonstration, and considered the proposition in my own way, I saw clearly that it must be true.' Another gentleman, of undoubted credit and judgment in these matters, who had part in this conversation, remembers it distinctly."

Saunderson we are told, though blind, could lecture on the prismatic spectrum, and on the theory of the rainbow. It is even conceivable, that by long habits of poetical reading, he might have become capable of producing such a description of their order in the spectrum, as is contained in the following lines of Thomson.*

There was scarcely any part of the science on which he had not composed something; but he discovered no intention of publishing any thing, till, by the persuasion of his friends, he prepared his "Elements of Algebra" for the press; which was published by subscription in two volumes, 4to, 1740.

He left many other writings, though none perhaps prepared for the press; among these were some valuable comments on Newton's Principia, which not only

---

* ——————————— " First, the flaming red
    Sprung vivid forth; the tawny orange next,
    And next delicious yellow, by whose side
    Fell the kind beams of all refreshing green;
    Then the pure blue that swells autumnal skies,
    Ethereal played, and then of sadder hue,
    Emerged and deepened indigo, as when
    The heavy-skirted evening droops with frost,
    While the last gleamings of refracted light,
    Died in the fainting violet away."

explain the more difficult parts, but often improve upon the doctrines. These are published in Latin, at the end of his posthumous " Treatise on Fluxions," a valuable work, published in 8vo, 1756.

His manuscript Lectures too, on most parts of natural philosophy, might make a considerable volume, and prove an acceptable present to the public, if printed.

Dr. Saunderson, as to his character, was a man of much wit and vivacity in conversation, and esteemed an excellent companion. He was endued with a great regard to truth, and was such an enemy to disguise, that he thought it his duty to speak his thoughts at all times with unrestrained freedom. Hence his sentiments on men and opinions, his friendship, or disregard, were expressed without reserve; a sincerity which raised him many enemies. A blind man moving in the sphere of a mathematician, seems to be a phenomenon difficult to be accounted for, and has excited the admiration of every age in which it has appeared. Tully mentions it as a thing scarcely credible of his own master in philosophy, Diodotus, that he exercised himself in it with more assiduity after he became blind; and, what he thought next to impossible to be done without sight, that he professed geometry, describing his diagrams so exactly to his scholars, that they could draw every line in its proper direction. But if we consider that the ideas of extended quantity, which are the chief objects of mathematics, may as well be acquired by the sense of touch, as by that of sight; that a fixed and steady attention is the principal qualification for this study, and that the blind are, by necessity, more abstracted than others, (for which reason it is said, that Democritus put out his eyes that he might think more intensely,) we shall perhaps find reason to suppose that there is no branch of science so much adapted to their circumstances. At first, Dr. Saunderson acquired most of his ideas by the sense of touch; and this, as is commonly the case with the blind, he enjoyed in great perfection. Yet he could not, as some are said to have done, distinguish colours by that sense; for after having made repeated trials, he used to say, it was pretending to impossibilities. But he could with great nicety and exactness perceive the smallest degree of roughness, or defect of polish, on a surface; thus, in a set of Roman medals he distinguished the genuine from the false, though they had been counterfeited with such exactness, as to deceive a connoisseur who had judged from the eye. By the sense of touch also, he distinguished the least variation; and he has been seen in a garden, when observations were making on the sun, to take notice of every cloud that interrupted the observation, almost as justly as others could see it. He could also tell when any thing was held near his face, or when he passed by a tree at no great distance, merely by the different impulse of the air on his face. His ear was also equally exact; he could readily distinguish the fourth part of a note by the quickness of this sense; and could judge of the size of a room, and of his distance from the wall. And if he ever walked over a pavement in courts or piazzas which reflected sound, and was afterwards conducted thither again, he could tell in what part of the walk he

had stood, merely by the note it sounded. Dr. Saunderson had a peculiar method of performing arithmetical calculations, by an ingenious machine and method, which has been called his " Palpable Arithmetic,
and is particularly described in a piece prefixed to the
first volume of his Algebra. That he was able to make
long and intricate calculations, both arithmetical and
algebraical, is a thing as certain as it is wonderful.
He had contrived for his own use, a commodious notation for any large numbers, which he could express
on his abacus, or calculating table ; and with which he
could readily perform any arithmetical operation by
the sense of touch only, for which reason it was called
his " Palpable Arithmetic."

His calculating table was a thin smooth board, a
little more than a foot square, raised upon a small
frame so as to lie hollow; which board was divided
into a great number of little squares by lines intersect-
ing one another perpendicularly, and parallel to the
sides of the table, and the parallel lines only one
tenth of an inch from each other, so that every square
inch of the table was thus divided into one hundred
little squares.

At every point of intersection, the board was per-
forated by small holes, capable of receiving a pin ;
for it was by the help of pins stuck up to the head
through these holes, that he expressed his numbers.
He used two sorts of pins, a larger and a smaller sort ;
at least, their heads were different, and might easily
be distinguished by touch. Of these pins he had a
large quantity in two boxes, with their points cut off,
which always stood ready before him when he calcu-

lated. The writer of that account describes particularly the whole process of using the machine, and concludes, "He could place and displace his pins with incredible nimbleness and facility, much to the pleasure and surprise of all the beholders; he could even break off in the middle of a calculation, and resume it when he pleased, and could presently know the condition of it, by only drawing his fingers gently over the table."

Saunderson's method of calculation deserves particular notice, not merely because it is the production of a blind man, but because it is calculated to be useful to such of the blind as may make mathematics their study.

Many blind philosophers of great eminence have derived advantages from Saunderson's invention ; it has enabled them to make out their long and difficult calculations, which they perhaps never would have been able to accomplish without its assistance. Among those I may mention the names of Grenville, Moyes, and Ward. For a more particular description of this curious contrivance, the reader is referred to the following letter from M. Diderot to a lady :—

"This Saunderson, madam, is an author deprived of sight, with whom it may not be foreign to our purpose to amuse you. They relate prodigies of him; and of these prodigies there is not one, which his progress in the Belles Lettres and his mathematical attainments do not render credible. The same instrument served him, for algebraical calculations, and for the construction of rectilineal figures. You would not, perhaps, be sorry that I should give you an explication of it, if you thought your mind previously qualified to understand it; and you shall soon perceive that it pre-supposes no intellectual preparations, of which you are not already mistress; and that it would be extremely useful to you, if you should ever be seized with the inclination of making long calculations by touch." *(See Transactions of the French Academy.)*

Mr. Saunderson, in mathematical learning, was equal to any of his time; and in the capacity of a teacher, perhaps superior to all. Whatever pieces, therefore, the world might be favoured with from so excellent a master, could not fail of meeting with a kind reception; and his work on the method of fluxions, though far from being a complete system of the fluxionary calculus, will prove of the utmost advantage to students in this branch of science. That perspicuity, that simple analysis and elegant construction, for which Dr. Saunderson was so remarkable and so justly celebrated, appear throughout this whole treatise. The consummate master and finished teacher are here fully displayed, in a judicious choice of examples, and the perspicuous method of solving and applying them.

"What the Doctor has given us," (says a learned writer very justly,) "upon Mr. Cotes's Logometria is particularly valuable, as by his intimate acquaintance with that extraordinary person, he may be presumed to have understood his writings better than any one at that time living, Dr. Smith only excepted, to whose superior genius and faithful care the world is so much indebted for the improvement, as well as the preservation of Mr. Cotes's Works.   But we are much mistaken if the latter part of this treatise, (we mean his explanation of the chief propositions of Sir Isaac Newton's Principia,) does not prove as valuable as what he has given us on the writings of Mr. Cotes. Every person who has attempted the arduous study of Sir Isaac's Principia, must be sufficiently acquainted with the difficulties of fully comprehending the demonstrations in that illustrious author. Dr. Saunderson has removed many of these difficulties ; and thereby rendered the study of the Principia much pleasanter and easier than it was before."

We have already observed, that this treatise is not a complete system of the Fluxionary Calculus ; its readers must therefore, be previously acquainted with the elementary parts of Fluxions, or be assisted, *viva voce*, by a master. With either of these helps, he will find it one of the most useful treatises that has hitherto appeared on the subject.

AUTHORITIES.

HUTTON's Mathematical Dictionary—NICHOLSON's Philosophical Journal—REID's Inquiry into the Human Mind—London Monthly Critical Review.

THE LIFE

OF

LEONARD EULER,

Professor of Mathematics in the Royal Academy of Saint Petersburgh, and Member of the Royal Societies of London, Berlin, Paris, Vienna, and Stockholm.

> " To him the motion of each orb was known,
> That wheels around the Sun's refulgent throne;
> He saw the Moon thro' Heav'n's blue concave glide,
> And into motion charm the expanding tide;
> While earth impetuous round her axis rolls,
> Exalts her watery zone and sinks the poles."

AMONG those eminent Philosophers who, by their lives and writings, have rendered so much service to mankind, is Leonard Euler; a man whose cultivated mind, and high intellectual attainments, and above all, his deep and unaffected piety, have rendered him the ornament of his country, and will transmit his name to posterity, not only as one of the greatest men but also as one of the best the world has ever yet produced.

LEONARD EULER was the son of a Clergyman in the neighbourhood of Basil, and was born on the 15th of April, 1707. His natural turn for mathematics soon appeared, from the eagerness and facility with which he became master of the elements, under the instruction of his father, by whom he was sent to the University of Basil at an early age. There, his abilities and his application were so distinguished, that he attracted the particular notice of John Bernoulli. That excellent mathematician seemed to look forward to the youth's future achievements in science, while his own kind care strengthened the powers by which they were to be accomplished. In order to superintend his studies, which far outstripped the usual routine of the public lectures, he gave him a private lesson regularly once a week ; when they conversed together on the acquisitions which the pupil had been making since the last interview, considered whatever difficulties might have occurred in his progress, and arranged the reading and exercises for the ensuing week. Under such eminent advantages, the capacity of Euler did not fail to make rapid improvements, and in his seventeenth year, the degree of Master of Arts was conferred on him. On this occasion, he received high applause for his probationary discourse, the subject of which was a comparison between the Cartesian and Newtonian systems.

His father having all along intended him for his successor, enjoined him now to relinquish his mathematical studies, and to prepare himself, by those of theology and general erudition, for the ministerial functions. After some time, however, had been consumed, this plan was given up. His father, a man of learning and liberality, abandoned his own views for those to which the inclination and talents of his son were so powerfully directed; persuaded that in thwarting the propensities of genius, there is a sort of impiety against nature, and that there would be real injustice to mankind, in smothering those abilities which were evidently destined to extend the boundaries of science. Leonard was permitted, therefore, to resume his favourite pursuits; and at the age of nineteen, having transmitted two Dissertations to the Academy of Sciences at Paris, one on the masting of ships, and the other on the velocity of sound, he commenced that splendid career, which continued for so long a period the admiration and glory of Europe.

About the same time he stood candidate for a vacant professorship in the University of Basil, but having lost the election, he resolved, in consequence of this disappointment, to leave his native country. In 1727, he set out for Petersburgh, where his friends the young Bernoullis had settled about two years before, and he flattered himself with prospects of literary preferment, under the patronage of Catharine the First. Those prospects, however, were not immediately realized ; nor was it till after he had been frequently and long disappointed, that he obtained any settlement. His first appointment appears to have been the chair of natural philosophy ; and when Daniel Bernoulli removed from Petersburgh, Euler succeeded him as professor of mathematics. In this situation he remained many years, engaged in the most laborious researches, enriching the academical collections of the Continent with papers of the highest value, and producing almost daily improvements in the various branches of physical, and more particularly analytical, science. In 1741, he complied with a pressing invitation from Frederic the Great, and resided at Berlin till 1766. Throughout this period he continued the same literary labours, directed by the same wonderful sagacity and comprehension of intellect. As he advanced with his own discoveries and inventions, the field of knowledge seemed to widen before his view, and new subjects still multiplied on him for further speculation. The toils of intense study only seemed to invigorate his future exertions, nor did the energy of Euler's mind give way, even when his bodily strength was overpowered; for in the year 1765, having completed in three days certain astronomical calculations which the academy called for in haste, but which several mathematicians of eminence had declared could not be performed within a shorter period than some months, the intense application threw him into a fever, by which he lost the sight of one eye. Shortly after his return to Petersburgh, he became totally blind. It was in this situation that he dictated to his servant, a tailor's apprentice, (who was absolutely devoid of mathematical knowledge,) his Elements of Algebra; which by their intrinsic merit in point of perspicuity and method, and the unhappy circumstances under which they were composed, have equally excited applause and astonishment. This work, though purely elementary, discovers the palpable characteristics of an inventive genius, and it is here alone we meet with a complete theory of the Analysis of Diophantes. About this time Euler was

elected by the Academy of Sciences at Paris one of
the foreign members of that learned body ; and after
this, the academical prize was adjudged to three of
his memoirs, concerning the inequalities in the motions of the planets. The two prize questions proposed by the same Academy for 1770 and 1772, were
designed to obtain from the labours of astronomers a
more perfect theory of the moon. Euler, assisted by
his eldest son, was a competitor for these prizes, and
obtained them both. In this last memoir he reserved
for farther consideration, several inequalities of the
moon's motion, which he could not determine in
his first theory, on account of the complicated calculations in which the method he then employed
had engaged him. He had the courage afterwards to
review his whole theory, with the assistance of his
son, and Messrs. Krafft and Lexell; and to pursue his
researches until he had constituted the new tables,
which appeared together with the great work, in 1772.
Instead of confining himself as before, to the fruitless
integration of three differential equations of the
second degree, which are furnished by mathematical
principles, he reduced them to the three ordinates,
which determine the place of the moon ; he divided
into classes all the inequalities of that planet as far as
they depend either on the elongation of the sun and
moon, or upon the eccentricity, parallax, or inclination
of the lunar orbit. All these means of investigation,
employed with such art and dexterity as could only be
expected from an analytical genius of the first order, were attended with the greatest success ; and it
is impossible to observe without admiration, such

immense calculations on the one hand, and on
the other the ingenious methods employed by this
great man to abridge them, and to facilitate their
application to the real motion of the moon. But
this admiration will be raised to astonishment, when
we consider at what period, and under what circumstances, all this was effected by Euler. It was when
he was totally blind, and consequently obliged to arrange all his computations by the sole powers of his
memory and genius. It was when he was embarrassed
in his domestic circumstances by a dreadful fire, that
had consumed a great part of his substance, and forced
him to quit a ruined house of which every corner was
so well known to him by habit, as in some measure
to supply the place of sight. It was in these circumstances that Euler composed a work which, alone, was
sufficient to render his name immortal. The heroic
patience and tranquillity of mind which he displayed
need no description; and he derived them, not only
from the love of science, but from the power of religion.
His philosophy was too genuine and sublime to end
its analysis in mechanical causes; it led him to that
divine philosophy of religion which ennobles human
nature, and can alone form a habit of true magnan-
imity, and patience in suffering.

Some time after this, the famous Wentzell, by
couching the cataract, restored Euler's sight; but
the satisfaction and joy that this successful operation
produced, were of short duration. Some instances
of negligence on the part of his surgeons, and his own
impatience to use an organ whose cure was not completely finished, deprived him of his sight a second

time ; and this relapse was accompanied with torment-
ing pain. He, however, with the assistance of his
sons, and Messrs. Krafft and Lexell, continued his
labours ; neither the loss of his sight nor the infirmities of an advanced age, could damp the ardour of
his genius. He had engaged to furnish the academy
of Petersburgh with as many memoirs, as would be
sufficient to complete its acts for twenty years after his
death. For the space of seven years he transmitted
to the academy, by Mr. Golswin, above two hundred
and seventy memoirs, which were revised and completed by his son. Such of these memoirs as were
of early date were separated from the rest, and form
a collection that was published in the year 1783,
under the title of Analytical Works. Euler's knowledge was more universal than could be well expected,
in one who had pursued, with such unremitting ardour, mathematics and astronomy as his favourite
studies. He had made a very considerable progress
in medical, botanical, and chemical science. What
was still more extraordinary, he was an excellent
scholar, and possessed what is generally called erudition in a very high degree. He had read with attention and taste, the most eminent writers of ancient
Rome ; the civil and literary history of all ages and
all nations was familiar to him ; and foreigners, who
had been only acquainted with his works, were astonished to find, in the conversation of a man whose
long life seemed solely occupied in mathematical and
physical discoveries, such an extensive acquaintance
with the most interesting branches of literature. In
this respect, no doubt, he was much indebted to a very

uncommon memory, which seemed to retain every idea that was conveyed to it, either from reading or from meditation. He could repeat the Æneid of Virgil from the beginning to the end, without hesitation, and indicate the first and last line of every page of the edition he used. Several attacks of a vertigo, in the beginning of September, 1783, which did not prevent his calculating the motions of the ærostatical globes, were, nevertheless, the forerunners of his mild and happy passage from this scene to a better. While he was amusing himself at tea with one of his grandchildren, he was struck with an apoplexy; which terminated his illustrious career, at the age of 76. His constitution was uncommonly strong and vigorous, his health was good, and the evening of his long life was calm and serene; sweetened by the fame that follows genius, the public esteem and respect that are never witheld from exemplary virtue, and domestic comforts which he was capable of feeling, and therefore deserved to enjoy.

In men devoted to study, we are not to look for those strong complicated passions, which are called forth amidst the vicissitudes and tumult of public life. To delineate the character of Euler requires no contrasts of colouring; sweetness of disposition, moderation in the passions, simplicity of manners, were its leading features. Susceptible of domestic affections, he was open to all their amiable impressions, and was remarkably fond of children. His manners were simple, without being singular; and seemed to flow naturally from a heart, that could dispense with those habits by which many must be trained to artificial mildness, and with the forms that are often necessary for concealment. Nor did the equability and calmness of his temper indicate a defect of energy, but the serenity of a soul that overlooked the frivolous provocations, the petulant caprices, and jarring humours of ordinary mortals.

Possessing a mind of such wonderful comprehension, and dispositions so admirably formed to virtue and to happiness, Euler found no difficulty in being a Christian; accordingly, "his faith was unfeigned," and his love was "that of a pure and undefiled heart." The advocates for the truth of revealed religion, therefore, may rejoice to add to the bright catalogue which already claims a Bacon, a Newton, a Locke, a Boyle, and a Hale, the illustrious name of Euler. Those early lessons of religion and virtue, which had been instilled into his infant mind by his pious father, were never departed from. Amidst his academic studies, he embraced every opportunity of improving them, both by reading and meditation. It was gratifying indeed, says one of his biographers, to see the good man surrounded by his amiable family in their devotional exercises; there, the Philosopher gave way to the Christian, and prayer and praise generally concluded the day. When no longer able to peruse the sacred volume on account of the loss of sight, one of his children read the chapter, and he explained it to them, and made such remarks as the nature of the subject required. On these occasions he would, by the most persuasive eloquence, impress on their minds the divine precepts which are contained in the inspired writings. Such was the life of Euler; but on this subject we must permit one of his learned and grateful pupils, (M. Fuss,) in his eulogy of his preceptor, to sum up the character of his venerable master. "His piety was rational and sincere, and his devotion was fervent; he was fully persuaded of the truths of Christianity, felt its importance to the dignity and happiness of human nature, and looked upon its detractors and opposers as the most pernicious enemies of man."

Euler was beloved and admired by every person of rank or talents, in the different countries in which he resided. Prince William of Prussia, while on a visit at St. Petersburgh, usually spent two or three hours every day in conversation with him. Catharine the First, with that munificence for which she was so justly distinguished, settled a pension on Euler, as a reward for the services he had rendered to the Russian Academy ; and, be it told to her honour, when Euler resigned the situation in the St. Petersburgh Academy, and left Russia in order to settle at Berlin, it was regularly paid, although the two countries were then in open hostilities. Frederic the Great was no less generous in rewarding his merit; for, on this occasion, besides a genteel salary, which he allowed this Philosopher, he made a present to him of a rich farm in Brandenburg.

The following circumstance, (taken from M. Fuss's Life of Euler,) which occurred about this period, it is presumed will not be deemed out of place here ; it shows the high respect entertained for the virtues and talents of this great man, not only by the first Princess in Europe, but by the soldier also, amidst the havoc of war; who, when he found he had set his unhallowed foot on the lands of Euler, which he deemed sacred, restrained his war-dogs; like Alexander, who, when he entered Thebes, amidst the general conflagration of the city, called to his soldiers to spare the house of Pindar. "The Russian forces having, in 1760, penetrated into the marshes of Brandenburg, plundered a farm of Euler's, near Charlottenburg; but General Tottleben had not come to make war on the sciences. Being informed of the loss which Euler had sustained, he hastened to repair it, by ordering payment beyond the real value of the property; and having communicated to the Empress Elizabeth an account of this involuntary disrespect, she was pleased to add a gratuity of four thousand florins to an indemnification already more than sufficient."

His death was considered as a public loss in the country which he inhabited. The Academy of Petersburgh went into deep mourning, and voted a marble bust of him, at their own expence, to be placed in their Assembly Hall. An honour still more distinguished had already been conferred on him, by that learned body, in his life-time. In an allegorical painting, a figure of Geometry is represented leaning on a table, exhibiting mathematical calculations, and the characters inscribed by order of the Academy are the formulas of his new theory of the moon. Thus, a country which at the beginning of the 17th century was considered as scarcely emerged from barbarism, is become the instructor of the most enlightened nations of Europe; doing honour to the lives of great men, embalming their memories, and setting those nations an example which some of them may blush to reflect, that they have had neither the virtue to propose, nor to imitate.

AUTHORITIES.

EULER's Life, prefixed to the first Volume of his Algebra, London, 1810—EULER's Letters to a German Princess, 2 vols. —Philosophical Magazine— AIKIN's General Biography.

THE LIFE

OF

EDWARD RUSHTON.

―――――――――

" Tho' train'd in boisterous elements, his mind
Was yet by soft humanity refin'd ;—
Brave, liberal, just, the calm domestic scene
Had o'er his temper breath'd a gay serene."

―――――――――

THERE is no history so useful *to* man, as the history *of* man; hence it is that Biography is considered not only one of the most pleasing sources of amusement that we can turn to, but it contains one of the best lessons of moral instruction that the human mind can possibly contemplate. In perusing the pages of Plutarch, how are we struck with the rich fund of intellectual knowledge, contained in the volumes of that inimitable Author ?—but why confine ourselves to the pages of antiquity ? The histories of all ages, and of every country, particularly that of our own, furnish many bright examples worthy our closest imitation. It is peculiarly pleasing to observe how many individuals in the middle and lower ranks of life, without the advantages of education, have raised themselves to a distinguished place in society, by the cultivation of their literary talents ; and among these

was Edward Rushton of Liverpool, who, though he
did not attain to the higher departments of literature,
was remarkable for the clearness and perspicuity of
his style, and for employing his pen in the cause of
humanity and of truth.

EDWARD RUSHTON was born on the 11th of Nov.
1756, in John-street, Liverpool. His education,
which he received at a free school, terminated with
his ninth year. At ten, he read Anson's Voyage,
resolved to be a sailor, was bound apprentice to Watt
and Gregson, and before he entered his eleventh year,
he was " a sea-boy on the high and giddy mast."
He performed the various duties of his station with
skill and credit, as was evinced by the following fact.
When he reached his sixteenth year, he received the
thanks of the Captain and crew of the vessel, for his
seaman-like conduct during a storm—having seized
the helm, and extricated the ship, when the Captain
and crew were wandering about in despair.

Before seventeen, whilst yet in his apprenticeship,
he signed articles as second mate of the vessel, in
which, a short time before, he entered as cabin boy.
When in this situation, in the West Indies, a circumstance occurred which is worthy of preservation. He
was dispatched from the ship with a boat's crew to the
shore, from which the vessel was then lying some
miles distant. When within about three miles of
Jamaica, the boat from some unknown cause upset,
and five or six individuals were consequently left to
struggle for life, depending only on their bodily
strength and skill for their preservation. The boat
in a short time presented itself keel upwards, upon

which they all speedily mounted; but no sooner had they seated themselves, and congratulated each other on their escape, than the boat slipped from under them, and they were again left to the mercy of the waves. In the boat among others was a negro, whose name was Quamina; between this individual and Rushton a friendship had for some time subsisted, for Rushton had taught Quamina to read. When the boat disappeared, Rushton beheld at some distance a small cask, which he knew contained fresh water; for this cask he made, but before he could reach it, it was seized by the negro, who, on seeing Rushton almost exhausted, thrust the cask towards him, turned away his head, bidding him good bye, and never more was seen. This cask saved Rushton's life. He has often told this story with tears in his eyes.

As second mate of the vessel he continued until the term of his apprenticeship was expired. At this period, the offer of a superior situation induced him to proceed to the coast of Africa on a slaving voyage. When he beheld the horrors of this disgraceful traffic he expressed his sentiments of it in strong and pointed language, with that boldness and integrity which characterized his every action, and, though in a subordinate situation, he went so far in that respect that it was thought necessary to threaten him with irons if he did not desist.

On this fatal voyage, whilst he was at Dominica, he was attacked by a violent inflammation of the eyes, which in three weeks left him with the left eye totally destroyed, and the right eye entirely covered by an opacity of the cornea. This misfortune was occa-

sioned by his exertions in assisting to relieve the necessities of his brethren of the sable race, among
whom an infectious fever had broken out.

Thus, in his nineteenth year, was he deprived of
one of the greatest blessings of nature. How much
he felt this privation, he has beautifully expressed in
the following little Poem.

ODE TO BLINDNESS.

Ah ! think if June's delicious rays,
The eye of sorrow can illume—
Or wild December's beamless days,
Can fling o'er all a transient gloom ;
Ah ! think if skies obscure or bright,
Can thus depress or cheer the mind :
Ah ! think 'midst clouds of utter night,
What mournful moments wait the blind !

And who shall tell his cause for woe,
To love the wife he ne'er must see,
To be a sire, yet not to know
The silent babe that climbs his knee !
To have his feelings daily torn,
With pain, the passing meal to find—
To live distressed, and die forlorn,
Are ills that oft await the blind !

When to the breezy upland led,
At noon, or blushing eve, or morn,
He bears the red-breast o'er his head,
While round him breathes the scented thorn ;
But Oh ! instead of Nature's face,
Hills, dales, and woods, and streams combin'd,
Instead of tints, and forms, and grace,
Night's blackest mantle shrouds the blind.

If rosy youth bereft of sight,
'Midst countless thousands pines unblest—
As the gay flower withdrawn from light,
Bows to the earth where all must rest;
Ah ! think, when life's declining hours
To chilling penury are consign'd,
And pain has palsied all his powers;
Ah ! think what woes await the blind.

In 1776, attended by his father, he visited London, and amongst other eminent men consulted the celebrated Baron Wentzell, oculist to the King, who declared him incurable. In this hopeless situation, poor Rushton returned to Liverpool, and resided with his father, with whom he continued but a short period, as the violent temper of his step-mother compelled him to leave the house and maintain himself on four shillings per week. An old aunt gave him lodgings, and for seven years he existed on this miserable, and considering the circumstances of his father, this shameful allowance. Whilst subsisting on this sum, he managed to pay a boy two pence or three pence per week, for reading to him an hour or two in the evening. He had a brooch, to which, as he has frequently been heard to declare he was often indebted for a dinner: nor was this brooch confined to himself; it was frequently lent to a friend for the self-same purpose.

From this state he was removed to one much more comfortable. His father placed one of his daughters with Rushton in a tavern, where he lived for about two years, and while in this situation he married. Finding, however, his pecuniary circumstances rather diminishing than increasing, he gave up the business.

He now entered into an engagement as editor of a newspaper called the " Herald," which for some time he pursued with much pleasure and little profit, until finding it impossible to express himself in that independent and liberal manner, which his reason and his conscience dictated, he threw up his situation and had to begin the world once more.

With an increasing family and very limited means, Rushton hesitated before he fixed on any particular course of life. He thought of several plans, but none seemed more agreeable to his taste than the business of a bookseller; his habits and his pursuits combined to render it more eligible than any other which presented itself to his thoughts. With thirty guineas, five children, and a wife to whose exertions he was greatly indebted, he commenced bookselling. This excellent wife laboured incessantly, and with attention and frugality the business succeeded, and Rushton felt himself more easy. At this time politics ran very high in Liverpool. Rushton had published several of his pieces, all in favour of the *Rights* of *Man*. He became a noted character, was marked and shot at ; the lead passed very close to the eyebrow, but did not do him the smallest injury. His timid friends, by whom he had been constantly visited while all was serene, now began to desert him ;—they were afraid of being seen near the house of a man who was looked upon as disaffected, because he boldly stepped forward in what he considered to be the cause of liberty and truth. Such are the prejudices with which a man has to struggle, whose determination it is to speak and act as his heart shall dictate. Difference of opinion respecting the best means of promoting a virtuous end, the good of mankind, is frequently the cause of disuniting friends who have long been warmly attached, and whose motives are, perhaps, equally pure.

Rushton, however, experienced the satisfaction of enjoying the steady attachment, and unremitting attention of a few tried and true friends, who with him had rejoiced in the triumphs of liberty in whatever land they were achieved. Whilst in business as a bookseller, the purses of the late Mr. W. Rathbone, and of Mr. W. Roscoe, were offered to him; he was invited to take what sum he might want, he refused them both, and he has often declared his feelings to have been those of satisfaction, when he reflected on this refusal. He was in poverty, nay, at the very moment he was struggling hard to gain a scanty pittance; yet he maintained his independence. His life for some years was but little varied, he continued successively to produce poetical pieces.

The premature death of the unfortunate Thomas Chatterton, or as Doctor Anderson has emphatically styled him the " Boy of Bristol," excited in every mind the deepest sorrow for his misfortunes. This poor neglected child of genius,* had scarcely reached his 18th year when he terminated his existence by

---

* TO THE MEMORY OF CHATTERTON.

Oh thou ! who many a silent hour,
  Satt'st brooding o'er thy plans profound ;
Oh Chatterton ! thou fairest flower,
  That ever graced poetic ground.

poison.   He had eaten nothing for three or four days before he committed this rash act; having no friend or patron to whom he could look up for encouragement, and being too proud to appeal to the charity of strangers, he adopted the dreadful alternative of quitting a world where he had met with nothing but poverty, disappointment, and neglect.   This melancholy catastrophe could not be overlooked by the

---

'Twas thine, in lyrics sweet and strong,
To bear th' enraptured soul along—
'Twas thine to paint domestic woe,
And bid the drops of pity flow !—
'Twas thine in Homer's glowing strain,
To sing contention's bloody reign ;
And oh ! 'twas thine, with unfledged wings to soar,
Upborne by native fire, to heights untried before.

In lonely paths, and church-yards drear,
    When shrouded, pale-eyed ghosts are seen ;
When many a wild note strikes the ear,
    From fairies rev'lling on the green.

Then didst thou oft with daring fire,
Sweep o'er the solemn gothic lyre ;
Then, whilst the broad moon lent her aid,
To times long past thy fancy stray'd ;
Then Hastings' field was heap'd with dead,
And Birtha mourn'd, and Baldwin bled ;
Yet, what to thee did poesy produce ?
Why—when on earth, neglect, when in the grave,
    abuse.

Ah penury ! thou chilling sprite,
    Thou pale depressor of the mind,
That with a cloud opaque as night,
    Veil'st many a genius from mankind.

humane-hearted Rushton. He has done justice to his memory in a copy of verses, which seem to be the effusion of a mind deeply imbued with the mournful subject. After speaking of his fine poetic genius, he proceeds to paint the horrid scene which preceded his death, in the most affecting language.

But it was not on this occasion alone, that Rushton's humanity was shewn;—his feelings were ever alive to the sufferings of his fellow-creatures; it was the same to him by what name they went, or to what country they belonged; whether they were burned by an Indian, or by an African sun! If he conceived they were injured or oppressed, he was ready at all times to vindicate their wrongs, with all that zeal and ability which Providence endued him with. It was this love for mankind, that induced him, in 1797, to write a letter to Washington, the then President of the United States on the subject of Negro Slavery, to whom it was transmitted in July, and a few weeks afterwards was returned under cover without one syllable in reply. As children who are crammed with sweetmeats have no relish for plain and wholesome food, so men in power who are seldom addressed but in the sweet tone of adulation, are apt to be disgusted with the plain and salutary language of truth; to offend was not the intention of the writer, yet the President was evidently irritated. To those who are acquainted with the philanthropic exertions of Rushton, which may be said to have characterized him from his youth, no apology for the subjoined extracts from that letter is necessary, and to those who have read thus far of his history, every demonstration of the amiable feelings which he retained to the last period of his existence, will I trust be acceptable. It must be farther observed, in favour of Rushton, that the letter now in question was not the result of any party feeling towards the American people. His political principle was that of a staunch republican; he venerated the name of Washington; he not only considered him one of the greatest, but one of the best men that ever appeared in the world! He also knew, at the same time, that he was but a human being, like himself, liable to err; —and that Washington did err, is a truth that none of his friends can deny; all his biographers acknowledged that he kept three hundred poor Africans in chains; it was this inconsistency that called forth Rushton's remarks.

Sometime afterwards he wrote to Thomas Paine on the same subject, but that pretended friend to mankind lent a deaf ear to his remonstrance. Among his poetical productions which appeared about this time, was that beautiful poem of " *Mary le More*," with several others on the same subject. The most particular occurrence in the latter years of his life, was a partial recovery of his sight; an event, which tended to make those years much more comfortable than any he had experienced since his youth. In the summer of 1805, hearing of the repeated successes of Dr. Gibson of Manchester, as an oculist, he was induced to obtain his opinion; that opinion was favourable, and after enduring, with his accustomed fortitude, five dreadful operations, he was, in the summer of 1807, ushered into that world from which, for more than thirty years, he had been excluded. His feelings on this occasion are truly recorded in the lines addressed to Gibson on this happy event.

During the last years of his life, Rushton did not write much, but those poems which he did produce, are excellent. "The Fire of English Liberty"— "Jemmy Armstrong," Stanzas addressed to Robert Southey, are all strongly in favour of those principles which, with fire unabated, he preserved till the last moment of his mental existence. For the few last years of his life, he was occasionally troubled with the gout, and his health visibly declined; but under all his afflictions he preserved his usual cheerfulness and gaiety till the last, and died on the 22d Nov. 1814, aged 58. The following view of his character was given by one of his intimate friends.

Edward Rushton was a public character, eminently distinguished by his actions, and by none more honourably than by his abhorrence of the doctrine of expediency, when opposed to the straight forward path of duty and principle. He thus put to shame many of "the puny danglers after wealth," and a false fame. Let it not be thought that this is the language of mere declamatory panegyric, as in many common-place encomiums of the dead, where, to bestow indiscriminate praise is the sole object. Such fulsome praise disgusts. The truth of the present attempt to describe worth, is felt by the writer, yet, he would not be thought to hold up Edward Rushton or any other man as the model of perfection. Every human being has his portion of alloy. But he wishes to prove by an eminent example, how much man may, by exercise of his faculties and moral capacities, advance himself in the practice and course of virtue. Examples of this kind, selected out of the middle walks of life, are cheering and animating, and may very materially assist by an honourable emulation, to incite to virtuous deeds, and tend to promote a closer attention to the dictates of unbending principle, a thing much wanting in the present day ; and therefore, essentially necessary to be more strongly inculcated.

Edward Rushton is praised, and justly praised, for the good qualities which he possessed ; but the great aim in penning the foregoing sketch is to advocate the cause of virtue, by exhibiting a bright example. The Roman poet exclaimed, Amicus Socrates! Amicus Plato! sed magis, Amicus veritas. So Edward Rushton was my friend, and I am proud to have enjoyed a share of his friendship, but the cause of virtue is dearer to me than any man, how much soever, like the subject of this memorial, he may have been distinguished by talents, and dignified by the proper employment of them.

The works of Rushton are not numerous, but they are truly valuable for their moral excellence. I have already observed that Rushton was not a first-rate genius, but as a man, he did honour to the age and country in which he lived.

Rushton's poetical pieces were not originally intended for publication, but being read and admired by his friends, they appeared first in the periodical journals of the day, and were afterwards collected together, and published in a small duodecimo volume, in London, in 1804 ; these, with his letters to General Washington, and Thomas Paine, are the only productions of his which were given to the public.

RUSHTON'S LETTER TO GENERAL WASHINGTON.

The following extracts from Rushton's letter to General Washington, will, I trust, be acceptable to my readers, as they will shew in what light he held this disgraceful traffic.

After paying some well-merited compliments to Washington's military talents, and patriotic exertions in the service of his country, during the Revolutionary war, he proceeds to animadvert on his conduct as a slave-holder, in the following terms.

" But it is not to the commander-in-chief of the American forces, nor to the President of the United States, that I have aught to address; my business is with George Washington of Mount-Vernon, in Virginia—a man, who, notwithstanding his hatred to oppression, and his ardent love of liberty, holds at this moment, hundreds of his fellow-beings in a state of abject bondage ; yes, you, who conquered under the banners of freedom ; you, who are now the first magistrate of a free people, are (strange to relate) a slave-holder. That a Liverpool merchant should endeavour to enrich himself by such a business, is not a matter of surprise, but that you, an enlightened character, strongly enamoured of your own freedom, you, who, if the British forces had succeeded in the Eastern states, would have retired with a few congenial spirits, to the rude fastnesses of the western wilds, there to have enjoyed that blessing, without which, a paradise would be disgusting, and with which the most savage region is not without its charms ; that you, I say, should continue to be a slave-holder, a

proprietor of human flesh and blood, creates in many
of your British friends, both astonishment and regret;
you, who are a republican, an advocate for the dis-
semination of knowledge, and for universal justice.
Where then are the arguments by which this shameful dereliction of principle can be supported? your
friend Jefferson has endeavoured to shew that the
Negroes are of an inferior order of beings, but surely
you will not have recourse to this subterfuge. Your
slaves, it may be urged, are well treated—that I deny,
man never can be well treated who is deprived of his
rights. They are well clothed, well fed, well lodged,
&c. Feed me with ambrosia, and wash it down with
nectar; yet, what are these if liberty be wanting?
you took arms in defence of the *Rights of Man ;*—
your Negroes are men:—Where then are the rights
of your Negroes?

It has been said by your apologists, that your feelings are inimical to slavery, and that you are induced
to acquiesce in it at present, merely from motives of
policy; the only true policy is justice, and he who
regards the consequences of an act, rather than the
justice of it, gives no very exalted proof of the greatness of his character. But if your feelings be actually repugnant to slavery, then are you more culpable
than the callous-hearted planter, who laughs at what
he calls the pitiful whinings of the abolitionists, because he believes slavery to be justifiable ! while you
persevere in a system which your conscience tells you
to be wrong. If we call the man obdurate, who
cannot perceive the atrociousness of slavery, what
epithet does he deserve, who, while he does perceive

its atrociousness, continues to be a proprietor of slaves ? Nor is it likely that your own unfortunate Negroes are the only sufferers, by your adhering to this nefarious business ; consider the force of an example like yours; consider how many of the sable race may now be pining in bondage, merely, forsooth, because the President of the United States, who has the character of a wise and good man, does not see cause to discontinue the long established practice. Of all the slave-holders under Heaven, those of the United States, appear to me the most reprehensible ; for man never is so truly odious as when he inflicts upon others that which he himself abominates. When the cup of slavery was presented to your countrymen, they rejected it with disdain, and appealed to the world, in justification of their conduct—yet, such is the inconsistency of man, that thousands upon thousands of those very people, with yourself amongst the number, are now sedulously employed in holding the self-same bitter draught to the lips of their sable brethren. From men who are strongly attached to their own rights, and have suffered much in their defence ;—one might have expected scrupulous attention to the rights of others ; did not experience show, that when we ourselves are oppressed, we perceive it with a lynx's eye ; but when we become the oppressors, no noon-tide bats are blinder ; you are boastful of your own rights; you are violators of the rights of others, and you are stimulated by an insatiable rapacity, to cruel and relentless oppression. In defending your own liberties, you undoubtedly suffered much, but if your Negroes, emulating the spirited example of their masters, were to throw off the galling yoke, and retiring peaceably to some uninhabited part of the Western region, were to resolve on liberty or death, what would be the conduct of the Southern planters on such an occasion? Nay; what would be your own conduct? you, who were " born in a land of liberty," who " early learned its value;" you, who " engaged in a perilous conflict to defend it;" you, who " in a word, devoted the best years of your life to secure its permanent establishment in your own country, and whose anxious recollection, whose sympathetic feelings, and whose best wishes are irresistibly excited; whensoever in any country you see an oppressed nation unfurl the banners of freedom."—Possessed of these energetic sentiments, what would be your conduct? would you have the virtue to applaud so just and animating a movement, as the revolt of your Southern Negroes? No; I fear both you and your countrymen, to gratify your own sordid views would scatter among an unoffending people, terror, desolation, and death. Harsh as this conclusion may appear, yet it is warranted by your present practice; for the man who can boast of his own rights, and hold two or three hundred of his fellow-beings in slavery, would not hesitate, in case of a revolt, to employ the most sanguinary means in his power, rather than forego that which the *truly* republican laws of his country are *pleased* to call his property. Shame! shame! that man should be deemed the property of man, or that the name of Washington should be found among the lists of such proprietors!

Should these strictures be deemed severe or unmerited on your part, how comes it, that while in the Northern or Middle states, the exertions of the Quakers, and other philanthropists, have produced such regulations as must speedily eradicate every trace of slavery in that quarter; how comes it, that from you, these humane efforts have never received the least countenance? If your mind have not sufficient firmness to do away that which is wrong, the moment you perceive it to be such, one might have expected that a plan for ameliorating the evil would have met with your warmest support; but no such thing. The just example of a majority of the states, has had no visible effect upon you; and as to the men of Maryland, of Virginia, of the two Carolinas, of Georgia, and of Kentucky, they smile contemptuously at the idea of Negro Emancipation, and with the States-constitution in one hand, and the cow-skin in the other, exhibit to the world such a spectacle, as every real friend to liberty must from his soul abominate.

"Then what is man, and what man seeing this, and having human feelings, does not blush and hang his head to think himself a man." Man does not readily perceive defects in that which he has been accustomed to venerate; hence it is, that you have escaped those animadversions, which your slave proprietorship has so long merited. For seven years you bravely fought the battles of your country, and contributed greatly to the establishment of her liberties; yet, you are a slave-holder. A majority of your countrymen have recently discovered, that slavery is an injustice, and are gradually abolishing the wrong; yet, you continue to be a slave-holder. You are a firm believer too, and your letters and speeches are replete with pious reflections on the Divine Being, Providence, &c. Yet you are a slave-holder! Oh Washington! ages to come will read with astonishment, that the man who was foremost to wrench the rights of America from the grasp of Britain, was the last to relinquish his own oppressive hold of poor and unoffending Negroes.

In the name of justice, what can induce you thus to tarnish your own well-earned celebrity, and to impair the fair features of American liberty with so foul and indelible a blot? Avarice is said to be the vice of age. Your slaves, old and young, male and female, father and mother, and child, might in the estimation of a Virginia planter, be worth from fifteen to twenty thousand pounds. Now, sir, are you sure that the unwillingness which you have shewn to liberate your Negroes, does not proceed from lurking pecuniary considerations? If this be the case, (and there are those who firmly believe it is) then there is no flesh left in your heart; and present reputation, future fame, and all that is estimable among the virtuous, are, for a few thousand pieces of paltry yellow dirt, irremediably renounced."

AUTHORITIES.

Belfast Magazine, vol. 5th and 7th—Liverpool Mercury, November, 1814.

THE LIFE

OF

JOHN GOUGH.

" On him fair science dawn'd in happier hours,
And waken'd into bloom young fancy's flowers."

Of all the surprising phenomena that have, in different ages, appeared among the human species, there is not one more difficult to be accounted for, than that of a blind man's excelling in the most diffi- cult and sublime parts of the mathematics; it seems, indeed, almost impossible, had we not the illustrious example before us of Professor Saunderson. We might, perhaps, have looked upon the instances of this kind related by authors, as fiction, or, at least, as exaggerated representations of the truth. The most remarkable of these instances, mentioned by his- torians, is that of Didymus, of Alexandria. The case of this extraordinary person was similar to that of our author, who, when twelve months old, was de- prived of his sight by the small pox, and retained no more idea of light and colours, than if he had been born blind.

John Gough was born on the 17th of January, in the year 1757, and was the oldest child of Nathan

Gough, shearman-dyer, of Kendal, and Susannah his wife. His father was the only child, by a first marriage, of Thomas Gough,* skinner and glover, of Wyersdale, in Lancashire; his mother was the oldest daughter of Mr. John Wilson, a respectable yeoman, who had a good estate on the west bank of Windermere lake. Of the subject of this biographical sketch, much might be said, even respecting the actions and pastimes of infancy; but this would be stepping beyond the necessary limits of these annals, and an improper interference with a work which, it is hoped, will not long be withheld from the public.† To all enquirers into the culture of enlargement of the human mind, such a work would be peculiarly acceptable, as unfolding the means by which he obtained a rich store of scientific knowledge, under difficulties and privations, apparently rendering such acquisitions nearly unattainable, if not impossible. At a very early age a misfortune befel him which, in his opinion, gave birth to the peculiarities of his character through life. Before the completion of his third year, he was

---

* Thomas Gough was the son of James Gough, who was not a native of Wyersdale, but the son of William Gough, a general in the Parliamentary army, and one of King Charles's judges. At the time of the Restoration he escaped the halter and axe of the executioner, by an early flight; after which he remained concealed many years in New England, with his friends and his father-in-law, Colonel Whaley, who not only faithfully secreted, but kindly supported him in his turn of fortune.

† The Prospectus of the Posthumous Works of John Gough was printed in 1826.

attacked with the small pox; this happened in December, 1759, and the virulence of the malady, joined to the injudicious treatment then in fashion, deprived him of his sight before the commencement of the next year. The loss indeed was not so total as to render him incapable of distinguishing day from night; but the slender ray of light which fell on the verge of the retina, was insufficient to afford him the least idea of colours, or the visible images of external objects which properly speaking constitute vision. Thus was "wisdom at one entrance quite shut out;" this proved the cause of opening others which, under different circumstances, might never have been explored. Into a detail of the exertions and contrivances by which he surmounted this great obstacle to mental improvement, we are precluded from entering, for the reason stated above; it must suffice, therefore, to notice briefly the progress of his early education, and the evidences of that distinction, which he attained in maturer life, as a man of science.*

At the age of six years he was placed under the care of Mr. Rebanks, at that time master of the school belonging to the society of Friends in Kendal. With this gentleman he began to study the princi-

---

* Gough is the friend alluded to in the following extract from Thomas Wilkinson's "Tours to the British Mountains."

" Ardent energies are not always crowned with wise achievements. I was once spending a few days at the foot of Blencathra. A party of six of us, on a midsummer morning, set off at four o'clock; to two of these individuals the ascent of such a high and rugged mountain might have seemed impracticable. The lame and the blind, without extraordi-

ples of the English language, prior to engaging with the Latin; but, as ought to have been expected at that early age, much time was consumed to little or no advantage. His subsequent attempts, however, to conquer the difficulties of the Latin grammar, were more successful; and under the tuition of Mr. George Bewly, who was appointed master of the school when Mr. Gough was about twelve years old, he made a rapid progress in the acquisition of that language. Mr. Bewly it appears was well prepared for his occupation, not only by his classical knowledge, but also by his attainments in the different branches of natural philosophy; and great were the advantages which Mr. Gough derived from the latter qualifications. From a very early period of infancy he had shewed a taste for zoology, and he now began to enlarge his knowledge of organic bodies, by extending his re-

---

nary minds, would not have hazarded the attempt amid the rocky steeps of this mountain; but the company of genius and science was courted, and not withheld on the occasion, and the first that was seen standing on the summit of the mountain, was the lame leaning on his crutch and staff. To the blind I attempted a description of the fearful precipices beneath us: but it was the first thing I repented of that day, —when I saw him fall on the ground with dizziness, and cling to the earth, and scream out, with the apprehension of tumbling down the rocks into the abyss below. Till then I thought that the idea of giddiness must be received at the eye; certainly it was as vivid in the mind of our learned and accomplished companion, from what he heard, as if he had seen the terrors around him. But we now moderated our descriptions, and only talked of extent, and the appearance of distant objects."

searches from the animal to the vegetable kingdom. To botanical pursuits, all his spare time from the necessary studies of the school was assiduously devoted; and as his ardour in cultivating this science never relaxed, he soon conquered the difficulties opposed to the gratification of his taste by the want of sight, and became enabled to discriminate and arrange, with great accuracy, the plants which came under his notice. Mr. Gough, indeed, possessed a power of discrimination and a retentiveness of memory, really astonishing.* His usual method of examining a plant, when particular accuracy was required, was by applying to its several parts the tip of his tongue; ordinary plants he could easily and readily recognise with the touch of his fingers. These pursuits, however, were not permitted to interfere with his classical studies; for it appears that, under the able instructions of Mr. Bewly, he not only gained a competent knowledge of the languages, but also a taste for the compositions of the ancients.

In the year 1772, Mr. Gough's attention was first turned to experimental philosophy; and perusing, with characteristic assiduity, the works of Mr. Boyle, he soon learned the nature of the phenomena arising from the difference in the specific gravity of fluids, and acquired correct notions respecting the doctrine of hydrostatics, and also pneumatics. He soon after-

---

*A circumstance occurred about four or five years before his death, which serves to illustrate this remark. A rare plant was at that time put into his hands, which he very soon called by its name; observing also, that he had never met with more than one specimen of it, and that was fifty years ago.

wards, but at what precise period is not clearly ascertained, entered upon the study of mathematics, under the tuition of Mr. John Slee, at that time residing at Mungrisdale, a sequestered part of Cumberland. As a teacher of mathematics, this gentleman's reputation stood deservedly high, and perhaps a more judicious choice of a tutor for such a pupil could not have been made. Whatever were the previous acquirements of the latter, still his deficiencies and disadvantages must have been many ; much therefore was to be done, and by the united skill and industry of both, much was accomplished. Of the particular mode of instruction adopted, a very particular and interesting account has been given by Mr. Slee himself; which, being intended for the work before referred to, cannot be here inserted. All that it is necessary in this brief memoir to state is, that the mode was so successful, as not only to give Mr. Gough a taste for mathematical knowledge, but to lay a foundation for those high attainments, which subsequently entitled him to rank among the most distinguished mathematicians of the age. In after life he was eminent as a teacher in that science, and out of the limited number of his pupils, some became senior wranglers at Cambridge, one of the highest honours to which the students in that University are encouraged to aspire.*   But

---

*Mr. Whewell, now tutor of Trinity College, Cambridge, was second wrangler in his year. Mr. Dawes, tutor of Downing College, Cambridge, was fourth wrangler.   Mr. King, now tutor of Queen's College, Cambridge, (esteemed one of the first mathematicians of the age,) was senior wrangler in his year.   Mr. Gaskin, tutor of Jesus' College, Cambridge,

to trace the subject of this brief memoir minutely, through the early exercise and gradual expansion of his mental powers, would lead us beyond our prescribed limits. To ascertain the extent of his acquirements, our readers must be referred to the essays, published in the "Memoirs of the Literary and Philosophical Society of Manchester," and in "Nicholson's Journal," of which a catalogue is subjoined. They have been highly valued by the most competent judges, and they certainly contain decisive evidence of the acuteness of his mind, and of the accuracy of his knowledge in various departments of science.

We have now only to add, that Mr. Gough was fully occupied in the duties of his employment as an instructor of youth, and in his usual philosophical investigations, to the close of the year 1823, when indications of declining powers began to be visible to his friends. Repeated attacks of epilepsy after inconsiderable intervals, though not materially injuring his mental faculties, gradually undermined his bodily health, and clearly pointed out the approaching termination of his earthly course. He died July 27th, 1825, in the sixty-eighth year of his age; and his remains were interred in the church yard of Kendal, on the Sunday morning after his decease, attended by his family, and a few select friends.

---

was second wrangler in his year. These gentlemen were all pupils of Mr. Gough. Mr. John Dalton, the eminent philosopher, and president of the Manchester Philosophical Society, was four or five years under Mr. Gough's instructions in mathematics and natural philosophy.

List of Essays, from the pen of Mr. Gough, communicated to the Manchester Philosophical Society.

1. (1790.) Reasons for supposing that Lakes have been more numerous than they are at present, with an attempt to assign the causes whereby they have been effaced.

2. The Laws of Motion of a Cylinder compelled by the repeated Strokes of a falling Block to penetrate an Obstacle, the Resistance of which is an invariable Force.

3. 4. Experiments and Observations on the Vegetation of Seeds.

5. (1796.) On the Variety of Voices.

6. (1801.) An Investigation of the Method whereby Men judge by the Ear, of the Position of sonorous Bodies, relative to their own Persons.

7. The Theory of Compound Sounds.

8. (1803.) A Description of a Property of Caoutchouc, or India Rubber, with some Reflections on the Cause of the Elasticity of this Substance.

9. An Essay on the Theory of Mixed Gases, and the State of Water in the Atmosphere.

10. (1804.) A Reply to Mr. Dalton's Objections to a late Theory of Mixed Gases.

11. Theorems and Problems intended to elucidate the Mechanical Principle called Vis Viva.

12. (1811.) Observations on the Ebbing and Flowing Well at Giggleswick, in the West Riding of Yorkshire, with a Theory of Reciprocating Fountains.

13. (1812.) Remarks on the Summer Birds of Passage, and on Migration in general.

14. The Laws of Statical Equilibrium analytically investigated.

List of Mr. Gough's communications, published in Nicholson's Journal.

1. On the supposed Revival of Insects after long immersion in Wine, or other intoxicating Liquor. Vol. iii.

2. A Statical Enquiry into the Source of Nutrition in succulent Vegetables. Ibid.

3. Instances of Suspended Animation in Vegetables. Ibid.

4. On the Exhibition of a Series of Primes, and the Resolution of a compound Number into all its Factors. Ibid.

5. Facts and Observations to explain the curious Phenomenon of Ventriloquism. Ibid.

6. Reply to Dr. Young's Letter on the Theory of Compound Sounds. Vol. iv.

7. On the Nature of Grave Harmonics. Ibid.

8. On the Nature of Musical Sounds, in Reply to Dr. Young. Ibid.

9. The Theory of Compound Sounds. Vol. v.

10. Experiments and Observations in Support of that Theory of Ventriloquism which is founded on the Reflection of Sound. Vol. vii.

11. Scoteography, or the Art of Writing in the Dark. Vol. viii.

12. On the Solution of Water in the Atmosphere; and on the Nature of Atmospherical Air. Vol. ix.

13. Narrative of some less common Effects of Lightning, by the Rev. Jonathan Wilson; with Remarks by Mr. Gough. Ibid.

14. Strictures on Mr. Dalton's Doctrine of Mixed Gases and an Answer to Mr. Henry's Defence of the same. Ibid.

15. Atmospherical Air not a mechanical Mixture of the Oxygen and Azotic Gases, demonstrated from the specific Gravities of these Fluids. Ibid.

16. Experiments proving the Necessity of Atmospherical Oxygen in the process of Vegetation. Vol. x.

17. Farther Observations on the Constitution of Mixed Gases. Ibid.

18. Experiments and Remarks on the Augmentation of Sounds. Ibid.

19. A Mathematical Theory of the Speaking Trumpet. Ibid.

20.   Theorems respecting the Properties of the Sides of Triangles, intersected by right Lines drawn from the three Angles, so as to meet in one Point.   Vol. xi.

21.   Investigation of the Properties of the Lines drawn in a Circle, by Mr. Boswell.   Vol. xii.

22.   On the division of an Arch of a Circle into two such Parts that their Sines, or Co-sines, or Versed-sines shall have a given Relation.   Vol. xiii.

23.   On the Cause of Fairy Rings.   Ibid.

24.   Experiments on the Magnetism of Slender Iron Wire. Ibid.

25.   Experiments on the Temperature of Water surrounded by Freezing Mixtures.   Ibid.

26.   Observations and experiments to shew that the Effects ascribed by Mr. Dispan to the perpendicular Descent of Hoar Frost, are not so general as to support his Theory.   Vol. xvi.

27.   Remarks on Torpidity in Animals.   In two letters. Vol. xviii.

28.   Description of a correct Chamber Barometer.   Vol. xx.

29.   An Essay on Polygonal Numbers, containing the Demonstration of a Proposition respecting whole Numbers in general.   Vol. xxi.

30.   A Mathematical Problem, with the Investigation. Ibid.

31.   Answer to Mr. Barlow's Remarks on the Essay on Polygonal Numbers.   Vol. xxii.

39.   An Abstract of a Meteorological Journal for the Years 1807 and 1808, kept at Middleshaw, near Kendal.   Vol. xxv.

33.   Experiments on the Expansion of moist Air raised to the boiling Temperature.   Ibid.

34.   An Inquiry, geometrical and arithmetical, into certain Properties of Solids in general; and of the five regular Bodies in particular.   Vol. xxx.

35.   On the Place of a Sound produced by a Musical String.   Vol. xxxii.

36. Remarks on the Perforations made in Paper by elec-
trical Batteries.   Vol. xxxv.

AUTHORITIES.

WILKINSON'S Mountain Rambles.—NICHOLSON'S Annals
of Kendal.

THE LIFE

OF

THOMAS HOLLAND,

OF MANCHESTER,

THE BLIND TEACHER.

"Yet he was kind, or, if severe in aught,
The love he bore to learning was his fault."

A few particulars in the history of this interesting character appeared in some of the periodical journals of the day; but, as all the accounts that I have seen were imperfect, I have been enabled, through the kindness of his family, to add a few additional facts, which have never been published. They will teach us that what appear to be misfortunes and privations, are appointed by our Heavenly Father for good, and may be turned to advantage by an active, intelligent, and pious mind.

Mr. Holland was born at Manchester, October 29, 1760, and spent his early years under the care of his parents, who long kept a flourishing boarding and day school for young ladies, in that town. At ten years of age he became a pupil of his uncle, the Rev. Philip Holland, of Bolton, whose eminence, as a teacher of youth, has still some living witnesses.

Here, his natural quickness of intellect, under such judicious direction, rendered the acquisition of knowledge extremely easy and rapid; he soon obtained a competent share of classical and French literature, and became particularly expert in arithmetic, and geography. Being designed for trade, he did not pursue the higher classics so far as several of his school fellows. He was intended to pursue the trade of a yarn merchant, which was his father's occupation, and with this design he was placed as an apprentice with Mr. Mort, of Cowbent; but, when about 18 years old, he was gradually, but totally, deprived of sight. He was now reduced to that helpless condition which Milton has so feelingly described, in the following pathetic lines,—

> "O dark, dark, dark, amid the blaze of noon,
> Irrecoverably dark, total eclipse,
> Without all hope of day!
> O first created beam, and thou great word,
> *Let there be light,* and light was over all!
> Why am I thus bereaved thy prime decree?
> The sun to me is dark,
> And silent."—

But happy is it for us, that we are constantly under the eye of a superintending Providence, who never fails to accommodate to the burden the strength appointed to bear it; and, in our distresses, affords not only those alleviations and needful aids which enable us to support them, but also makes those sufferings frequently instrumental in producing the means by which they are mitigated. This is peculiarly the case with respect to the blind; for though nothing beneath the skies can compensate their loss, yet they derive from it advantages which those who are blessed with sight do not possess, which make the loss of it supportable, and furnish a needful supply of intellectual consolation.

This privation prevented Mr. Holland from pursuing the business for which he was originally intended; and he, at first, endeavoured to prepare himself for the musical profession; but his attention being directed to teaching, in a school kept by his mother, he afterwards became master of one of the most distinguished ladies' schools in Manchester, and attended a great number of private pupils in that town and neighbourhood. In this profession, he was particularly distinguished for his power of exciting the attention, and cultivating the understandings of his pupils; and his examinations for ascertaining whether they understood their lessons, were remarkably accurate and discriminating. In conjunction with his brother, the Rev. John Holland, of Bolton, he published three editions of " Exercises for the Memory and Understanding," partly selected and partly original. His original contributions to this book were dialogues and pieces of poetry, well adapted to convey instruction; such were the supposed "Dialogues between the Severn and the Wye," and the "Ouse and the Trent;" giving a complete account of the parts of England and Wales through which those rivers flow, and of events in the history of England which happened there; the work also contained descriptions of birds and their notes, and of animals and their food. His peculiar infirmity led him to carry on his plan of instruction very much by conversation, and close questioning on the books which he gave his pupils to read;

and he may be said to have been the father of the "Interrogative System," which has since been claimed by another, whose merit, however, in promoting its extension, it is not here intended to question. His great skill in ready calculation, rendered him also a most valuable and efficient member of the committees of several of the canals, railways, and water-works, connected with the important district in which he resided.

In these useful labours he spent a long life, highly esteemed among an extensive circle of friends, for mental qualities of no common kind, extensive knowledge, and great cheerfulness; qualities which continued to the last, amidst much bodily infirmity, under which he laboured during several of the latter years of his life. He died on the 11th of June, 1829, calm and resigned; and, at the close, so easily, that the moment of his departure was not perceived, by those of his numerous family who surrounded his bedside. He was a constant attendant of the chapel in Mosley Street, where his funeral sermon was preached by the excellent Minister, the Rev. J. J. Taylor, who has permitted the following well merited character of him to close this tribute to his memory. "Early in his career, our departed friend was visited by one of the severest privations which could have befallen an intelligent and inquiring mind, a privation which for ever closed up one of the principal avenues to knowledge, and compelled the sufferer to resort more entirely to his internal resources. He once observed to me, with a rational and cheerful piety, which forcibly struck me at the time, and which I therefore wish not to omit mentioning, that this privation, by the kind arrangement of Providence, had been converted into one of the chief blessings of his existence ; had procured for him innumerable friends, and had been a principal means of his great usefulness in life; had directed his time and thoughts to the pursuit of knowledge, and the cultivation of the human mind ; and had thus saved him, by the quiet and unambitious course of life into which it had induced him to enter, from very distressing embarrassments and misfortunes, to which others, whose early prospects were far more flattering, had ultimately fallen victims. My friends, let us turn this good man's example to our own account. Like him, let us devote our lives to useful, honourable, and active employment; like him, let us be forward to promote rational instruction and rational entertainment among the young; like him, let us find a blessing in every dispensation of Providence, and extract the elements of improvement and thankfulness even from privation and suffering ; like him, let our Christianity be seen in deeds of active usefulness, and in faithfully using the gifts and opportunities that we enjoy ; like him, let us lean on the God of our fathers, and wait in patience His merciful signal of release. That friend is gone ! Gone, as we hope and trust, through the mercy of God, to the just man's reward. That friend is gone, and hath left the place which he so long and so usefully filled in society, to be filled by the young and rising generation."

AUTHORITIES.

Monthly Repository, and Review of Theology and general Literature. No. 722.

SOME ACCOUNT OF

DAVID McBEATH,

TEACHER AT THE ASYLUM FOR THE BLIND,

IN EDINBURGH.

THIS ingenious and very interesting person was born at Dalkeith, in 1792. He lost his sight at an early age, by a severe disease, which so enfeebled his frame,that his stature, appearance, and voice, continued to the last to be those of a mere youth. His abilities were great, and his mind was cultivated far beyond what is commonly to be found in one of his order in society. He had a powerfully inventive genius, as is exemplified in his maturing a mode of communication for the blind, by means of a string alphabet, now used in the Asylum at Glasgow, and elsewhere. This was considered by the learned editors of the " Edinburgh Philosophical Journal," of such importance as to demand a full description in that work. He also contrived a board for the study of music, arithmetic, algebra, and other branches of the mathematics. His success as a teacher of his companions in misfortune, was greatindeed; and frequently called forth the approbation of the public in Edinburgh, at the various examination of the pupils in the Asylum, which took place year after year. He had the satisfaction of sending one of his pupils to Glasgow, as teacher in the Asylum there; by whose exertions that institution has been since distinguished. And two others were established in America, in the same capacity, in flourishing schools, recently instituted, for the blind. The latter teachers were selected by a gentleman sent to Europe to visit all the institutions for the blind fort hat purpose; that in Edinburgh being the last he visited. The newspaper press, (perhaps little aware, at the time, of the important and valuable results that were to arise from the full accounts given of the examinations at Edinburgh,) has been the means of calling forth christian benevolence, both in Great Britain, and on the continents of Europe and America; and, while the publications gratified those immediately concerned, they have been the means, under divine providence, of diffusing a spirit of pure philanthrophy, which can never be abused or misdirected; rescuing a valuable portion of suffering humanity from a state of misery and indigence, and exchanging their sad condition for one of comfort and benefit, both as to time and eternity. David McBeath died in Edinburgh, on the 7th of November, 1834, in the 42nd year of his age.

The following short account of his curious contrivance, (the string alphabet,) may not be uninteresting to the reader. The twenty-six letters of the alphabet are divided into seven classes, proceeding from A to Z; each class consists of four letters, with the exception of the last, which comprehends but two. The first four letters, or A, B, C, D, are each formed by a large round knot; the second four, E, F, G, H, by a knot projecting from the string; the third, I, J, K, L, by a knot vulgarly called a drummer's plait; the fourth, **M, N, O, P,** by a simple noose; the fifth, **Q, R, S, T,** by a noose with the string drawn through it; the sixth, **U, V, W, X,** by a noose with a netting knot formed upon it; and the seventh class, or **Y** and **Z,** by a twisted noose. Thus there are seven different kinds of knots to indicate the whole letters of the alphabet; but to distinguish each of the four letters in a class from the others, the expedient is adopted, of adding a common small knot, at a less or greater distance from the letter to which it belongs. By this plan, the letter **A** is indicated only by the knot of the class to which it belongs; **B** is the same knot repeated, but close to it is a small common knot; **C** is the same knot repeated, with the small knot, half an inch distant; and **D** is the same knot repeated, with the small knot an inch distant. The same plan goes on throughout, so that by first feeling the kind of knot, and then feeling whether it has a small knot attached, and at what distance, any letter may be instantly told. The length of the string alphabet is little more than three feet, and any blind person, with the ordinary sense of touch, may learn the whole in an hour.

AUTHORITIES.

Scottish Guardian, November 7, 1834.— Chambers's Edinburgh Journal, April, 1834.

Mr. NELSON,
THE BLIND PROFESSOR.

In the remains of the late Reverend D. Edmund Griffin, of New York, there is a very interesting account of a blind gentleman, named Nelson. This accomplished scholar was the classical professor in Rutger's College, New Jersey, and is mentioned by the learned editor of Griffin's' Memoirs in the following passage.

" At the age of fourteen, Master Griffin was placed at a school just then rising into great celebrity. This was kept in the city of New York, by Mr. Nelson, distinguished at that time as *the Blind Teacher*, but afterwards more widely known as the learned classical professor, in Rutger's College, New Jersey. The mention of his name recalls to the writer, who was his college class-mate, the merits of this singular man; and as death has now turned his misfortune into an instructive lesson, he may be permitted to dwell for a moment upon his eventful story. The life of Mr. Nelson was a striking exemplification of that resolution which conquers fortune. Total blindness, after a long and gradual advance, came upon him about his twentieth year, when terminating his college course. It found him poor, and left him, to all appearance, both pennyless and wretched, with two sisters to maintain ; without money, without friends, without a profession, and without sight. Under such an accumulation of griefs, most minds would have sunk, but with him it was otherwise ; at all times proud and resolute, his spirit rose at once, into what might well be termed, a fierceness of independence, and he resolved within himself to be indebted for support to no exertions but his own. His classical education, which, owing to his feeble vision, had been necessarily imperfect, he now determined to complete; and immediately entered upon the apparently hopeless task, with a view to fit himself as a teacher of youth. He instructed his sisters in the pronunciation of Greek and Latin, and employed one or other constantly, in the task of reading aloud to him the classics usually taught in the schools. A naturally faithful memory, spurred on by such strong excitement, performed its oft-repeated miracles, and in a space of time incredibly short, he became master of their contents, even to the minutest points of critical reading. In illustration of this, the author remembers on one occasion, that a dispute having arisen between Mr. N. and the Classical Professor of the College, as to the construction of a passage in Virgil, from which his students were reciting, the Professor appealed to the circumstance of a comma in the sentence, as conclusive of the question. 'True,' said Mr. N., colouring with strong emotion; 'but permit me to observe,' said he, turning his sightless eyeballs towards the book he held in his hand, 'that, in my *Heyne's* edition, it is a colon, and not a comma.'

"At this period, a gentleman, who incidentally became acquainted with his history, in a feeling somewhat between pity and confidence, placed his two sons under his charge, with a view to enable him to try the experiment of teaching. A few months' trial was sufficient; he then fearlessly appeared before the

public, and at once challenged a comparison with the
best established classical schools in the city.*   The
novelty and boldness of the attempt attracted general
attention ; the lofty confidence he displayed in himself excited respect ; and soon, his untiring assiduity,
his real knowledge, and a burning zeal, which, knowing no bounds in his own devotion to his scholars,
awakened somewhat of a corresponding spirit in their
minds, completed the conquest.   His reputation
spread daily; scholars flocked to him in crowds;
competition sunk before him ; and, in the course of a
few years, he found himself in the enjoyment of an
income superior to that of any college patronage in
the United States, with, to him, the infinitely higher
gratification of having risen above the pity of the

---

* Sir Kenelm Digby mentions a blind man who lived in his
house, and was preceptor to his sons, the loss of whose sight
seemed to be overpaid by his other abilities. He could beat
the cleverest chess players, and would play at cards and tables,
as well as most men ; and likewise at bowls, shuttleboard, and
other games, wherein one would imagine a clear sight to be
absolutely requisite. When he taught his scholars to declaim,
represent a tragedy, or the like, he knew, by their voice, whether
they stood up or sat down, and all the different gestures and
situations of their bodies; so that they behaved themselves
before him with the same propriety as if he had seen them
perfectly. He could feel in his body, and chiefly in his head,
(as he himself affirmed,) a certain effect, whereby he knew
when the sun was up, and could discern a clear from a cloudy
day. That he frequently told without being mistaken, when,
for trial's sake, he was lodged in a close chamber, into which
the sunshine had no admittance, nor did any body come to
him, to give notice of the state of the weather.

world, and fought his own blind way to honourable independence. Nor was this all ; he had succeeded in placing classical education on higher ground than any of his predecessors or contemporaries had done, and he felt proud to think that he was, in some measure, a benefactor to that college which, a few years before, he had entered in poverty, and quitted in blindness.

"The examination of candidates for admission into Columbia College, was, at that time, long and rigid, continuing for several days, and terminating in an arrangement of their names in order of merit. The older schools were not willing to yield pre-eminence to a blind competitor, and their choice scholars were therefore studiously drilled for the occasion; most of the teachers, and many anxious fathers, were in close attendance, to encourage their sons or pupils by their presence, or perhaps to become judges of the impartiality of the decision. ' Among these,' says Professor Mc. Vicker, ' Mr. Nelson might always be distinguished, the first to come, the last to go; the most anxious, and yet the most confident; his blind steps, as he entered the hall, being followed, rather than directed, by the youth who attended him, so singularly resolute was he in all his motions.' His beloved pupil, Edmund Griffin, on this occasion triumphed over all competitors, though some of them were much his seniors, and of more than ordinary talents and attainments."

AUTHORITY.

Blackwood's Magazine, for July, 1832.

RELIGION

WHEN religion was an integral part of tribal society life, the blind were often important figures. Elderly blind people were prophets, soothsayers, and religious leaders. With the advent of organized religion, the blind tended to be excluded from religious leadership. As William Artman and L. V. Hall point out in their 1853 book, *Beauties and Achievements of the Blind,* "As ministers of the gospel, the blind have in every age and branch of the Christian church received but little encouragement, if they have not always been indiscriminately rejected. . . . In [ancient] Judaism under the law of Moses, blindness was a disqualification for priestly office."

While other traditions excluded blind people from their priestly ranks, Islam—even if it did not fully embrace the blind—accepted them for certain roles. Blind Muslims became teachers, singers, and workers in the mosques, calling the faithful to prayer from minarets.

Ishbel Ross in her 1950 book, *Journey into Light: The Story of the Education of the Blind* mentions that in the ninth century the blind in Japan were divided into two classes—the Todo, or blind lay people who looked after the welfare of the sightless in the feudal system, and the Moso, or blind monks, who were organized by the Buddhist Kakai (774–835), a sculptor and calligrapher who studied and founded the sect

known as Shingon-shu. The blind monks had
their music, known as *biwa*.

By Wilson's time, a few notable blind ministers could be found in Protestant churches and
universities. Wilson mentions that although
Joan Wast (?–1553) was blind from birth, she
learned at an early age to knit stockings and
sleeves and to assist her father in the business of
rope making. During the reign of Queen Mary,
Wast was put to death for her religious beliefs.

Rev. John Troughton (1637–81) was a Puritan
and prominent blind religious figure. He became
blind from smallpox at the age of four. In 1655 he
went to Oxford University and earned a bachelor
of arts degree. He lost his teaching fellowship at
Oxford after the restoration of Charles II and became a teacher in Bichester. According to John
Kitto in his 1845 book, *The Lost Senses,* when the
Declaration for Religious Toleration was issued
in 1671 Troughton and other bachelors in divinity
proceeded to the city of Oxford to begin preaching. Troughton was deemed by far the best
teacher. When Troughton died in 1681, Abraham
James, a blind minister of the free church in
Woodstock, preached his funeral sermon.

Rev. Richard Lucas (1648–1715) is mentioned
by both Wilson and Kitto. He became blind
when he was a young man and went on to be a
minister. Although completely blind, he "dis-
charged the duties of his holy calling with zeal

and fidelity that would have done him credit, even if he had possessed all his bodily powers in the highest perfection."

Rev. Edward Stokes (1705–98) was blinded at the age of nine when his brother accidentally shot him. He later went to the university and became a minister. Wilson notes that despite his blindness, Stokes performed the service of his church for many years, with only the assistance of a person to read the lessons.

The story of the Reverend Thomas Blacklock (1721–91) appears in all four editions of Wilson's *Biography*. Blacklock was blinded by smallpox at the age of one. As a young man he was a friend of Robert Burns and Sir Walter Scott. Berthold Lowenfeld in his 1975 book, *The Changing Status of the Blind: From Separation to Integration*, mentions that he began to write poetry and studied for the ministry. Although he achieved fame as a preacher and was an ordained minister, the prejudice of his contemporaries prevented him from a parish-church career. Ross says that "Blacklock was an important link in the long chain of circumstance that pushed ahead the training of the blind. Like Dr. Samuel Gridley Howe many years later in America, he mingled with men and women of letters who drew attention in their writings and conversations to the state of the blind. He was not only a notable sightless man himself but he worked quietly for the benefit of his fellow sufferers. His translation of Valentin Haüy's essay was widely read and studied. It was a factor in the sudden rise of schools for the blind throughout Britain." He helped establish the school for the blind in Edinburgh, although it was not opened until 1793, after his death.

"The Blind Clergyman," Dr. Guyse, is mentioned only by Wilson. The account he cites is taken from the *Morning Chronicle* of January 21, 1791, and tells the story of a man who, while rambling on the borders of Wales, meets a sixty-year-old man also on horseback. On following him across a ford he finds to his astonishment that the guide he has been following is blind. Each week the old pastor rode his horse eight "long Welsh miles" from his home to the village church to conduct services. "As we entered the church yard, the respectful 'How do you do?' of the young, and the hearty shakes by the hand of the old, and the familiar gambols of the children, showed how their old pastor reigned in the hearts of all."

In the nineteenth century some of the first works translated into line type (embossed letter systems) for the blind were parts of the Bible. A blind minister, the Reverend William Moon (1818–94), invented the embossed-letter system that bears his name, "Moon Type," and first used it to carry out his missionary work.

Today many blind people serve their religious communities in various capacities, including blind ministers who have used the radio. Most of the great religious works and texts are now available to the blind and visually impaired. Listed in the American Foundation for the Blind's *Directory of Services for the Blind and Visually Impaired Persons in the United States and Canada* (24th edition, 1993) are more than twenty producers and publishers of religious materials. These are produced in braille, large print, and cassette tapes and range from music and hymn books to religious magazines, teaching aids, texts, devotional materials, translations of Bibles into other languages, and recordings of radio and television services. Churches increasingly have people who are willing to record for the blind as well as computers with a software program that translates print into braille. These advances make it possible for blind ministers and lay people to obtain the latest changes in services, hymns, texts, readings, and announcements.

JOAN WAST,

THE BLIND MARTYR.

"Superstition, still to reason blind,
With iron sceptre rules the darken'd mind."

I am now about to introduce to my readers a female, who though she was not distinguished for rank, talents, or education, yet deserves particular notice, as being one of that noble army of the reformation, who counted not their lives dear unto themselves. Thousands and tens of thousands of these worthies finished their course with joy, at the stake, or on the scaffold; "these are they which came out of great tribulation, and have washed their robes, and made them white, in the blood of the Lamb."

Among many who glorified God by suffering martyrdom, in the reign of Queen Mary of bloody memory, Joan Wast, a poor woman, deserves never to be forgotten. Though blind from her birth, she learned, at an early age, to knit stockings and sleeves, and to assist her father in the business of rope makind; always discovering the utmost aversion to idleness or sloth. After the death of her parents, she lived with her brother; and, by daily attendance at church, and hearing divine service read in the vulgar tongue, during the reign of King Edward, she became deeply imbued with religious principles. This rendered her desirous of possessing the word of God, so that having, by her own labour, at length earned and saved as much money as would purchase a New Testament,* she procured one, and as she could not read it herself, got others to read it to her; among these was an old man, seventy years of age a prisoner for debt in the Common-hall at Derby, and clerk of the parish, who read a chapter to her almost every day. She would also sometimes give a penny or two, as she could spare the money, to those who would not read to her without payment. By these means she became well acquainted with the New Testament, and could repeat

---

* In the reign of Edward I., the price of a Bible was £30, a most enormous sum; for, in 1272, the pay of a labouring man was only three half-pence a day, so that such a work would have cost him more than fifteen years' labour. In the reign of Edward III., the New Testament of Wickliffe's version sold for four marks and forty pence, or £2. 16s. 8d. From 1461 to 1483, just at the time when the art of printing was discovered, Faust (or Faustus) sold his printed copies at Paris for sixty crowns, while the scribes demanded five hundred; but in the latter end of Richard III.'s reign the price was reduced to thirty crowns. " In the reign of Henry VIII.," says the good old Martyrologist, " the desire that the people had for knowledge, may appear by their sitting up all night in reading or hearing; also, by their expenses and charges in buying of books in English, of whom some gave five marks, some more, some less, for a book, and some gave a load of hay for a few chapters of St. James, or of St. Paul, in English." An act of Parliament was subsequently obtained by the enemies of truth, in which it was enacted, "that no artifycers, prentices, journeymen, servingmen, husbandmen, or labourers," were to read the Bible or New Testament in English, to themselves or to any others, privately or openly, on pain of death.

many chapters without the book; and daily increasing in sacred knowledge, she exhibited its influence on her life, till, when she was about twenty-two years of age, she was condemned for not believing the doctrine of transubstantiation, and was burned at Derby, August 1, 1553.

During the reign of the gloomy bigot Mary, one Thomas Edwards, a boy of seventeen years of age, and also blind, was burnt alive in Smithfield, for asserting that the Scriptures were the only authority we ought to acknowledge. From the above facts, the reader will see the honourable share the blind had in that glorious struggle between light and darkness, liberty and slavery, which in the end produced the great moral revolution that took place in the 16th century, to which, under God, we owe all the civil and religious liberties we now enjoy.

———

AUTHORITY.
Townly, page 193.

THE LIFE

OF

THE REV. JOHN TROUGHTON.

"Unskilful he to fawn, or seek for power,
By doctrines fashion'd to the varying hour."

THIS eminent divine lived in the seventeenth century. He was what was then called a Puritan; a poor,
despised, persecuted class of men, of whom the world
was not worthy. Wood, author of the "Athenæ Oxonienses," although greatly opposed to the Puritans,
speaks very favourably of Troughton, and he is also
mentioned by Calamy and Palmer, as a man of great
learning and talents, and of much moderation. I
prefer Wood's account of him, which I shall insert
here, to those of the other two.

"John Troughton, son of Nathan Troughton, a
clothier, was born in the city of Coventry, and educated in the free-school there, under Samuel Frankland,
he became scholar of St. John's College, 1655, and
afterwards a Fellow, and Bachelor of Arts. Upon the
restoration of King Charles II. he was, however, ejected, to make room for one who had been expelled by
the visitors in 1648, and retired to a market town in
Oxfordshire, commonly called Bicester; where, living

a moderate nonconformist, he read academical learning to young men, and sometimes preached in private, whereby he got a comfortable subsistence. Upon the issuing out of his Majesty's declaration for the toleration of religion, dated 15th of March, 1671, this Mr. Troughton was one of those four, (Dr. Henry Langley, and Thomas Gilbert, and Henry Cornish, Bachelor of Divinity, being the other three,) who were appointed by the principal heads of the brethren, to carry on the work of preaching within the city of Oxford. The place where they held their meetings was in Thames-street, without the north gate, in a house which had been built a little before the civil war began, by Thomas Punn, alias Thomas Aires; where each person endeavouring to shew his parts, this our author Troughton was, by the auditory of scholars, (who came among them merely out of novelty,) held the best, and was by them most applauded. The truth is, though the man had been blind, occasioned by the small-pox, ever since he was four years old, yet he was a good school divine and metaphysician, and was much commended while he was in the University for his disputations. He was not of so busy, turbulent, and furious a spirit, as those of his persuasion commonly are, but very moderate. And although he often preached, as occasions offered themselves, in prohibited assemblies, yet he did not make it his business, by employing all the little tricks and artifices, too frequently practised by other hot-headed zealots of his fraternity, viz. vilifying and railing at the established ordinances of the church, libelling the conformable ministry, keeping their meetings at the very time when the services and administration of the church are regularly performing, &c.—he did not, I say, by these and such like most unwarrantable contrivances, endeavour to withdraw weaker persons from the sacred bosom of the church, in order to fix and herd them in associated, defying conventicles. He was respected by, and maintained an amicable correspondence with some of the conformable clergy, because of his great knowledge and moderation. He hath written and published, as follows:

"Lutherus Redivivus; or, the Protestant Doctrine of Justification by Faith only, vindicated; and the plausible opinion of justification by faith and obedience, proved to be Arminian and Popish, and to lead unavoidably to Socinianism. Part I. London, 1667. This is reflected on by Thomas Hotchkis, in his preface to the second part of 'A Discourse concerning Imputed Righteousness, &c.' London, 1678.

"Lutherus Redivivus; or, the Protestant Doctrine of Justification by Christ's Righteousness imputed to Believers, explained and vindicated. Part II. London, 1678.

"Letter to a Friend touching God's Providence about sinful actions; in answer to a Letter, entitled, 'The Reconcileableness of God's Presence, &c.' and also to a Postscript of that letter. London, 1678.

"Popery the Grand Apostasy; being the substance of certain Sermons preached on 2 Thess. ii chap. from verse 1 to 12, on occasion of the desperate plot of the Papists against the King, kingdom, and Protestant Religion. To which is added, a Sermon on Rev. xviii. 4. preached on the 5th. of Nov. 1678. London, 1680

" An Apology for the Nonconformists, shewing their reasons, both for their not conforming, and for their preaching publicly, though forbidden by law. London, 1681, quarto.

" An Answer to Dr. Stillingfleet's Sermon and his Defence of it, so much as concerneth the Nonconformists' preaching. Printed with the Apology.

"This learned and religious person, Mr. John Troughton, died in a house of one of the brethren, situate and being in All-Saint's parish within the city of Oxford, on the 20th of August, 1681, aged 44 years ; whereupon his body was carried to Bicester before mentioned, alias Burchester, and buried in the church there. At which time Abraham James, a blind man, master of the free-school at Woodstock, (sometime of Magdalen Hall,) preaching his funeral sermon, did take occasion not only to be lavish in the commendations of the defunct, but to make several glances on the government established by law ; so that an auditor there, named Samuel Blackwell, M.A. and vicar of Bicester, (a zealous man for the Church of England,) complaining to the diocesan of him, James was glad to retract what he had said before him, to prevent an ejection from his school, which otherwise would inevitably have come to pass."

AUTHORITY:

Calamy's Life of Baxter—Palmer's Lives of the Nonconformists—Wood's Athenæ Oxonienses.

THE LIFE

OF

REV. RICHARD LUCAS, D.D.

" Ana as a bird each fond endearment tries,
To tempt its new fledged offspring to the skies,
He tried each art, reproved each dull delay,
Allured to brighter worlds, and led the way."

THERE is no period of our history, that has produced such a number of polemic writers, as appeared
in the 17th century. Among the burning and shining
lights of those spirit stirring times, lived Richard
Lucas. This eminent divine was of Welsh extraction,
the son of Mr. Richard Lucas, of Presteign, in Rad-
norshire, and was born in that county, in the year
1648. After a proper foundation of school learning,
he was sent to Oxford, and entered a student of Jesus
College, in 1664. Having taken both his degrees in
arts, he entered into holy orders, about the year 1672;
and was afterwards master of the free school at Aber-
gavenny; but being much esteemed for his talents
in the pulpit, he was chosen vicar of St. Stephen's,
Coleman-street, London, and lecturer of St. Olave,
Southwark, in 1683. His sight began to fail him in
his youth, but he lost it totally about this time. This

melancholy catastrophe is alluded to by the author
himself, in his preface to the first volume of his
"Treatise on Happiness." In these pages he has described his helpless condition, in language which
must affect the reader even to tears; and he gives
the names of a number of distinguished individuals,
who had laboured under the same affliction.   He
concludes by observing, that he was not equal to the
least of those worthies in fame, but, that he was equal
to the greatest in misfortune.   And it may be here
remarked, that the greater part of his valuable works
were composed after he lost his sight; and, therefore,
he is entitled to a place in this collection. This eminent christian, in alluding to his loss of sight, proceeds
with the following pious remarks.   "It has pleased
God, that in a few years I should finish the more pleasant and delightful part of life, if sense were to be the
judge and standard of pleasure, being confined, (I will
not say condemned) to retirement, and solitude.   In
this state, conversation has lost much of its former air
and briskness ; study, which is the only employment left me, is clogged with this weight and in-
cumbrance, that all the assistance I can receive from
without, must be conveyed by another's sense, not my
own ; which, it may easily be believed, are instruments, or organs, as ill fitted and awkwardly managed
by me, as wooden legs and hands, by the maimed.
Should I ambitiously affect to have my name march
in the train of those, although not all equally great
ones, Homer, Appius, Aufidius, Didymus, Walkup,
Pare, Jean C. Aveugle, &c. all of them eminent
for their service and usefulness, as well as for their

affliction, of the same kind with mine; even this might seem almost a commendable infirmity; for the last thing a mind truly great and philosophical puts off, is, the desire of glory. But the truth is plainly this, the vigour and activity of my mind, the health and strength of my body, (being now in the flower of my age,) continuing unbroken under this affliction, I found, that if I did not discover some employment that might entertain it, it would weary out itself with fruitless desires of, and vain attempts after, its wonted objects. That the life of man is to be esteemed by its usefulness and serviceableness in the world, a sober reflection upon this, wrought me up to a resolution, strong enough to contemn all the difficulties the loss of my sight could represent to me, in an enterprize of this nature. Thus you see on what principles I became engaged in this work ; I thought it my duty to set myself some task, which might serve at once to divert my thoughts from a melancholy application on my misfortune; and entertain my mind with such a rational employment as might render me most easy to myself, and most serviceable to the world." Notwithstanding this great privation, Mr. Lucas continued to discharge the duties of his holy calling, with a zeal and fidelity that would have done him credit, even if he had possessed all his bodily powers in the highest perfection. His learning, his talents, and his misfortunes, procured for him the patronage of some of the leading men of the times, who were anxious to reward such uncommon merit. He took the degree of doctor in divinity, and was installed prebendary of Westminster, in 1696. He died in June, 1715, and was in-

terred in Westminster Abbey, but no stone or monument marks his grave. He was greatly esteemed for his
piety, and learning, and his writings will preserve his
fame. He wrote " A Treatise on Practical Christianity;" "An Enquiry after Happiness;" "The Morality
of the Gospel;" " Christian Thoughts for every Day of
the Week;" " A Guide to Heaven;" "The Duty of
Servants;" and " Sermons;" in five volumes. He also
made a Latin translation of the " Whole duty of man,"
which was published in 1680. He left a son of his
own name, who was bred at Sydney College, Cambridge, where he took his Master of Arts degree, and
published some of his father's sermons. Of Dr. Lucas,
Mr. Orton, has given the following character from
Dr. Doddridge's MSS.

"His style is very peculiar, sometimes exceedingly
fine, nearly approaching to conversation; sometimes
grand and sublime; generally very expressive. His
method not clear, but his thoughts excellent; many
are taken from attentive observation of life; he wrote,
as entirely devoted to God, and superior to the world.
His "Practical Christianity," is most valuable, and
also his "Enquiry after Happiness," especially the
second volume." Orton speaks of reading the latter
work a sixth time. The pious Mr. Hervey, in speaking of this work says, "May I be permitted to recommend as a treasure of inestimable value, and a treatise
particularly applicable to my subject, " Dr. Lucas's
Enquiry after Happiness;" that part, especially,
which displays the method, and enumerates the advantages of improving life, or living much in a little
time; chapter III. page 158 of the 6th edition.—An

author, in whom, the gentleman, the scholar, and the christian, are most happily united; a performance, which in point of solid argument, unaffected piety, and a vein of thought amazingly fertile, has, perhaps, no superior. Nor can I wish my reader a more refined pleasure, or a more substantial happiness, than that of having the sentiments of this entertaining and pathetic writer, woven into the very texture of his heart."

The treatise on " Practical christianity," is earnestly recommended also, by Sir Richard Steele, in the Guardian, No. LXIII.

To these great names, I must add that of the Rev. John Wesley, who warmly recommends the Treatise on happiness, to his people, as one of the most valuable books a christian can read. I will close this imperfect sketch of Dr. Lucas's life, by one short quotation from his inimitable work. In this passage will be seen, how much this great and good man felt, under this greatest of all privations, the loss of his sight.

" I am sensible that these heads of remark occur often ; and though it be under different aspects, yet, 'tis possible that I may sometimes light upon the same thoughts, nay, peradventure the very same words; 'tis against my will if I do ; *but I want sight*, to revise my papers, and am glad to disburden my memory as fast as I can; and therefore charge it with nothing that I have once entrusted to writing ; and the toil of recollecting my thoughts, scattered up and down like Sybils oracles in dispersed leaves, by a hand which 'tis impossible for me to direct, or animate, is most intolerable ; if therefore, I slip into any error of this kind I cannot but presume of pardon, having so just an excuse."

AUTHORITIES:

Lucas upon Happiness, Vol. 1.—Chalmers's Biographical Dictionary, Vol. 20.—Hervey's Meditations.

THE REV. EDWARD STOKES,

THE BENEVOLENT BLIND CLERGYMAN.

" His house was known to all the vagrant train,
He chid their wanderings, but reliev'd their pain;
The long remember'd beggar was his guest,
Whose beard descending swept his aged breast;
The broken soldier, kindly bade to stay,
Sat by his fire, and talk'd the night away;
Wept o'er his wounds, or tales of sorrow done,
Shoulder'd his crutch, and show'd how fields were won.
Pleased with his guests, the good man learn'd to glow,
And quite forgot their vices and their woe,
Careless, their merits or their faults to scan,
His pity gave ere charity began."

The Rev. Edward Stokes was born in 1705.
When nine years old, he and his elder brother were
sent to school, but an accident occurred about this
time, which almost proved fatal to him. As his brother was amusing himself with a loaded pistol, it suddenly went off, and a portion of its contents lodged in
Edward's face : in consequence of this misfortune he
entirely lost his sight. As soon as his health was
sufficiently established, he returned to school, where
he pursued his studies with great success. From
school he went to the University, at which place he
remained till he took his degree of Master of Arts;
he was then admitted into holy orders, and shortly
afterwards was appointed to a living in Leicestershire
as the parish minister. He was beloved by the peo-

ple among whom he lived, his benevolence knew no difference between one sect and another, but his bounty was equally experienced by all. Notwithstanding his blindness, he performed the service of his church for many years, with the assistance of a person to read the lessons. At his death, the poor of his parish had to lament a most liberal benefactor, who had expended among them nearly the whole of a very handsome private fortune. He died at the Rectory House, at Blaby, in Leicestershire, June, 1796, in the 93rd year of his age, and the 50th of his incumbency.

AUTHORITY.

Biographical Anecdotes, vol. 2.

THE LIFE

OF

THOMAS BLACKLOCK, D.D.

"In manners gentle, in affection mild,
"In wit a man, simplicity a child."

THE Life of BLACKLOCK has a claim to notice beyond that of most of the Poets of our nation, with
whom he is now associated. He who reads his Poems
with that interest which their intrinsic merit deserves,
will feel that interest very much increased, when he
shall be told the various difficulties which their author
overcame in their production, the obstacles which
nature and fortune placed in his way to the possession of those ideas which he acquired, to the
communication of those which his poetry unfolds.

The facts stated in the present account, are chiefly
taken from the learned and ingenious Dr. Anderson's
narrative, which is written with such copiousness of
intelligence as leaves little to be supplied, and such
felicity of performance as precludes the most distant
hope of improvement. Among the few additional

particulars detailed here, the present compiler has endeavoured to give a complete account of his writings.

Dr. Thomas Blacklock was born at Annan, in the county of Dumfries, November 10, 1721. His parents were natives of the county of Cumberland; his father was by trade a bricklayer, his mother the daughter of a considerable dealer in cattle; both respectable in their characters and, it would appear, possessed of considerable knowledge and urbanity, which, in a country where education was cheap, and property a good deal subdivided, was often the case with persons of their station. Before he was six months old, he was totally deprived of his sight by the small pox, and reduced to that forlorn situation, so feelingly described by himself in his soliloquy. This rendered him incapable of any of those mechanical trades in which his father might naturally have been inclined to place him; and his circumstances prevented his aspiring to the higher professions. The good man, therefore, kept his son in the house; and, with the assistance of some of his friends, fostered that inclination which he early showed for books, by reading to amuse him; first the simple sort of publications which are commonly put into the hands of children, and then several passages out of some of our poets. His companions (whom his early gentleness and kindness of disposition, as well as their compassion for his misfortune, strongly attached to him,) were very assiduous in their good offices, in reading to instruct and amuse him. By their assistance, he acquired some knowledge of the Latin tongue; but he never was at a grammar school till at a more advanced period of life. Poetry was even then his favorite reading, and he found an enthusiastic delight in the works of Milton, Spencer, Prior, Pope, and Addison, and in those of his countryman Ramsay. From loving and admiring them so much, he soon was led to endeavour to imitate them, and when scarcely twelve years of age he began to write verses. Among these early essays of his genius, there was one addressed to a little girl whom he had offended, which is preserved in his works, and is not perhaps inferior to any of the premature compositions of boys assisted by the best education, which are only recalled into notice by the future fame of their authors.

He had attained the age of nineteen, when his father was killed by the accidental fall of a malt-kiln belonging to his son-in-law. This loss, heavy to any one at that early age, would have been, however, to a young man possessing the ordinary advantages of education, comparatively light; but to him, thus suddenly deprived of the support on which his youth had leaned, destitute almost of any resource which industry affords to those who have the blessings of sight, with a body feeble and delicate from nature, and a mind congenially susceptible, it was not surprising that this blow was doubly severe, and threw on his spirits that despondent gloom to which he then gave way, and which sometimes overclouded him in the subsequent period of his life.

Though dependent, however, he was not destitute of friends, and heaven rewarded the pious confidence which he expressed in its care, by providing for him protectors and patrons, by whose assistance he obtained advantages which, had his father lived, might perhaps never have opened to him.

He lived with his mother about a year after his father's death, and began to be distinguished as a young man of uncommon talents and genius. These were at that time unassisted by learning; the circumstances of his family affording him no better education than the smattering of Latin which his companions had taught him, and the perusal and recollection of the few English authors, which they or his father, in the intervals of his daily labour, had read to him.

Poetry, however, though it attains its highest perfection in a cultivated soil, grows perhaps as luxuriantly in a wild one. To poetry he was devoted from his earliest days, and about this time several of his poetical productions began to be handed about, which considerably enlarged the circle of his friends and acquaintances.

Some of his compositions being shown to Dr. Stephenson, an eminent physician in Edinburgh, who was accidentally at Dumfries on a professional visit, he formed the benevolent design of carrying him to the metropolis, and giving to his natural endowments the assistance of classical education.

" He came to Edinburgh in 1741, and was enrolled," says Mr. Mackenzie, " a Student of Divinity in the University there, though at that time without any particular view of entering into the Church." But this account may be reasonably doubted ; for in the University of Edinburgh, no student is admitted into the theological class, till he has completed a course of languages and philosophy. Besides, it appears by the following letter from the Rev. Richard Batty of Kirk Andrews, (whose wife was Blacklock's cousin,) to Sir James Johnson, Bart. of Westerhall, dated January 21, 1794, and printed in the Scottish Register, that he continued at the grammar school in Edinburgh, till the beginning of 1745.

"I had a letter some time ago from Mr. Hogan, at Comlongan, signifying that Lady Annandale had spoke to you about a bursary for one Thomas Blacklock, a blind boy, who is now at the grammar school in Edinburgh. He is endowed with the most surprising genius, and has been the author of a great many excellent poems. He has been hitherto supported by the bounty of Dr. Stephenson, a gentleman in Edinburgh. I understand that there will be a bursary vacant against Candlemas; if, therefore, you would please to favour him with your interest, it will be a great charity done to a poor lad, who may do a great deal of good in his generation."

The effect of this application is not known; but he seems to have continued his studies under the patronage of Dr. Stephenson, till the year 1745.

Of the kindness of Dr. Stephenson, he always spoke with the greatest warmth of gratitude and affection; and addressed to him his " Imitation of the first Ode of Horace."

After he had followed his studies at Edinburgh for four years, on the breaking out of the Rebellion in 1745, he returned to Dumfries, where he resided with Mr. Mc Murdo, his brother-in-law, in whose house he was treated with kindness and affection; and had an opportunity, from the society which it afforded, of considerably increasing the store of his ideas. In 1746, he published a small collection of his poems, at Glasgow.

After the close of the Rebellion, and the complete restoration of the peace of the country, he returned to Edinburgh, and pursued his studies there for six years longer.

In 1754, he published at Edinburgh a second edition of his poems, very much improved and enlarged, in 8vo, to which was prefixed, " an Account of his Life, in a letter to the publisher," from Mr. Gordon of Dumfries. On the title page he is designated " student of philosophy in the university of Edinburgh;" so that he was not then, as Mr. Mackenzie supposes, " enrolled a student of Divinity."

This publication attracted the attention of Mr. Spence, the patron of Dodsley, Duck, and Richardson. and of other persons of indigent and uncultivated genius, who conceived a great regard for Blacklock, and formed the benevolent design of recommending him to the patronage of persons in affluence or power, by writing a very elaborate and ingenious " Account of his Life, Character, and Poems," which he published in London, in 8vo. 1754.

During his last residence in Edinburgh, among other literary acquaintance, he obtained that of the celebrated David Hume, who, with that humanity and benevolence for which he was distinguished, attached himself warmly to Blacklock's interests. He wrote a letter to Dodsley, March 12, 1754, containing a very favourable representation of the " goodness of his disposition, and the beauty of his genius," which contributed to promote the subscription for an edition of his poems, in 4to, which was published in London in 1756, under the superintendance of Mr. Spence, together with his "Account of the Life, Character, and Poems of Mr. Blacklock," which had been printed separately in 1754. He testified his obligations to Mr. Spence, to whom he was personally unknown, in an epistle written at Dumfries in 1759.

In the course of his education at Edinburgh, he acquired a proficiency in the learned languages, and became more a master of the French tongue than was common there, from the social intercourse to which he had the good fortune to be admitted in the house of Provost Alexander, who had married a native of France.

At the university he obtained a knowledge of the various branches of philosophy and theology, to which his course of study naturally led; and acquired at the same time a considerable fund of learning and information in those departments of science and belles lettres, from which his loss of sight did not absolutely preclude him. In 1756, he published at Edinburgh, "an Essay towards Universal Etymology, or the Analysis of a Sentence," in 8vo.

In this pamphlet, the general principles of grammar, and the definitions of the several parts of speech are given in verse; and illustrations in the form of notes constituting the greatest part of it, are added in prose. The notes and illustrations are concise, but judicious; the verses are not remarkable for learning or poetical embellishment; the subject did not allow it; the concluding lines, however, on the advantages of grammar, are in a style more worthy of Blacklock.

In 1757, he began a course of study, with a view to give lectures on Oratory to young gentlemen intended for the bar or the pulpit. On this occasion, he wrote to Mr. Hume, informed him of his plan, and requested his assistance in the prosecution of it. But Mr. Hume doubting the probability of its success, he abandoned the project; and then adopted the decided intention of going into the church.

After applying closely for a considerable time to the study of theology, he passed the usual trials in the presbytery of Dumfries; and was, by that presbytery, licensed a preacher of the gospel in 1759.

As a preacher, he obtained high reputation, and was fond of composing sermons. In 1760, when the nation was alarmed by a threatened invasion from the French, he published "The Right Improvement of Time," a sermon, 8vo. He seems to have imbibed pretty deeply the apprehensions of his countrymen. The sentiments it contains are just and solid; and the advice is calculated to be useful at all times, particularly in the prospect of national danger or distress.

The same year he contributed several poetical pieces to the first volume of Donaldson's "Collection of Original Poems, by Scotch gentlemen," 12mo.

Mrs. Blacklock ascribes the "Epistle on Taste," printed in this volume as Mr. Gordon's, to Blacklock, excepting the lines relating to himself.

In 1761, he published "Faith, Hope, and Charity compared," a sermon, 8vo. Though this cannot be called a first rate performance, it abounds with just and elegant remarks, and his favourite topic of charity, is agreeably and forcibly illustrated.

In 1762, he married Miss Sarah Johnston, daughter of Mr. Joseph Johnston, surgeon, in Dumfries, a man of eminence in his profession, and of a character highly respected ; a connection which formed the great solace and blessing of his future life, and gave him, with all the tenderness of a wife, all the zealous care of a guide and friend. This event took place a few days before his being ordained minister of Kirkcudbright, in consequence of a presentation from the crown, obtained for him by the Earl of Selkirk, a benevolent nobleman, whom Blacklock's situation and genius had interested in his behalf. But the inhabitants of the parish, whether from an aversion to patronage, so prevalent among the lower ranks in North Britain ; or from some political disputes which at that time subsisted between them and Lord Selkirk ; or from those prejudices which some of them might naturally entertain against a person deprived of sight; or perhaps from all those causes united, were so extremely disinclined to receive him as their minister, that, after a legal dispute of nearly two years, it was thought expedient by his friends, as it had always been wished by himself, to compromise the matter, by resigning his right to the living, and accepting a moderate annuity in its stead.

The following anecdote of Blacklock is mentioned in Dr. Cleghorn's "Thesis de Somno." It happened at the inn in Kirkcudbright, on the day of his ordination, and is authenticated by the testimony of Mrs. Black-

lock, who was present with Mr. Gordon and a numerous company of his friends, who dined with him on
the occasion. It merits notice, both as a curious fact
relative to the state of the mind in sleep, and on account of the just and elegant compliment with which
it concludes.

"Dr. Blacklock, one day, harrassed by the censures
of the populace, whereby not only his reputation but
his very existence was endangered, and fatigued with
mental exertion, fell asleep after dinner. Some hours
after, he was called upon by a friend, answered his
salutation, rose and went with him into the dining
room, where some of his companions were met. He
joined with two of them in a concert, singing, as
usual, with taste and elegance, without missing a note,
or forgetting a word; he then went to supper, and
drank a glass or two of wine. His friends, however,
observed him to be a little absent and inattentive; by-
and-by he began to speak to himself, but in so low
and confused a manner as to be unintelligible. At
last, being pretty forcibly roused, he awoke with a
sudden start, unconscious of all that had happened, as
till then he had continued fast asleep." Dr. Cleghorn
adds with great truth, after relating this fact : "No
one will suspect either the judgment or the veracity
of Dr. Blacklock. All who knew him bear testimony
to his judgment ; his fame rests on a better foundation
than fictitious narratives ; no man more delights in, or
more strictly adheres, to the truth on all points."

With a very slender provision, he removed, in 1764,
to Edinburgh; and to make up by his industry a more
comfortable and decent subsistence, he adopted the

plan of receiving a certain number of young gentlemen, as boarders, into his house; whose studies in languages and philosophy he might, if necessary, assist.
In this situation he continued till 1787; when he
found his time of life and state of health required a
degree of repose, which induced him to discontinue
the receiving of boarders.

In the occupation which he thus exercised for so
many years of his life, no teacher was perhaps, ever
more agreeable to his pupils, no master of a family
to its inmates, than Blacklock. The gentleness of his
manners, the benignity of his disposition, and that
warm interest in the happiness of others, which led
him so constantly to promote it, were qualities that
could not fail to procure him the love and regard of the
young gentlemen committed to his charge; while the
society, which esteem and respect for his character and
genius often assembled at his house, afforded them
an advantage rarely to be found in establishments of
a similar kind. In the circle of his friends, he appeared entirely to forget the privation of sight, and the
melancholy which at other times it might produce.

He entered, with the cheerful playfulness of a
young man, into all the sprightly narrative, the sportive fancy, and the humorous jest that rose around
him. It was highly gratifying to philanthropy, to
see how much a mind endowed with knowledge,
kindled by genius, and above all lighted up with inno-
cence and piety like Blacklock's, could overcome the
weight of its own calamity, and enjoy the content, the
happiness, and the gaiety of others. Several of those
inmates of his house were students of physic from

England, Ireland, and America, who retained, in future life, all the warmth of that impression which his friendship at this early period had made upon them; and in various quarters of the world he had friends and correspondents, from whom no length of time nor distance of place, had ever estranged him. Among his favourite correspondents may be reckoned Dr. Tucker, Author of "The Bermudian," a poem, and "The Anchoret;" and Dr. Downman, author of "Infancy" a poem, and other ingenious performances.

In 1766, upon the unsolicited recommendation of his friend Dr. Beattie, the degree of Doctor of Divinity was conferred on him by the University of Aberdeen.

In 1767, he published "Paraclesis, or Consolation deduced from Natural and Revealed Religion," in two dissertations. The first, supposed to have been composed by Cicero, now rendered into English; the last originally written by Thomas Blacklock, D.D. in 8vo.

His motive (he tells, in a letter to a friend prefixed to this work,) for translating the first, and writing the last treatise on Consolation was to alleviate the pressure of repeated disappointments, to soothe his anguish for the loss of departed friends, to elude the rage of implacable and unprovoked enemies, and to support his own mind, which for a number of years, besides its literary difficulties, and its natural disadvantages, had maintained an incessant struggle with fortune. Of the Dissertation ascribed to Cicero, he endeavours to prove the authenticity; but his arguments are by no means satisfactory. The generality of critics have questioned its authenticity. Dr.

Middleton, in his Life of Cicero, says it is undoubtedly spurious. The translation is well executed ; it is both faithful and elegant. The second Dissertation is mostly taken up with a clear and succinct view of the evidence of Christianity, the professed subject of it; the consolation derived from revealed religion is touched upon towards the conclusion, though at no great length.

In 1768, he published, without his name, two Discourses on the Spirit and Evidences of Christianity. The former preached at the Hague, the 8th Sep. 1762 ; the latter delivered in the French Church at Hanau, on the occasion of the late peace, to a congregation composed of Catholics and Protestants. It was translated from the original French of the Rev. James Armand, Minister of the Walloon Church in Hanau, and dedicated by the translator to the Rev. Moderator of the General Assembly. The Dedication, which is a long one, is chiefly intended for the perusal of the Clergy of the church of Scotland, but deserves the attentive consideration of all who are intended for, or engaged, in the work of the ministry. The observations it contains are judicious and pertinent; the style is sprightly and animated ; and the spirit it breathes, though sometimes remote from that charity which on other occasions he so eloquently enforced and so generally practised, is the spirit of benevolence and love to mankind. The discourses themselves are lively and animated, and the style of the translations clear, nervous, and spirited.

In 1773, he published at Edinburgh a poem entitled, " A Panegyric on Great Britain," in 8vo. This poem, which is a kind of satire on the age, exhibits shrewdness of observation, and a sarcastic vein, which might have fitted him for satirical composition, had he chosen to employ his pen more frequently on that branch of poetry.

In music, both as a judge and a performer, his skill was considerable; nor was he unacquainted with its principles as a science. Whether he composed much is uncertain, but there is published in the Edinburgh Magazine and Review, for 1774, " Absence," a Pastoral, set to music by Dr. Blacklock; and those who have heard him sing will, upon perusal of this little piece, have the idea of his manner and taste strikingly recalled to their recollection.

The same year he published the " Graham," a heroic ballad, in four Cantos, 4to. It was begun, he tells us in the advertisement prefixed to it, and pursued by its author to divert wakeful and melancholy hours, which the recollection of past misfortunes, and the sense of present inconveniences, would otherwise have severely embittered.

The professed intention of his " Graham," is to cherish and encourage a mutual harmony between the inhabitants of South and North Britain. To this end he has exhibited, in strong colours, some parts of those miseries which their ancient animosities had occasioned. His " Graham" is an affecting story, in which love and jealousy have a principal share. The narration is animated and agreeable; the fable is beautifully fancied, and sufficiently perspicuous; the characters are boldly marked; the manners he paints suit the times to which he refers, and the moral is

momentous   We perceive, scattered through the
whole piece, those secret graces, and those bewitching
beauties, which the critic would in vain attempt to
describe; but it is perhaps too far spun out, and the
stanza in which it is written is not the best chosen
nor the most agreeable to the ear.

This was the last publication which he gave to the
world with his name : from this time the state of his
health, which had always been infirm and delicate,
began visibly to decline.   He frequently complained
of lowness of spirits, and was occasionally subject to
deafness, which, though he seldom felt it in any great
degree, was sufficient, in his situation, to whom the
sense of hearing was almost the only channel of communication with the external world, to cause very
lively uneasiness.   Amidst indisposition of body,
however, and disquietude of mind, the gentleness of
his temper never forsook him, and he felt all that
resignation and confidence in the Supreme Being,
which his earliest and latest life equally acknowledged.
In summer, 1791, he was seized with a feverish disorder, which at first seemed of a slight, and never
rose to a very violent kind; but a frame so little
robust as his was not able to resist; and after about a
week's illness it carried him off on the 7th of July,
1791, in the 70th year of his age.   He was interred
in the burying-ground of the Chapel of Ease, in the
parish of St. Cuthbert, where a decent monument was
erected to his memory by his widow, who survived
him several years.   There is something in the character of this great man, which the good will value above
every other consideration ; that was, his deep and un-

affected piety, and his resignation to the Divine will; which was evinced through his long and useful life, and shone conspicuously in the man and in the christian, and added an additional lustre to his other virtues.

The article Blind, in the Encyclopædia Britannica, published at Edinburgh in the year 1783, was written by him. In this little treatise, (which I will venture to recommend, not only on account of its peculiarity, as being the production of a blind man, but of its intrinsic merit,) there are no marks of any extraordinary conception of visible objects, nor any allusion to those mental images which ingenuity might suppose deducible from the descriptive passages with which his poetry abounds. It contains chiefly reflections on the distresses and disadvantages of blindness, and the best means of alleviating them: directions for the education of the blind, and a description of various inventions for enabling them to attain and to practise several arts and sciences, from which their situation might seem to exclude them. The sympathy and active benevolence of Blacklock prompted him to this composition, as well as to a translation of M. Hauy's Account of the charitable Institution for the blind at Paris. "To the blind," (says this article in the Encyclopædia,) "the visible world is totally annihilated: he is perfectly conscious of no space but that in which he stands, or to which his extremities can reach. All the various modes of delicate proportion, all the beautiful varieties of light and colours, whether exhibited in the works of nature or art, are to the blind irretrievably lost! Dependent for every thing, but mere existence, on the good offices of others; from every point obnoxious to injury, which they are neither capacitated to perceive, nor qualified to resist; they are, during the present state of being, rather to be considered as prisoners at large, than citizens of nature." In that part which relates to the education of the blind, one direction is rather singular, though it seems extremely proper.

The author strongly recommends to their parents and relations to accustom them to an early exertion of their own active powers, though at a risk of their personal safety. "Parents and relations ought never to be too ready in offering their assistance to the blind in any office which they can perform, or in any acquisition which they can procure for themselves, whether they are prompted by amusement or necessity. Let a blind boy be permitted to walk through the neighbourhood without a guide, not only though he should run some hazard, but even though he should suffer some pain. If he has a mechanical turn, let him not be denied the use of edged tools; for it is better that he should lose a little blood, or even break a bone, than be perpetually confined to the same place, debilitated in his frame, and depressed in his mind. Such a being can have no enjoyment but to feel his own weakness, and become his own tormentor; or to transfer to others all the malignity and peevishness arising from the natural, adventitious, or imaginary evils which he feels. Scars, fractures, and dislocations in his body, are trivial misfortunes compared with imbecility, timidity, or fretfulness of mind. Besides the sensible and dreadful effects which inactivity must have in relaxing the nerves, and consequently in depressing the spirits, nothing can be more productive of jealousy, envy, peevishness and every passion that corrodes the soul to agony, than a painful impression of dependence on others, and of our insufficiency to our own happiness. This impression, which even in his most improved state, will be too deeply felt by every blind man, is redoubled by that utter incapacity of action, which must result from the officious humanity of those who would anticipate or supply all his wants, who would prevent all his motions, who would do or procure every thing for him without his own interposition."

This direction was probably suggested from the author's own feeling of the want of that boldness and independence, which the means it recommends are calculated to produce.*

" If you talk to a blind boy of invisible beings, let benevolence be an inseparable ingredient in their character. You may, if you please, tell him of departed spirits, anxious for the welfare of their surviving friends ; of ministering angels, who descend with pleasure from Heaven to execute the purposes of their Maker's benignity ; you may even regale his

---

*"If the limbs of your blind child or pupil are tremulous; if he is apt to start, and is easily susceptible of surprise; if he finds it difficult to sleep; if his slumbers, when commenced, are frequently interrupted, and attended with perturbation; if his ordinary exercise appears to him more terrible and more insuperable than usual; if his appetite becomes languid, and his digestion slow ; if agreeable occurrences give him less pleasure and adverse events more pain than they ought to inspire this is the crisis of vigorous interposition."

imagination with the sportive gambols and innocent
frolics of fairies ; but let him hear as seldom as possible, even in stories which he knows to be fabulous, of
vindictive ghosts, vindictive fiends, or avenging fu-
ries.   They seize and pre-occupy every avenue of
terror which is open in the soul, nor are they easily
dispossessed.   Sooner should we hope to exorcise a
ghost, or appease a fury, than to obliterate their
images in a warm and susceptible imagination, where
they have been habitually impressed, and where those
feelings cannot be dissipated by external phenomena.
If horrors of this kind should agitate the heart of a
blind boy, (which may happen, notwithstanding the
most strenuous endeavours to prevent it,) the stories
which he has heard will be most effectually discredited
by ridicule.   This, however, must be cautiously applied, by gentle and delicate gradations."

The following descriptive strokes, most of which,
with a great many others, Mr. Spence has collected,
are as finely drawn, and as justly coloured as sight
could have made them.

" Mild gleams the purple evening o'er the plain."

" Ye vales, which to the raptured eye,
Disclosed the flowery pride of May ;
Ye circling hills, whose summits high,
Blushed with the morning's earliest ray."

" Let long-lived pansies here their scents bestow,
The violets languish and the roses glow ;
In yellow glory let the crocus shine—
Narcissus here his love-sick head recline ;
Here hyacinths in purple sweetness rise,
And tulips tinged with beauty's fairest dyes."

" On rising ground, the prospect to command,
Untinged with smoke, where vernal breezes blow,
In rural neatness let thy cottage stand;
Here wave a wood, and there a river flow."

"Oft on the glassy stream, with raptured eyes,
Surveys her form in mimic sweetness rise;
Oft as the waters pleased reflect her face,
Adjusts her locks, and heightens every grace."

——————————" Oft while the Sun
Darts boundless glory through the expanse of Heaven,
A gloom of congregated vapours rise;
Than night more dreadful in his blackest shroud,
And o'er the face of things incumbent hang,
Portending tempest; till the source of day
Again asserts the empire of the sky,
And o'er the blotted scene of nature throws
A keener splendour."

In producing such passages as the above, the
genius of the author must be acknowledged. Whatever idea or impression those objects of sight produced
in his mind, how imperfect soever that idea, or how
different soever from the true, still the impression
would be felt by a mind susceptible and warm like
Blacklock's, that could not have been so felt by one
of a coarser and more sluggish mould. Even the
memory that could treasure up the poetical attributes
and expressions of such objects, must have been assisted and prompted by poetical feeling; and the very
catalogue of words which was thus ready at command,
was an indication of that ardour of soul, which, from
his infancy, led him,—

——————————"Where the Muses haunt—
Smit with the love of sacred song."

As the unmeaning syllables which compose a name give to the lover or the friend emotions, which in others it were impossible they should excite, it was not on the whole surprising, that a learned foreigner, on considering Blacklock's Poems relatively to his situation, should have broken out into the following panegyric, with which I shall not be much accused of partiality if I close this account.

" Blacklock will appear to posterity a fable, as to us he is a prodigy. It will be thought a fiction, a paradox, that a man blind from his infancy, besides having made himself so much a master of various foreign languages, should be a great Poet in his own ; and without having hardly ever seen the light, should be so remarkably happy in description."

AUTHORITIES.

ANDERSON's Lives of the Poets—MACKENZIE's Life of BLACKLOCK—SPENCE's Life of BLACKLOCK.

THE BLIND CLERGYMAN.

"The service past, around the pious man,
With steady zeal, each honest rustic ran;
E'en children followed, with endearing wile,
And plucked his gown, to share the good man's smile."

"In my rambles last summer," says the writer from whom this account is taken, "on the borders of Wales, I found myself one morning alone on the banks of the beautiful river Wye, without a servant or a guide. I had to ford the river, at a place where, according to the instructions given me at the nearest hamlet, if I diverged ever so little from the marks, which the rippling of the current made as it passed over a ledge rock, I should sink twice the depth of myself and horse. While I stood hesitating on the margin, viewing attentively the course of the ford, a person passed me on the canter, and the next instant I saw him plunge into the river; presuming on his acquaintance with the passage, I immediately and closely followed his steps. As soon as we had gained the opposite bank, I accosted him with thanks for the benefit of his guidance; but, what was my astonishment, when, bursting into a hearty laugh, he observed, that my confidence would have been less, had I known that I had been following a blind guide. The manner of the man, as well as the fact, attracted my curiosity. To my expressions of surprise at his venturing to cross the river alone, he answered, that he, and the horse he rode, had done the same every Sunday morning for the last five years; but that, in reality, this was not the most perilous part of his weekly peregrination, as I should be convinced, if my way led over the mountain before us. My journey had no object but pleasure; I therefore resolved to attach myself to my extraordinary companion, and soon learned, in our chat, as we wound up the steep mountain's side, that he was a clergyman, and of that class which is the disgrace of our ecclesiastical establishment; I mean the country curates, who exist upon the *liberal* stipend of thirty, twenty, and sometimes fifteen pounds a year! This gentleman, aged sixty, had, about thirty years before, been engaged in the curacy to which he was now travelling, and, though it was at the distance of eight long Welch miles from the place of his residence, such was the respect of his flock towards him, that, at the commencement of his calamity, rather than part with him, they sent regularly, every Sunday morning, a deputation to guide their old pastor on his way. The road, besides crossing the river we had just passed, led over a craggy mountain, on whose top innumerable and uncertain bogs were constantly forming, but which, nevertheless, by the instinct of his Welch poney, this blind man has actually crossed alone for the last five years, having so long dismissed the assistance of guides. While our talk beguiled the way, we insensibly arrived within sight of his village church, which was seated in a deep and narrow vale. As I looked down upon it, the bright verdure of the meadows, which were here and there chequered with patches of yellow corn ; the moving herd of cattle; the rich foliage of the groves of oak, hanging irregularly over its sides ; the white houses of the inhabitants, which sprinkled every corner of this peaceful retreat; and above all, the inhabitants themselves, assembled in their best attire, round their place of worship : all this gay scene, rushing at once on the view, struck my senses and imagination more forcibly than I can express. As we entered the churchyard, the respectful 'how do you do ?' of the young the hearty shakes of the old, and the familiar gambols of the children, shewed how their old pastor reigned in the hearts of all. After some refreshment at the nearest house, we went to the church, where my veteran priest read the prayers, psalms, and chapters of the day, and then preached a sermon, in a manner that could have made no one advert to his loss of sight.* At dinner, which it seems that four of the most substantial farmers of the vale provide

---

* The late Dr. Guyse lost his eye-sight in the pulpit, while he was in prayer, before the sermon. Having finished his prayer, he was, consequently, unable to make use of his written papers, but preached without notes. As he was led out of the meeting, after service was over, he could not help lamenting his sudden and total blindness. A good old gentlewoman, who heard him deplore his loss, said to him; " God be praised that your sight is gone ; I think I never heard you preach so powerful a sermon in my life. Now we shall have no more notes. I wish, for my own part, that the Lord had taken away your eye-sight twenty years ago, for your ministry would have been more useful by twenty degrees."

Toplady's Works, vol. 4, page 166.

in turn, he related the progress of his increased powers of memory. For the first year, he attempted only the prayers and sermons, the best readers of the parish making it a pride to officiate for him in the psalms and chapters ; he next undertook the labour of learning these by heart, and, at present by continual repetition, there is not a psalm or chapter, of the more than two hundred appointed for the Sunday service, that he is not perfect in. He told me also, that having in his little school two sons of his own, intended for the university, he has, by hearing them continually, committed the greatest part of Homer and Virgil to memory."

AUTHORITY.

Morning Chronicle of January 21, 1791.

SCIENCE AND MEDICINE

Science

THE field of science has not traditionally attracted many blind people because it has been thought to require sight. The people Wilson features prove that with ingenuity and perseverance, blind people can develop ways of observing and drawing conclusions that are as accurate as traditional methods.

"The Blind Engineer," (1604–65) referred to as Count de Hagan by Wilson and as François Blaise Pagan by other writers, became blind in one eye while serving as a soldier in the siege of Montanban in 1621. He rose to the rank of field marshal and, while serving in Portugal, lost sight in the other eye because of an illness. During the next twenty years he wrote a number of publications. Among his well-known works are *Geometrical Theorems, Astronomical Tales,* and *An Historical and Geographical Account of the River of the Amazons.*

G. E. Rumph (Rumpfius) (1627–1702), a self-educated botanist, was born in Germany in 1627 and as a young man settled in what was then the Dutch East Indies. Nelson Coon, in an article in *New Outlook for the Blind* (April 1958), says that during much of Rumph's productive life he was visually impaired. At the age of forty he developed cataracts. Despite his visual impairment he was able to explore the plant life of the island of Amboina with the assistance of his son. At the age of sixty-five and totally blind he completed the manuscript of his great work, *Herbarium Aboinense.* A print on the title page of his book depicts him examining the leaves of a plant with his fingers. Coon quotes Elmer D. Merrill, a leading authority on the botany of the Far East, who said of Rumph in 1917 that he would especially "emphasize the ability, energy, and broad interests of the man, for his record as an investigator is a most remarkable one, more especially when we take into consideration the period in which he lived and worked, and the great handicap under which he struggled."

John Metcalf (1717–1810), commonly known as "Blind Jack of Knaresborough," was a remarkable person. He played the violin, was a horse trader, innkeeper, wool and fish merchant, and peddler. Blind from smallpox at six years old, he was self-sufficient early on. In his travels he walked widely around England using a long staff and noticed the poor condition of the roads. He was later contracted as an engineer to build roads and bridges in the north of England. According to Richard French in his book *From Homer to Helen Keller: A Social and Educational Study of the Blind* (1932), "He seems to have been one of the first to use crushed stone for making roadbeds."

From early childhood Henry Moyes showed an interest in mechanical items such as windmills, but as an adult his affinity for science developed in the area of philosophy. Although smallpox left him blind at the age of three, as a schoolboy he studied mathematics as well as music. Margaret Caldwell in an article in *The New Beacon* (March 1965) says that Moyes "became eminent in scientific fields long before braille, with its inestimable benefits to sightless students, came into general use." Cardwell mentions that he "left Scotland in 1779 and came to England for a time, but grew restless and, fond of traveling, decided to visit America. There he met many notable scientists of that day, and there, too, he lectured on optics. Because of his blindness, the Americans were greatly surprised at his choice of subject. On his return he traveled in Ireland and finally settled down in Manchester, England. He joined the Manchester Philosophical Society at which he read at its meeting several notable papers on chemistry and other branches of physical science."

François Huber (1750–1831), according to Wilson, suffered from cataracts and became blind by the age of fifteen. As a result of ill health he moved to the country and became a naturalist, specializing in studying the life of bees. C. Warren Bledsoe, in his article "History and Philosophy of Work for the Blind" in *Social and Rehabilitation Services for the Blind* (1992) remarks that with Huber's wife, son, and perceptive servant acting as his eyes, he was able to draw revolutionary conclusions regarding the habits of the queen and the other bees in the hive. According to Wilson, Huber's wife told him the color of the insects, whose form and size he afterwards perceived by touch. He could also easily identify bees by listening to their buzzing as they flew. His book *New Observations of the Bees* (1792) is a classic on the subject.

Gustaf Dalén (1869–1937), the Swedish inventor of the automatic marine light and winner of the Nobel Prize for physics, was blinded by an explosion in 1912, yet he continued to perfect his inventions. Another inventor, Ralph Teetor (1890–1982), became blind at the age of five, yet he earned a bachelor of science degree in engineering in 1912 from the University of Pennsylvania. In 1957 he invented cruise control, which has since become standard in many cars.

Medicine

MEDICINE is not generally recognized as a field accessible to blind people. Doctors who lose their sight while already practicing medicine are usually unable to continue. In Wilson's time this attitude seems to have been less pronounced. Hugh James (1771–1817), who became totally blind in 1806 after several years of eye problems, continued to practice medicine "with increased success," reports Wilson.

One of the few exceptions, Dr. Robert Babcock

(1851–1930), who was totally blind all his life, had a distinguished career as a specialist in lung and heart diseases. According to Lorraine Rovig in her 1995 speech to the National Federation of the Blind, "JOB—A Unique Resource with a Realistic Appraisal of Blindness," he earned numerous degrees and awards. "The real handicap I had to overcome was not blindness," Babcock said. "It was the danger of thinking that blindness was insuperable."

David Hartman (1949–), who became blind from glaucoma at the age of eight, received his degree in psychiatry from Temple University School of Medicine in 1976. He was the first blind person in more than one hundred years to enter medical school. He, like others, has proven that blind people can aspire to professional employment in the field of medicine.

THE BLIND ENGINEER.

To the preceding instances we may add that of the Count de Hagan, who was born in the beginning of the seventeenth century. Having entered the army at the early age of twelve years, he lost his left eye before he was seventeen, at the siege of Montauban; he still, however, pursued his profession with unabated ardour, and distinguished himself by many acts of brilliant courage. At last, when about to be sent into Portugal, with the rank of Field Marshal, he was seized with an illness which deprived him of sight in his remaining eye. He was yet only in his thirty-eighth year, and he determined that the misfortunes he had already sustained in the service of his country, should not prevent him from re-commencing his public career in a new character. He had always been attached to mathematics; and he now devoted himself assiduously to the prosecution of his favourite study, with a view, principally, to the improvement of the science of fortification, for which his great experience in the field particularly fitted him. During twenty years after this, which he passed in a state of total blindness, he gave a variety of publications to the world; among which may be mentioned, besides his well-known and important work on fortification, his "Geometrical Theorems" and his "Astronomical Tables." He was also the author of a rare book, called, "An Historical and Geographical Account of the

River of the Amazons;" which is remarkable as containing a chart, asserted to have been made by himself, after he became blind. It is said not to be very correct, although a wonderful production for such an artist.

G. E. RUMPH, OR RUMPFIUS,

THE BLIND PHYSICIAN OF HANAU.

―――――――
" If one sense be suppressed,
But retires to the rest."
―――――――

The phenomena of mind are at all times interesting, and many curious theories have been started on the value of the different senses. In the mental powers of the Blind, of which our anecdotes give such extraordinary proof, we see the loss of one sense compensated by the superior intensity and perfection of the remaining ones ; and, as nature ever designs well, if she chance in some respects to fail in her good intentions, she generally takes care in others to atone for such deficiencies. Where the mind is properly constituted, says Lieut. Holman, " the diminution of one faculty naturally calls others into more extensive action: in short, there are very few obstacles which man's perseverance may not enable him to overcome, if he will but rightly exercise those faculties with which the beneficence of his Creator has endowed him.'

G. E. RUMPH, OR RUMPFIUS, Doctor of physic in the University of Hanau, and a member of the Academy of Naturalists, was born at Hanau, 1637. He went to Amboyna, and became consul and senior merchant there, which did not prevent his employing his time in collecting the plants of the country.

Although he lost his sight at the age of forty-three, he could discover the nature and shape of a plant, by his taste and feeling. He comprised the history of all the plants which he had collected in the country where he settled, in twelve books: they were not, however, printed then; but John Burman published them, betwixt 1740 and 1750, in 7 vols. fol., under the title of "Herbarium Amboinense," 1755. Burman has added an Auctuarium, with the table usually bound at the end of vol.. vi. The work has some faults, or rather misfortunes, of a posthumous publication; but it must be observed, that the figures, far inferior to those of the "Hortus Malabaricus," are generally not more than half the size of nature. The original drawings, still in existence, are said to be very fine. Rumph also left "Imagines Piscium Testaceorum," Leyden, 1751, fol., reprinted 1769; the former is much valued for the plates. He wrote, besides, "The Political History of Amboyna," which has never been printed; but a copy is deposited in the India Company's chest at Amsterdam, and another at Amboyna.

Ireland, in the Chalcographimania (most probably on the authority of Tommy Coram), says, that Rumpfius, although quite blind, gave £1000 for a shell; and that there is a print of him handling the shell. The only known portrait of Rumpfius, is one before he lost his sight; it is a small oval, with an inscription.

AUTHORITY.

General Biographical Dictionary.

THE LIFE

OF

JOHN METCALF,

Commonly called "Blind Jack" of Knaresborough.

" The fell disease deprived him of his sight,
And left to grope his way in endless night."

We almost invariably find that Nature, in with-
holding from man the benefit of one sense, compen-
sates the deficiency by the superior perfection in which
she bestows others. The extraordinary particulars related in the following pages strikingly exemplify this
observation, and shew to what a degree the power of
habit, and a good understanding, are capable of overcoming impediments apparently insurmountable. For
instance, who would expect to find a man totally
blind from his infancy, superintending the building
of bridges and the construction of high roads; occupations for which his defect would seem to have
wholly disqualified him. These, however, were undertakings that Metcalf successfully executed; and
which, together with many singular adventures in
which he engaged, cannot fail to excite no small degree of astonishment and admiration.

JOHN METCALF was born in 1717, at Knaresborough, in Yorkshire; when four years of age his
parents, who were labouring people, put him to school,
where he continued two years. At the expiration of
that time, he was seized with the small pox, which
deprived him of his sight, in spite of all the means
that were employed for its preservation.   About
six months after his recovery, he was able to go from
his father's house to the end of the street, and to return, without a guide; and in about three years he
could find his way alone to any part of Knaresborough.   About this period he began to associate with
boys of his own age, among whom he acted a distinguished part in the juvenile pranks of taking birds'
nests, and robbing orchards.   As his father kept
horses, he learned to ride, and soon became a good
horseman, a gallop being his favourite pace.   At the
age of thirteen he was taught music, in which he
made great proficiency, though the cry of a hound or
a harrier was more congenial to his taste, than the
sound of an instrument.   He kept hounds of his own,
and frequently hunted with a Mr. Woodburn* of

* Metcalf, with some other young men, expressed a great
desire for a day's sport; and knowing that Mr. Woodburn
the master of the Knaresborough pack of hounds, had often
lent them to Metcalf for the same purpose, they doubted not
of the success of his application. On the evening before the
appointed day Metcalf went, flushed with hope, to Mr.
Woodburn, requesting him to lend the pack for the next day.
This was a favour out of his power to grant, having engaged
to meet Squire Trapps with the hounds next morning, upon
Scoton Moor, for the purpose of entering some young fox
hounds. Chagrined at this, Metcalf debated with himself

Knaresborough, who kept a pack, and was always very desirous of Metcalf's company in the chase. When about fourteen years old, his activity and the success with which his enterprises were usually attended, led him to imagine that he might undertake any thing without danger, and greatly consoled him for the want of sight; but he was taught to regret its loss by a severe wound he received, in consequence of a fall into a gravel-pit, while making his retreat from a plum-tree in which he had been surprised by the owner.

---

whether the disappointment should fall to Mr. Woodburn's friends, or his own: determining that it should not be the lot of the latter, he arose the next morning before day break, and crossed the high bridge, near which he had the advantage of the joint echoes of the old castle and Belmont-wood. He had brought with him an extraordinarily good hound of his own, and taking him by the ears, made him give mouth very loudly, himself giving some halloos at the same time. This device had so good an effect, that in a few minutes he had nine couple about him, as the hounds were kept by various people about the shambles, and were suffered to lie unkennelled. Mounting his horse, away he rode with the dogs to Harrowgate, where he met his friends ready mounted and in high spirits. Some of them proposed going to Bilton Wood, near Knaresborough, but this was opposed by Metcalf, who preferred the Moor; in fact, he was apprehensive of being followed by Mr. Woodburn, and wished to be farther from Knaresborough on that account. Pursuant to his advice, they drew the Moor at the distance of five miles, when they started a hare, killed her after a fine chase, and immediately put up another; just at this moment came up Mr. Woodburn, very angry, threatening to send Metcalf to the house of correction, and his passion rising to the utmost he rode up with an intention to

About this period he learned to swim, and soon bceame so very expert that his companions did not choose to come near him in the water, it being his custom to seize and plunge them to the bottom, and then swim over them by way of diversion. In this year two men being drowned in the deeps of the river Nid, Metcalf was employed to seek for their bodies, and succeeded in bringing up one of them.

A friend of his named Baker, having carried two packs of yarn to wash at the river, they were swept away by a sudden swelling of the current, and carried through the arches of the bridge, which is founded on a rock. A little below there is a piece of still water,

---

horse-whip him, which Metcalf prevented by galloping out of his reach. Mr. Woodburn then endeavoured to call off the hounds, but Metcalf, knowing the fleetness of his own horse, ventured within speaking, though not within whipping distance of him, and begged that he would not spoil them by taking them off, and that he was sure they would (as they actually did,) kill in a very short time. Metcalf soon found that Mr. Woodburn's anger had begun to abate, and going nearer to him, pleaded in excuse a misunderstanding of his plan, which he said he thought had been fixed for the day after. The apology succeeded with this good natured gentleman who, giving the hare to Metcalf, desired he would accompany him to Scoton Moor, whither, though late, he would go, rather than wholly disappoint Mr. Trapps. Metcalf proposed to his friend to cross the river Nid at Holm bottom; and Mr. Woodburn not being acquainted with the ford, he again undertook the office of guide, and leading the way, they soon arrived at Seoton Moor, where Mr. Trapps and his company had waited for them several hours. Mr. Woodburn explained the cause of the delay, and being now able to participate in the joke, the affair ended very agreeably.

supposed to be about twenty-one feet in depth ; as soon as the yarn came to this place it sunk.   Metcalf promised to recover the yarn for his friend, but the latter smiled at the supposed absurdity of the attempt; he, however, procured some long cart ropes, fixed a hook at one end, and leaving the other to be held by some persons on the high bridge, he descended, and by degrees recovered the whole of the yarn.

He continued to practice on the violin, till he was able to play country dances.   During the winter season, he performed as a wait at Knaresborough, with three others ; he likewise attended the assemblies which were held every fortnight, and frequented many other places where there was public dancing.   Notwithstanding these engagements, he found opportunity for playing his neighbours a number of mischievous tricks, and for a long time escaped suspicion.   At length, however, his expertness became known, and when any arch trick had been played, it was always the first inquiry, where Metcalf had been at that time.

Though he was fully engaged, he still retained his fondness for hunting, and also began to keep game cocks.   Whenever he went to a cock-pit, it was his custom to place himself on the lowest seat, near some friend who was a good judge, and who, by certain motions, enabled him to bet, hedge, &c.

In 1732, he was invited to Harrowgate to play at the assembly, as successor to a poor old man, who, borne down by the weight of one hundred years, began to play too slowly for country dances.   Here he was well received by the visiting nobility and gentry. In this employment he passed his evenings, and the mornings he spent in cock fighting, hunting, and coursing. About this period also he bought a horse, and often ran him for small plates; and his musical engagements increasing, he took a partner who was likewise a good performer.

In summer he often played at bowls, and, singular as it may seem, was frequently the winner. Cards likewise began to engage his attention, and he generally won the majority of the games. But these achievements were far from limiting his ambition or capacity, for he now began to attend the races at York, and other places. At the race ground he commonly rode in among the crowd, and was often successful in his bets, in which he was, however, assisted by several gentlemen to whom he was known. Having once matched one of his horses to run three miles for a considerable wager, and the parties agreeing each to ride his own horse, they set up posts at certain distances on the Forrest Moor, describing a circle of one mile, having consequently to go three times round the course. Under the idea that Metcalf would be unable to keep the course, great odds were laid against him, but his ingenuity furnished him with an expedient in this dilemma. He procured some bells, and placing a man with one at each post, was enabled by the ringing to judge when to turn; by this contrivance, and the superior speed of his horse, he came in winner amidst the applause of all present, except those who had betted against him. At different times he bought horses to sell again, which he often did with a large profit, so accurate was his judgment.

In 1738, Metcalf attained the age of twenty-one;

he was extremely robust, and six feet one inch and a half in height. About this time he acquired considerable celebrity as a pugilist, from the following circumstance. A friend of his being insulted in a public house by a man who, from his ferocious temper and great strength, was the general dread of the neighbourhood, Metcalf bestowed on him such discipline as soon extorted a cry for mercy.

Returning one day on foot from Harrowgate, he had proceeded about a mile, when he was overtaken by a Knaresborough man on horseback, who proposed, for two shillings' worth of punch, to let him ride in turn, dividing the distances equally. Metcalf agreed, on condition that he should have the first ride, to which his townsman assented on these terms; that he should ride a little beyond Poppleton field, where he would see a gate on his right hand, to which he should fasten the horse. Metcalf, however, rode forward to Knaresborough, which was seventeen miles from the place where he left his fellow traveller. The latter was greatly enraged at being obliged to walk so far, but Metcalf pleading in excuse that he never saw the gate, the man found it his interest to join in the laugh.

He was now in the prime of life, and possessed a peculiar archness of disposition, with an uncommon flow of spirits, and unparalleled contempt of danger ; and though his conduct was long marked by a variety of mischievous tricks, yet he afterwards planned and brought to perfection several schemes, both of private and public utility.

When the Harrowgate season was over, Metcalf

always remained a few days, and passed his evenings at one or other of the different inns. At the Royal Oak, now the Granby, he attracted the notice of Miss Benson, the landlady's daughter, whose constant attention and kindness soon inspired him with a reciprocal affection ; knowing, however, that her mother would oppose their union, various successful devices were employed to conceal their mutual partiality, and frequent meetings. An event, however, occurred, which obliged Metcalf to quit not only the object of his attachment, but likewise that part of the country. During his absence a Mr. Dickenson had paid his addresses to Miss Benson, and now urged his suit with such ardour, that the banns were published and the wedding-day appointed, to the no small mortification of Metcalf, who thought himself secure of her affection ; but though he loved her tenderly, his pride prevented him from manifesting his feelings, or attempting to prevent the match. On the day preceding that on which the nuptials were to be celebrated, Metcalf, riding past the Royal Oak, was accosted with, "one wants to speak with you." He immediately turned towards the stables of the Oak, and there to his joy and surprise, he found the object of his love, who had sent her mother's servant to call him. After some explanation, an elopement was resolved upon, which Metcalf, with the assistance of a friend, effected that night, and the next morning they were united. The confusion of his rival, who had provided an entertainment for two hundred people, may easily be conceived. Mrs. Benson, being much enraged at her daughter's conduct, refused either to see her or give up her clothes; nor was she reconciled to her till she was delivered of her second child, on which occasion she stood sponsor for it, and presented Metcalf with his wife's fortune.   It now became a matter of wonder that she should have preferred a blind man to Dickenson, she being as handsome a woman as any in the country. A lady having asked her why she refused so many good offers for Blind Jack, she answered, " because I could not be happy without him."   And being more particularly questioned, she replied, " his actions are so singular, and his spirit so manly and enterprising, that I could not help liking him."

He now purchased a house at Knaresborough, and continued to play at Harrowgate in the season; and set up a four wheeled chaise and a one horse chair for public accommodation, there having been nothing of the kind there before.   He kept these vehicles two summers, when the inn-keepers beginning to run chaises, he gave them up, as he also did racing and hunting; but still wanting employment, he bought horses, and went to the coast for fish, which he took to Leeds and Manchester.   So indefatigable was he that he frequently walked for two nights and a day, with little or no rest, for as a family was coming on, he was as eager for business as he had been for diversion ; still keeping up his spirits, as Providence endowed him with good health.   Going from Knaresborough to Leeds in a snow storm, and crossing a brook, the ice gave way under one of his horses, and he was under the necessity of unloading to get him out; but the horse, as soon as free, ran back to Knaresborough, leaving him with two panniers of fish, and

three other loaded horses, which, together with the
badness of the night, greatly perplexed him; after
much difficulty, however, he divided the weight
amongst the other three, and pursuing his route, he
arrived at Leeds by break of day. But the profits of
this business being but small, and the fatigue excessive, he soon abandoned it.

At the commencement of the rebellion, in 1745,
he exchanged his situation as violin player at Harrowgate, for the profession of arms. This singular event
was brought about in the following manner; William
Thornton, Esq. of Thornville, having resolved to
raise a company at his own expense, asked Metcalf,
who was well known to him, whether he would join
the company about to be raised, and whether he knew
of any spirited fellows likely to make good soldiers.
Upon his replying in the affirmative, he was appointed
assistant to a sergeant, and in two days raised one
hundred and forty four men, out of which the Captain
drafted sixty four, the number of privates he wanted.
With this company, among whom was Metcalf as
musician, Captain Thornton joined the army under
General Wade. In the first battle in which they
were engaged twenty of the men, with the Lieutenant
and Ensign, were made prisoners, and the Captain
himself very narrowly escaped. Metcalf, after a variety of adventures, rejoined his patron, and was
always in the field during the different engagements
which succeeded. After the battle of Culloden, he
returned to his family at Knaresborough, and had the
happiness to find his faithful partner and children in
good health. His wife confessed that she had enter-

tained many fears for her poor blind adventurer, yet knowing that a spirit of enterprise made a part of his nature, she was often comforted by the hope that he would, in some degree, signalize himself, notwithstanding the misfortune under which he laboured. This declaration, following a most cordial reception, gave full confirmation to an opinion which Metcalf had ever held, that the caresses and approbation of the softer sex are the highest reward that a man can receive.

Being again at liberty to choose his occupation, he attended Harrowgate as usual. During his Scotch expedition, he had become acquainted with various articles manufactured in that country, and judging that he might dispose of some of them to advantage in England, he repaired in the spring to Scotland, and furnished himself with a variety of cotton and worsted articles, for which he found a ready sale in his native country; among a thousand articles he knew what each cost him, from a particular mode of marking them. He not only frequently dealt in horses, directing his choice by feeling the animal,* but he also engaged pretty deeply in contraband trade, the profits of which were at that time much more

*The Queen's Bays at this time were quartered at Durham, and four horses were to be sold from each troop. Metcalf had notice sent him of the sale, but did not receive the letter until the day before it commenced; he set off, however, that afternoon from Durham, and riding all night, got there by day break. His first business was to become acquainted with the farriers, whom he began to question as to the horses which were to be sold. Amongst the number to be disposed of was a grey

considerable than the risk. One time in particular
having received a pressing letter from Newcastle-
upon-Tyne requiring his speedy attendance, he set
out on horse-back at three in the morning, and got
into Newcastle in the evening about six o'clock, the
distance being nearly seventy-four miles, and without
much fatigue. Having received some packages, he
employed a few soldiers to convey them to a carrier,
supposing that men of their description were least
liable to suspicion. After sending off his goods,
he staid two nights with some relations he had

---

one belonging to one of the drums; the man who had the
charge of him not having been sufficiently careful in trimming
him, had burnt him severely, which caused a prodigious
swelling. Had this careless conduct been known to his superi-
ors, he would have been punished for it, and upon that account the matter was hushed up. Metcalf, however, apprised
of the real cause in the course of his conversation with the
farriers, determined to purchase him, supposing that they
would be desirous to part with him at any price; and in this
supposition he was not mistaken. The sale began by bringing
out seven bay horses, six of which a gentleman bought for a
carriage, and Metcalf purchased the seventh ; they then
brought forward the grey horse, which our chapman bought
at the very low price of three pounds fifteen shillings, which
was first affixed by the auctioneer, but which, however, the
people said was very much beyond the value. Having used
such applications as he thought efficacious for his recovery,
by the time he had got him home, he had the satisfaction to
find him perfectly recovered, and within a week afterwards
refused fifteen guineas for him ; he kept him many years as
a draught horse, and the other horse also was sold to a profit,
by which he thought himself very well paid for his trip to
Durham.

there, and then set out home. He had with him about a hundred weight of tea, cased over with tow, and tightly corded up; this he put into a wallet which he laid across his saddle. Coming to Chester-le-street, about half way between Newcastle and Durham, he met at the inn an exciseman, who knew him as soon as he had dismounted, and asked him what he had got there. Metcalf answered, "It is some tow and line for my aunt, who lives a few miles distant; I wish she was far enough for giving me the trouble to fetch it." The officer asked him to bring it in, but he replied, " For the time I shall stay, it may as well remain on the horsing stone." By this seeming indifference about his package, he removed suspicion from the mind of the exciseman, who assisted in replacing it across the saddle; he then pursued his journey and got home in safety. Once, having disposed of a string of horses, he bought with the produce, a quantity of rum, brandy, and tea, to the amount of £200, put them on board a vessel for Leith, and travelled over land on foot, to meet the vessel there ; he had about thirty miles to walk, and carried near five stone weight of goods which he did not choose to put on ship board. At Leith he had the mortification to wait six weeks, without receiving any tidings of the vessel, which many supposed to have been lost, there having been a storm in the interval. The distress of mind resulting from this, induced him once to say; "if she is lost, I wish I had been in her; for she had all my property on board." Soon after, however, the ship got into Leith harbour; he then went on board, and set sail for Newcastle, but another

storm arising, the mate was washed overboard, the
mainsail carried away, and the ship was driven near
the coast of Norway. Despair became general, and
the prospect of going to the bottom seemed almost
certain. It now appeared to him a dreadful thing to
leave the world in the midst of health and vigour ;
he reflected on the impiety of his wish respecting the
former storm, and so effectually was his way of thinking changed, that had he had all the wealth in the
universe, he would have given it to have been on shore.
The wind however changing, hope began to return,
and the Captain put about for the Scotch coast, intending to reach Aberbrothick. A signal of distress
was put up, but the sea ran so high, that no boat
could venture out with a pilot ; he then stood in for
the harbour, but struck against the pier end, owing
to the unmanageable state of the vessel, from the loss
of her mainsail. She narrowly escaped being bilged,
but having got to the back of the pier, was towed
round into the harbour, with near five feet water in
the hold. Her escape from the merciless elements,
however, did not seem to terminate her dangers, the
country people shewing a disposition to seize the
ship as a wreck, and plunder her ; but fortunately
there was at hand a party consisting of an officer and
twenty men, of Pulteney's regiment, who had been
in pursuit of some smugglers, and Metcalf knowing
them well, as Captain Thornton's company was attached to that regiment, the officer sent three files of
men to protect the vessel, while the crew were removing the goods to a warehouse. As the vessel
stood in need of repairs, Metcalf put his goods on

board another, and sailed for Newcastle. There he met with an acquaintance, and from the seeming cordiality of the meeting, he thought he might have trusted his life in the hands of this man. With this impression, Metcalf opened to him the state of his affairs; informing him that he had got four hundred gallons of gin and brandy, for which he had a permit, and about thirty gallons for which he had none, and which he wanted to land; telling him, at the same time, of the harrassing voyage he had just finished. But it seems his misfortunes were only about to commence; for in a quarter of an hour, he found that the man whom he had taken for a friend, had gone down to the quay side, and giving information of what he knew, all the goods were seized and brought on shore. Metcalf imagined that none were seizable but the small part for which he had not obtained a permit; but was soon undeceived, the whole being liable to seizure as not agreeing with the specified quantity. He then repaired to the Custom House, and applied to Mr. Sunderland, the collector; this gentleman, being in the habit of visiting Harrowgate, knew Metcalf, and received him very kindly, but informed him that it was not in his power to serve him, the captors being the excise officers, and not under his control. He, however, suggested that some good might result from an application to Alderman Peireth, with whom Metcalf was acquainted, and who was particularly intimate with the collector of the excise. The good alderman gave him a letter to the collector, representing, as instructed by Metcalf, that the bearer had bought 400 gallons of spirits at the

Custom-house at Aberdeen; and that the extra quantity was for the purpose of treating the sailors and other friends, as well as for sea-stock for himself. At first the collector told him that he could do nothing for him, until he should write up to the board, and receive an answer; but Metcalf remonstrating on the inconvenience of the delay, and the other re-considering the letter, he agreed to come down to the quay at four o'clock in the afternoon, which he accordingly did, and released every thing without expense.

In 1751, he commenced a new employment; he set up a stage waggon betwixt York and Knaresborough, being the first on that road, and drove it himself, twice a week in the summer, and once in winter. This business, with the occasional conveyance of army baggage,* employed his attention till the

---

* A short time after the regiment, called the Queen's Bays, was raised, it was quartered at Knaresborough and the adjacent towns; but after a short stay, it was ordered to the North. The country people seemed extremely unwilling to supply carriages for conveying the baggage, the King's allowance being but nine-pence a mile per ton; that of the county, one shilling in the West-riding, and fifteen pence in the North-riding. Metcalf having two waggons, (one of them covered,) had a mind to try this business; and, to make sure of a journey, got the soldiers to press his two carriages, which were accordingly loaded, himself attending them to Durham. Previously to loading, however, the country people, who knew the advantage of carrying for the army, and who had kept back in hopes of an advance in the price, came forward with their waggons in opposition to Metcalf, but the soldiers would have no other. Arriving at Durham, he met Bland's Dragoons, on their march from the North to York; they loaded his waggons again for Northallerton, and would wil-

period of his first contracting for the making of roads, which engagement suiting him better, he relinquished every other pursuit. During his leisure hours, he had studied mensuration in a way peculiar to himself; and when certain of the girth and length of any piece of timber, he was able accurately to reduce its contents to square feet and inches, and could bring the dimensions of any building into yards or feet. The first piece of road he made, was about three miles of that between Fearnsby and Minskip, and the materials for the whole were to be produced from one gravel-pit; he therefore provided deal boards, and erected a temporary house at the pit; took a dozen horses to the place; fixed racks and mangers, and hired a house for his men, at Minskip. He often walked to Knaresborough in the morning, with four or five stones of meal on his shoulders, and joined his men by six o'clock. He completed the road much sooner than was expected, to the entire satisfaction of the surveyor and rustees.† Soon after this, he contracted for building

lingly have engaged them to York, but this he was obliged to decline, having promised to bring twenty three wool-packs to Knaresborough. He was just six days in performing this journey, and cleared, with eight horses and the one he rode, no less a sum than twenty pounds; though many people were afraid to travel with soldiers.

† "The blind projector of roads would reply to me, when I expressed myself surprised at the accuracy of his discriminations, that there was nothing surprising in the matter; 'you, sir,' says he, 'can have recourse to your eye sight whenever you want to see or examine any thing, whereas I have only my memory to trust to. There is, however one advantage, that I possess; the readiness with which at pleasure you view an

a bridge at Boroughbridge, which he completed with credit to his abilities. The business of making roads, and building and repairing bridges, in Yorkshire, Lancashire, Derbyshire, and Cheshire, he continued with great success until the year 1792, when he returned to his native county.

In the summer of 1788, he lost his wife, in the sixty first year of her age, and the fortieth of their union, leaving four children. She was interred in the church-yard of Stockport, in Cheshire, where they then resided.

After some unsuccessful speculations in the cotton trade, Metcalf returned to Yorkshire; and for want of other engagements, he bought hay to sell again. He measured the stacks with his arms, and having learned the height, he could readily tell what number of square yards were contained, in a stack of any value between one and five hundred pounds. Sometimes he bought a little standing wood, and if he could get the girth and height, would calculate the solid contents.

---

objects, prevents the necessity of fixing the ideas of it deeply in your mind, and the impressions, in general, become quickly obliterated. On the contrary, the information I possess, being acquired with greater difficulty, is on that very account, so firmly fixed on the memory, as to be almost indelible.' I made some inquiries respecting this new road he was now making; it was really astonishing, to hear with what accuracy he described the courses and nature of the different soils, through which it was conducted. Having mentioned to him a boggy piece of ground it passed through, he observed that that was the only place he had doubts concerning; and that he was apprehensive they had, contrary to his directions, been too sparing of their materials." *From Dr. Bew's account.*

In addition to this brief history of the life of this singular character, the reader will not be displeased to find the following anecdotes, which are of a nature too extraordinary to be omitted. Metcalf had learned to walk and ride very readily through all the streets of York, and being once in that city, as he was passing the George Inn the landlord called to him, and informed him that a gentleman in the house wanted a guide to Harrowgate, adding, "I know you can do as well as any one." To this proposal Metcalf agreed, upon condition that his blindness should be kept secret from the gentleman, who might otherwise be afraid to trust him. The stranger was soon ready, and they set off on horse-back, Metcalf taking the lead. When they came to Allerton, the gentleman inquired whose large house that was on the right, to which Metcalf replied without hesitation. A little further, the road is crossed by that from Wetherby to Boroughbridge, and runs along by the lofty brick wall of Allerton Park. A road led out of the Park, opposite to a gate upon the Knaresborough road, which Metcalf was afraid of missing; but perceiving the current of wind that came through the Park gate, he readily turned his horse towards the opposite one. Here he found some difficulty in opening the gate, in consequence, as he imagined, of some alteration that had been made in the hanging of it, he having not been that way for several months; therefore, backing his horse, he exclaimed, "Confound thee, thou always goest to the heel of the gate instead of the head." The gentleman then observed, his horse seemed rather awkward, but that his own mare was good at coming up to a gate ; on which Metcalf cheerfully permitted him to perform that office. Passing through Knaresborough they entered the forest, which was then uninclosed, nor was there yet any turnpike road upon it. Having proceeded a little way, the gentleman observed a light, and asked what it was. Metcalf took it for granted that his companion had seen what is called a *Will o' the Wisp*, which frequently appears there in a low and swampy spot, near the road ; but fearful of betraying himself, he did not ask in what direction the light lay. To divert his attention from this object, he asked him if he did not see two lights, one to the right, and one to the left ; the stranger replied, that he saw but one, to the right, "Well then, sir," says Metcalf, "that is Harrowgate." Having arrived at their journey's end, they stopped at the house now called the Granby, where Metcalf, being well acquainted with the place, led both the horses into the stable ; he then went into the house, where he found his fellow traveller comfortably seated over a tankard of negus, in which he pledged his guide. Metcalf took it very readily from him the first time, but the second he was rather wide of his mark. He soon after withdrew, leaving the landlord to explain what his companion was yet ignorant of. The latter hinted to the landlord his suspicion, that his guide must have taken a great quantity of spirits since their arrival ; upon which the landlord inquiring his reason for entertaining such an opinion, "I judged so," replied the traveller, "from the appearance of his eyes." "Eyes! Bless you, sir, do you not know that he is blind ?" " What do you mean by that?" "I mean, sir, that he cannot see." "Blind"! he exclaimed with astonishment; "Yes sir, as blind as a stone." The stranger desired Metcalf to be called, and upon his confirming the landlord's account, "Had I known that," said he, "I would not have ventured with you for a hundred pounds." "And I, sir," said Metcalf, " would not have lost my way for a thousand." The services of the evening were rewarded with two guineas, and a plentiful entertainment the next day by the gentleman, who considered this circumstance as the most extraordinary he had ever met with.

Metcalf happened once to be at Scriven, at the house of one Green, an inn-keeper, where two persons had a dispute concerning some sheep, which one of them had put into the penfold. The owner of the sheep, a townsman of Metcalf's, appeared to be ill-treated by the other party, who wished to take an unfair advantage ; Metcalf perceiving that they were not likely to agree about the damages, departed. It being about midnight, he resolved to perform a good turn for his friend, before he went home. The penfold being walled round, he climbed over, and laying hold of the sheep one after the other, he threw them over the wall; the difficulty of the undertaking increased, however, as the number diminished, because they were not so easily caught ; but not deterred by that circumstance, he completed the business. On the return of day, when the penfold was found untenanted, though the door was fast locked, a considerable degree of surprise was excited, and various conjectures were formed relative to the rogues who had liberated the sheep; but Metcalf passed unsuspected, and enjoyed the joke in silence.

Passing once through Halifax, he stopped at an inn called the Broad Stone. The landlord's son and some others who frequented Harrowgate, having heard of Metcalf's exploits, expressed a wish to play at cards with him, to which he consented, and a pack was sent for, which he requested permission to examine. They then began, for as the landlord was his friend, he could rely on him to prevent any deception. And Metcalf beat four of them in turn, playing for liquor only; not satisfied with this, some of the company proposed playing for money, and at shilling whist, Metcalf won fifteen shillings. The losing party then proposed playing double or quit, but he declined playing more than half guinea points; at length, however, yielding to their importunity, he engaged for guineas, and being favoured by fortune he won ten, and a shilling for liquor each game. The loser taking up the cards went out, and soon returned with eight guineas more, which speedily followed the other ten.

Among the numerous roads which Metcalf contracted to make, was part of the Manchester road, from Blackmoor to Standish Foot. As it was not marked out, the surveyor, contrary to expectation, took it over deep marshes, out of which it was the opinion of the trustees, that it would be necessary to dig the earth till they came to a solid bottom. This plan appeared to Metcalf extremely tedious and expensive, and liable to other disadvantages; he therefore argued the point privately with the surveyor, and several other gentlemen, but they were all immoveable in their former opinion. Metcalf attended their next meeting, and addressed them in the following manner; "Gentlemen, I propose to make the road over the marshes after my own plan, and if it does not answer, I will be at the expense of making it over again after yours." To this proposal they assented. Having engaged to complete nine miles in ten months, he began in six different parts, nearly four hundred men being employed. One of the places was peat, and Standish Common was a deep bog, over which it was thought impracticable to make any road. Here he cast it fourteen yards wide, raising it in a circular form, and the water, which in many places ran across the road, was carried off by drains; but he found the greatest difficulty in conveying stones to the spot, on account of the softness of the ground. Those who passed that way to Huddersfield market, were not sparing in their censure of their undertaking, and even doubted whether it would ever be completed. Having, however, levelled the piece to the end, he ordered his men to collect heather or ling, and bind it in round bundles which they could span with their hands; these bundles were placed close together, and another row laid over them, upon which they were well pressed down, and covered with stone and gravel. This piece, being about half a mile in length, when completed was so remarkably fine, that any person might have gone over it in winter unshod, without being wet; and, though other parts of the road soon wanted repairing, this needed none for twelve years. Dr. Bew, speaking of Metcalf, says; "With the assistance only of a long staff, I have several times met this man traversing the road, ascending precipices, exploring valleys, and investigating their extent, form, and situation, so as to execute his designs in the best manner. The plans which he designs, and the estimates he makes, are done in a method peculiar to himself, and of which he cannot well convey the meaning to others. His abilities in this respect are, nevertheless, so great, that he finds constant employment. Most of the roads over the Peak, in Derbyshire, have been altered by his directions, particularly those in the vicinity of Buxton; and he is at this time constructing a new one betwixt Wilmslow and Congleton, with a view to open a communication to the great London road, without being obliged to pass over the mountains."

These particulars, concerning this extraordinary man and useful member of society, are taken from a narrative published by himself, after his return to his native county. He there, with a daughter and a son-in-law who kept his house, fixed his residence at Spofforth, near Wetherby, happy in the enjoyment of the fruits of his industry, when his advanced age prevented him from engaging in the more active occupations to which he had been accustomed. He died in the year 1802.

AUTHORITIES.

The Life of METCALF. Liverpool edition, 1802—Eccentric Mirror, vol. the 2nd—Transactions of the Manchester Philosophical Society.

THE LIFE

OF

DR. HENRY MOYES.

"When but a stripling, with fond alarms
His bosom danced to Nature's boundless charms."

AMONG the many illustrious characters, whose
names adorn the pages of British Biography, Dr.
Henry Moyes claims our particular attention. His
virtues, his genius, and his scientific acquirements,
have been the admiration of every country which he
has visited. This distinguished individual, was born
at Kirkaldy, in Fifeshire, and lost his sight by the
small-pox,* before he was three years old, so that he

---

* Every operation of the mind is greatly facilitated by the
employment of sensible symbols, especially the process of acquiring, apprehending, and recollecting knowledge, as well
as of pursuing long and intricate calculations or deductions.
Our faculties receive such important assistance from these lines,
figures, letters, and other marks, which may be made to present the record of every thought faithfully to the eye, that we
are justified in quoting any remarkable case of progress, even
in abstract science, attained without the aid of this invaluable
organ, as a noble example of what perseverance may accomplish in the face of the most formidable difficulties.

scarcely retained in after life, any recollection of having ever seen, yet he used to say, that he remembered having once observed a water-mill in motion; and
it is characteristic of the tendencies of his mind, that
even at that early age, his attention was attracted by
the circumstance of the water flowing in one direction,
while the wheel turned round in the opposite, a mys-
tery on which he reflected for some time before he
could comprehend it. Blind as he was, he distinguished himself when a boy, by his proficiency in all
the usual branches of a literary education, but "mechanical exercises," were the favorite employments of
his infant years. We have no information respecting
him from this period, till the time of his leaving College. He commenced, at Edinburgh, a series of lectures on the theory and practice of music, but not
meeting with that encouragement which he expected,
he relinquished this design. He next turned his attention to a subject which was more congenial to his
feelings—natural and experimental philosophy presented an extensive field for the exercise of his talents.
He was the first blind man who had proposed to lecture on chemistry; as a lecturer he acquired great
reputation; his address was easy and pleasing, his
nguage correct, and he performed his experiments
in a manner which always gave great pleasure to his
auditors. He left Scotland in 1779, and travelled into
England, where he was well received. His audience
was generally composed of the most respectable people of the towns through which he passed; but being
of a restless disposition and fond of travelling, he in
1785, visited America. In the summer of that year

he made a tour of the Union, and conversed with such men as were distinguished, either for their learning or love of science. The following paragraph respecting him, appeared in one of the American newspapers of that day. "The celebrated Dr. Moyes, though blind, delivered a lecture upon optics,* delineated the properties of light and shade, and gave an astonishing illustration of the power of touch. A highly polished plane of steel was presented to him, with a stroke of an etching tool so minutely engraved

---

* In no part of the human fabric, or even throughout the whole of nature, with which we are acquainted, are there more evident marks of exquisite perfection and wisdom, than in what relates to the sense of seeing; whether we direct our attention to the wonderful regularity, order, minuteness, and velocity of the rays of light, which minister to this sense, or to the structure and formation of the little organ, in which this faculty is destined to reside. With a ball and socket, (as a learned and elegant philosopher beautifully observes) of an inch diameter, we are enabled, in an instant of time, without changing our place, to perceive the disposition of an army, the figure of a palace, and the variety of a landscape; and not only, as he further remarks, to find our way through the pathless ocean, traverse the globe of the earth, determine its figure and dimensions, and delineate every region of it; but,

> "Breaking hence, we take our ardent flight
> Thro' the blue infinite,"

ascertain the order, revolutions, and distances of the planetary orbs, and even form probable conjectures on

> " .... every star,
> Which the clear concave of a winter's night,
> Pours on the eye or astronomic tube,
> Far stretching, snatches from the dark abyss."
> *Thompson.*

on it, that it was invisible to the naked eye, and only
discoverable with a powerful magnifying glass—with
his fingers he discovered the extent, and measured the
length of the line. This gentleman informed me,
that being overturned in a stage coach, one dark
rainy evening, in England, and the carriage and four
horses thrown into a ditch, the passengers and driver
with two eyes a-piece, were obliged to apply to him,
who had no eyes, for assistance, in extricating the
horses. As for me, said he, after I had recovered
from the astonishment of the fall, and discovered that
I had escaped unhurt, I was quite at home in the
dark ditch. The inversion of the order of things was
amusing, I, that was obliged to be led about like a
child in the glaring sun, was now directing eight
persons to pull here and haul there, with all the dexterity and activity of a man-of-war's boatswain."

On his return from America, he took a house
in Edinburgh, where he resided for some time, beloved and admired, not only by his countrymen, but
also by strangers, who resorted to that ancient metropolis. But he had not yet finished his travels. Before
his American expedition he had formed the design of
coming over to Ireland, and when he had now returned, he determined to carry his favourite project
into execution, and accordingly in 1790, he crossed
the channel, and arrived in Belfast. He visited all
the principal towns in the island; he was every
where received with that respect which was due
to his great merit. He remained a few months
in Dublin, where he was visited by some of the most
respectable individuals in that metropolis. Among

his Irish friends was the ingenious Mr. Kirwan of
Dublin, a name well known in the scientific world.
Between these two great men a friendship commenced
which only ended with their lives. Dr. Moyes was
highly gratified with his journey through Ireland;
the hospitable manner in which he was every where
received, and the friendship he experienced, were the
theme of his eulogiums on that people. He now took
up his residence at Manchester, and there determined
to spend the remainder of his life. He was here in
his native element, or to use his own words, "quite
at home." In one of the most enlightened neighbour-
hoods in the empire, surrounded by a circle of chosen friends—distinguished by their taste, their talents,
and their love of science; and with access to the
numerous and well selected libraries, it was no wonder that these advantages induced Dr. Moyes to prefer Manchester to any other place he had been in.
He was elected a member of the Manchester Philosophical Society, and enriched its collection by several
valuable papers on chemistry, as well as the other
branches of physical science. The following particulars of our philosopher's character, come from the
classic pen of Dr. Bew.

"Dr. Henry Moyes, who occasionally read lectures on philosophical chemistry at Manchester, lost
his sight by the small-pox in early infancy. He
never recollected to have seen; but the first traces of
memory, I have, (says he) are in some confused ideas
of the solar system. He had the good fortune to be
born in a country where learning of every kind is
highly cultivated, and to be brought up in a family

devoted to learning. Possessed of native genius, and ardent in his applications, he made rapid advances in various departments of erudition, and not only acquired the fundamental principles of mechanics, music, and the languages, but likewise entered deeply into the investigation of the profounder sciences, and displayed an acute and general knowledge of geometry, optics, algebra, astronomy, chemistry, and in short, of most of the branches of the Newtonian Philosophy : *
At a very early age, he made himself acquainted with the use of edged tools so perfectly, that notwithstanding his entire blindness, he was able to make little wind-mills ; and even constructed a loom with his own hands, which still show the marks of wounds he received in the execution of these juvenile exploits. By a most agreeable intimacy and frequent intercourse, which I enjoyed with this accomplished blind gentleman, whilst he resided at Manchester, I had an opportunity of repeatedly observing the peculiar manner in which he arranged his ideas, and acquired his

* " Moyes possessed all that extreme delicacy in the senses of touch and hearing, for which the blind have usually been remarkable, we have been told that having been one day accosted in the street by a young friend, whom he had not met with for a good many years, his instant remark, on hearing his voice, was, how much taller you have grown since we last met! He contrived for himself, a system of palpable arithmetic, on a different principle from that of Saunderson, and possessing the advantage in point of neatness and simplicity. Dr. Moyes, must have been a person of extraordinary mental endowments, and affords us certainly, next to Saunderson, the most striking example on record, of attainments in the mathematics, made without any assistance from the eye.

information. Whenever he was introduced into company, I remarked that he continued some time silent. The sound directed him to judge of the dimensions of the room, and the different voices, of the number of persons that were present; his distinctions in these respects were very accurate, and his memory so retentive, that he was seldom mistaken. I have known him instantly to recognize a person on first hearing him speak, though more than two years had elapsed since the time of their last meeting. He determined pretty nearly the stature of those he was speaking with, by the direction of their voices; and he made tolerable conjectures respecting their temper and dispositions, by the manner in which they conducted their conversation. It must be observed that this gentleman's eyes were not totally insensible to intense light. The rays refracted through a prism, when sufficiently vivid, produced certain distinguishable effects on them. The red gave him a disagreeable sensation, which he compared to the touch of a saw; as the colours declined in violence, the harshness lessened, until the green afforded a sensation that was highly pleasing to him, and which he described as conveying an idea similar to what he felt in running his hand over polished surfaces. Polished surfaces, meandering streams, and gentle declivities, were the figures by which he expressed his ideas of beauty; rugged rocks, irregular points, and boisterous elements, furnished him with expressions for terror and disgust. He excelled in the charms of conversation; was happy in his allusions to visual objects; and discoursed on the nature, composition, and beauty of colours, with pertinence and precision.

"Dr. Moyes was a striking instance of the power the human soul possesses, of finding resources of satisfaction, even under the most rigorous calamities. Though involved in ever-during darkness, and excluded from the charming views of silent, or animated nature; though dependent upon an undertaking for the means of his subsistence, the success of which was very precarious; in short, though destitute of other support than his genius, still Dr. Moyes was generally cheerful and apparently happy. Indeed, it must afford much pleasure to the feeling heart, to observe this hilarity of temper prevail almost universally with the blind. Though cut off from the cheerful ways of men and the contemplation of the human face divine, they have this consolation—they are exempt from the discernment, and contagious influence of those painful emotions of the soul, that are visible on the countenance, and which hypocrisy itself cannot conceal. This disposition likewise, may be considered as an internal evidence of the native worth of the human mind, that thus supports its dignity and cheerfulness under one of the severest calamities that can possibly befall us."

This good man, after a life of 57 years, spent in learned labours and inglorious ease, paid the debt of nature, August 10th, 1807. As he never had entered into the married state, he was enabled by prudence and œconomy to amass a considerable sum, which he bequeathed to his brother. In his manner of living he was abstemious. He was entirely unacquainted with the use of ardent spirits, or fermented liquors. He had a natural dislike to animal food of

every description ; consequently his meals were plain
and simple. He was very partial to a sea-weed, well
known by the name of dulse, this he would boil, and
dress up with a little butter, which, with a crust of
bread, and a draught of spring-water, was the only
luxury in which he indulged.   Well might Dr. Moyes
say with Goldsmith's hermit—

> " No flocks that range the valley free,
> To slaughter I condemn,
> Taught by that power which pities me,
> I learn to pity them;
> But from the mountain's grassy side,
> A guiltless feast I bring;
> A scrip with herbs and fruit supplied,
> And water from the spring."

AUTHORITIES.

Transactions of the Manchester Philosophical Society—Encyclopædia Britannica—Select Anecdotes, vol. the 2nd.

THE LIFE

OF

M. HUBER,

THE BLIND PHILOSOPHER OF GENEVA.

" Of all the race of animals, alone
The bees have common cities of their own ;
And, common sons, beneath one law they live,
And with one common stock their traffic drive.
Each has a certain home, a sev'ral stall ;
All is the state's, the state provides for all.
Mindful of coming cold, they share the pain,
And hoard for winter's use the summer's gain.
Some o'er the public magazines preside,
And some are sent new forage to provide.
Their toil is common ; common is their sleep ;
They shake their wings when morn begins to peep,
Rush through the city gates without delay,
Nor ends their work but with declining day.
Then having spent the last remains of light,
They give their bodies due repose at night ;
When hollow murmurs of their ev'ning bells
Dismiss the sleepy swains, and toll them to their cells."

OF all the deprivations to which man is subject,
there is not one which to a greater degree shuts him
out from the sources of pleasure, and the means of
usefulness, than the loss of sight. He may lose the
perception of odours, and taste, without any diminution of the higher order of enjoyments; he may also
be deprived of hearing, and yet may still have access
to the widest field of instruction and delight. But

he who has lost the power of vision is debarred, by the most formidable obstacles, from the perusal of that "book of knowledge," written by the fair hand of nature herself, in which are to be found, not the pictures of things, drawn by other minds, but the originals themselves. And yet there have been men, who have struggled with and overcome the difficulties of this affliction, to a degree which would be incredible, if it did not rest on the most indubitable proofs. How many instances have there been of blind persons, who have pursued knowledge with ardour and success, and have accomplished undertakings which would have done them honour, even if they had possessed all the bodily senses in the highest degree of perfection! The truth of the above remarks will be strikingly illustrated in the following pages.

Francis Huber was born at Geneva, in July, 1750, of an honourable family, in which quickness of intellect and a lively imagination seemed hereditary. His father, John Huber, had the reputation of being one of the wisest men of his time, and in this light is often mentioned by Voltaire, who highly appreciated his original conversation; he was also an agreeable musician, and wrote verses which were praised even at Ferney. The predilections of the father were inherited by the son. In his early years he attended the public lectures of the college, and, under the guidance of good masters, acquired a taste for literature, which was matured by the conversation of his father, to whom he was also indebted for his love of natural history. He was initiated in the physical sciences, by attending the lectures of M. de Laussure, and by making experiments in the laboratory of a relative, who ruined himself in the search for the philosopher's stone. Endowed with great warmth of feeling, his precocity was very remarkable, and he commenced the study of natural objects, at an age when others are only beginning to be conscious of their existence. He was shortly to suffer the most grievous of all privations, and, as if instinctively, he laid up a store of recollections and feelings for the remainder of his life.

About the age of fifteen, his general health and also his eye-sight began to be impaired; his ardour in the pursuit of knowledge and amusement,—the passionate eagerness with which he followed his studies by day, and the reading of romances by night, (sometimes by no stronger light than that of the moon,) were the causes, it is said, which threatened the ruin both of his sight and of his constitution. His father at that period took him to Paris, in order to consult Tronchin on his health, and Wenzel on the state of his eyes. Tronchin, with the view of removing a tendency to consumption, sent him to pass some time at Stein, a village in the environs of Paris, that he might be out of the reach of every species of agitation: there he lived the life of a mere peasant, followed the plough, and occupied himself wholly in agricultural pursuits. This plan was completely successful so far as regarded his general health, which was ever afterwards unshaken, while he acquired a taste for the country, and a tender recollection of its pleasures, which never forsook him. The oculist Wenzel con-

sidered his sight, however, as incurable ; he thought
it unsafe to risk the operation for cataract, which was
then not so well understood as it is now, and announced to Huber the probability of his shortly becoming completely blind.

His eyes, however, in spite of their weakness had,
both before his departure and after his return, encountered those of Marie-Aimèe Lullin, the daughter
of one of the Syndics of the republic. They had met
each other frequently at the dancing master's ; an
affection, such as is felt at the age of seventeen, sprang
up between them and became part of their existence,
and neither of them believed it possible that their fates
could be disunited. The speedy approach, however, of
Huber's blindness, determined M. Lullin to refuse
his consent to their union, but as the misfortune of
him whom she had chosen as her future partner, became more certain, Marie regarded herself as bound
never to forsake him. " But," said she, " now that
he requires a guide to be every moment with him,
nothing shall prevent me from being united to him."
Her early attachment was rivetted by time, and afterwards became a species of generous heroism ; and she
resolved to wait till she had attained her majority,
(then fixed at twenty-five years,) in order to be united
to Huber. To all the temptations, and even to all
the persecutions, by which her father endeavoured to
shake her resolution, she remained impregnable ; and
the moment she attained her majority, she presented
herself at the altar, with the spouse whom she had
chosen when he was happy and attractive, and to cheer

whose melancholy fate she was now resolved to devote her life.

Being united to the object of her disinterested affection, their mutual good conduct soon obtained pardon for their disobedience. The constancy of Madame Huber was, in all respects, worthy of the juvenile energy which she had displayed, and during the forty years' continuance of their union, she never ceased to bestow the tenderest care on her blind husband ; she was his reader, and his secretary, made observations for him, and spared him every embarrassment that his situation was likely to produce. This excellent woman soon discovered a thousand means of alleviating her husband's unfortunate calamity. During the war she formed whole armies with pins of various sizes, and thus enabled him to distinguish the positions of the different corps ; she likewise stuck the pins in a map, which gave him a correct idea of the movement of the troops ; and she formed plans, in relief of the places they occupied. In a word, she had but one occupation, that of making the life of her husband happy, and to such a point did this amiable woman carry her attentions, that M. Huber asserted, that he should be miserable were he to cease to be blind. "I should not know," said he, "to what extent a person in my situation could be beloved ; besides, to me, my wife is always young, fresh, and pretty, and that is no light matter." This affectionate instance of conjugal attachment has been mentioned by celebrated writers; Voltaire frequently alludes to it in his correspondence, and the episode of the Belmont family in Delphine, is a true picture, although somewhat veiled, of that of Huber and his wife.

We have seen blind men excel as poets; some have distinguished themselves as philosophers, and others as arithmeticians; but it was reserved for Huber to become illustrious, in a science requiring the examination of objects so minute, that the most clear sighted observers find a difficulty in distinguishing them. The perusal of the works of Reaumur and Bonnet, and the conversations of the latter, directed his curiosity to the study of bees; his constant residence in the country inspired him, first, with the desire of verifying some facts, and afterwards of supplying some deficiencies in the history of these insects. But, for this kind of observation, it was not only necessary that he should have an instrument such as the labours of the optician might supply, but also an intelligent assistant, whom he could instruct in the use of it. At this time, he had a servant in his family, named Francis Burnens, equally remarkable for his sagacity, and for his attachment to his master. Huber drilled him in the art of observing, directed him in his inquiries by questions dexterously proposed, and by means of his own youthful recollections, and the confirmatory testimony of his wife and friends, he corrected the reports of his assistant, and in this way succeeded in acquiring a clear and accurate idea of the most minute facts. "I am much more certain," he said to a friend one day, laughing, " of what I relate than you are yourself, for you publish only what you have seen with your own eyes, whereas I take a medium among

the testimony of many." This, indeed, is very plausible reasoning, but will induce no one to quarrel with
his eyes.

Huber discovered that the mysterious and remarkably prolific nuptials of the queen bee, the single mother of all her tribe, are celebrated, not in the hive,
but in the open air, at an elevation sufficiently great
to escape ordinary eyes, but not to elude the researches of a blind man, aided by a peasant; and he
described in detail the consequences of the early or
late celebration of this aërial hymen. He confirmed,
by repeated observation, the discovery of Schirach,
at that time disputed; that bees can at their pleasure
transform, by an appropriate kind of food, the eggs
of working bees to queens, or, to speak more correctly,
neuters to females; he showed also how some working
bees can lay productive eggs. He described with
great care the combats of the queen bees with each
other, the massacre of the drones, and all the singular circumstances that take place in the hive, when a
foreign queen is substituted for the indigenous one.
He showed the influence produced by the size of the
cells, on the growth of the insects reared in them, and
how the larvæ of the bees spin the silk of their cells.
Huber proved to demonstration that the queen is ovi-
parous; he studied the origin of swarms, and was the
first who gave an accurate history of the flying colonies. He pointed out the use of their antennæ in enabling the bees to distinguish each other; and, finally,
from the knowledge he had acquired of their policy,

he drew up good rules for their economical superintendance. For the greater part of these delicate observations, on hitherto unnoticed facts, he was indebted
to his invention, under various forms, of glass hives;
one description of which he termed *ruches en livre*
or *en feuillettes*, book or sheet hives, and the other
ruches plates, flat hives, which allowed the labours of
the community to be witnessed in their minutest
details.

These discoveries were greatly facilitated by Burnens, who in his zeal for the discovery of truth, would
brave without shrinking the wrath of an entire hive,
in order to discover the most insignificant fact, and
was even seen to seize an enormous wasp, in spite of
the grievous stings of a whole nest of hornets. From
this, we may judge of the enthusiasm with which his
master (and I use the term here, not in the sense of
employer but instructor,) inspired all his agents in
the pursuit of truth. The publication of his labours
took place in 1792, in the form of letters to Charles
Bonnet, and under the title of " Nouvelles Observations sur les Abeilles." Naturalists were much struck,
not only with the novelty of the facts, detailed in
this work, but with their rigorous accuracy, and the
extraordinary difficulties which the author had com-
bated so successfully.

The activity of his researches suffered no interrup-
tion, either from this first success, which might have
satisfied his personal vanity, or from the embarras-
sing changes occasioned by the revolution, and his

separation from his faithful Burnens.   Another assistant was necessary to him, and this office his wife
performed for some time.   His son Peter, who afterwards acquired considerable celebrity by his history
of ants and other insects, next commenced his apprenticeship as observer to his father; and it was
principally by his assistance, that Huber made new
and laborious researches into the history of bees.
These researches form the second volume of the second edition of his work, published in 1814, and
partly edited by his son.

The origin of wax was then a disputed point among
naturalists, some affirming, but without sufficient proof,
that it was formed with the honey ; Huber, who had
successfully cleared up the origin of the propolis,
confirmed this opinion by numerous observations, and
in particular, showed, with the assistance of Burnens,
how the wax escapes in the shape of flakes between the
rings of the abdomen.   He devoted himself to laborious researches on the formation of the bee-hive, and
followed step by step its wonderful construction, which
seems to resolve, by its perfection, the most delicate
problems of geometry ; he also pointed out the part
which each class of bees takes in forming the hive, and
followed their labours from the rudiments of the first
cell, until the completion of the honey comb.   Huber
first made known the ravages of the *sphinx atropos* in
the hives which it enters.   He even attempted to clear
up the history of the senses in bees, and in particular
to ascertain the locality of the sense of smell, the ex-

istence of which is proved by the whole history of insects, but the seat of which, their structure has not
yet enabled us to fix with certainty. He also undertook curious researches on the respiration of bees,
and proved, by numerous experiments, that they
absorb oxygen like other animals. The question,
however, arose, how could the purity of the air be
maintained, in a hive plastered with mastic, and
closed in all its parts, except at the narrow orifice
which serves as the entrance ? This problem required
all the sagacity of our observer, and he finally arrived at the conclusion, that the bees, by a particular
movement of their wings, agitate the air in such a
manner as to produce its renovation; after having assured himself of this by direct observations, he further proved it, by means of the experiment of an artificial ventilation. These experiments on respiration required some analysis of the air in bee-hives,
and this brought Huber into correspondence with Senebier, who was then occupied with similar researches on vegetables. Among the means that Huber
had at first devised, for discovering the nature of the
air in bee-hives, was that of producing the germination of various kinds of seeds, in accordance with the
notion, that they never germinate in an atmosphere
that has not its due quantity of oxygen. This experiment, although inadequate to the end proposed,
suggested to the two friends the idea of occupying
themselves with inquiries on germination; and the
most curious part of this association is the fact, that

very frequently it was Senebier who suggested the
experiments, and Huber, deprived of sight, who executed them. Their labours have been published in
their joint names, under the title of "Memoires
sur l'Influence de l'Air dans la Germination des
Graines."

The style of Huber is, in general, clear and elegant,
and while not destitute of the precision required in
didactic compositions, it is blended with that charm
which a poetical imagination is capable of diffusing
over all objects. That, however, by which it is particularly distinguished, is what would be least expected, the description of facts in so graphic a manner, that in the perusal we seem ourselves to see the
objects which the author, alas, had not seen. In considering this singular quality of the style of a blind
person, I have accounted for it, by the efforts it must
have cost him to connect the accounts of his assistants,
in order to form a complete idea.

His taste for the fine arts, being deprived of the
power of expatiating on form, was led to sounds.
He loved poetry but music, had the greatest charms
for him: his taste for it might be called innate, and
he was greatly indebted to it throughout his whole
life, as a source of delightful recreation; his voice also
was agreeable, and he had been initiated from his
earliest youth in the beauties of Italian music.

The wish to keep up acquaintance with absent
friends, without recourse to a secretary, suggested
to him the idea of having a printing press for his

own use ; it was made for him by his servant, Claude Lechet, whom he had inspired with a taste for mechanics, in the same way that he had formerly instructed Burnens in natural history. A series of numbered cases contained small printing types, executed in bold relief, which he arranged in his hand. On the lines thus composed, he placed a sheet of paper blackened with a particular kind of ink, and above that a sheet of white paper ; with a press, set in motion by his foot, he succeeded in printing a letter, which he folded and sealed himself, greatly delighted with the idea of that independence of others, which he hoped to acquire by this means. The difficulty, however, of putting the press into action made him soon abandon the use of it ; but the letters, and the algebraic characters of burnt earth, which his son, ever zealous and ingenious in his service, had made for him, were a source of occupation and amusement for upwards of fifteen years. He enjoyed also the pleasure of walking in the fields, and was even able to do this alone ; by means of strings in his hand, and small knots made at intervals, he always knew where he was, and would direct himself accordingly. The activity of his mind made it necessary that he should have such occupations, or he might have been amongst the most miserable of mankind ; his friends around him also had no other wish than to please and assist him, and it therefore ceases to be a wonder how he preserved that happy disposition, which is so often destroyed by collision with mankind.

The conversation of Huber was generally of an amiable and pleasant cast ; his wit was gay and

lively ; and to few departments of knowledge was he
a stranger.   He delighted in elevating his thoughts
to the contemplation of the most lofty and important
subjects, and he could also descend to the most playful
and familiar.   He was not learned, in the usual ac-
ceptance of the term, but, like a skilful diver, he explored the depths of every question with extraordinary
tact and sagacity.   When the conversation turned on
subjects in which he felt more than common interest,
his fine countenance became peculiarly animated ; the
vivacity of his physiognomy, by some mysterious
charm, seemed to give expression even to his eyes, so
long condemned to darkness, and the tones of his voice
then became more solemn and impressive.   To extensive knowledge, M. Huber also joined an extraordinary memory : he related, in a most graceful style,
a great variety of interesting anecdotes, and nothing
could be more affecting than to hear him sing the words
of the scene between Œdipus and his daughter.

This extraordinary man passed the latter years of
his life at Lausanne, under the care of his daughter,
Madame de Molin, and from time to time he resumed
his early pursuits.   The discovery of stingless bees in
the neighbourhood of Tampico, by Captain Hall, excited his interest, and his joy was great when his
friend, Professor Prevost, was able to send him, first a
few specimens, and afterwards a whole hive of these
insects.   This was the last attention he paid to that
favourite pursuit, to which he had been indebted for
his fame, and, what was more, for his happiness.
Naturalists, who have followed in his track, although
enjoying the benefit of sight, have found nothing

of importance to add to the observations of one who was deprived of vision.

Huber preserved his faculties, and was both amiable and beloved to the last. At the age of eighty-one he thus wrote to one of his dearest friends ; " There are moments when it is impossible to keep one's arms folded, and it is then, in unbracing them a little, that we can repeat to those whom we love, all the esteem, the affection, and the gratitude with which they inspire us ;" further on, he added, "I can only say to you, that resignation and serenity are blessings that have not been denied to me." He wrote these lines on the 20th of December, and on the 22nd he was no more, having calmly breathed his last in the arms of his daughter.

AUTHORITIES.

Memoirs of the Empress Josephine, vol. 1—Foreign Quarterly Review, vol. 10. p 561—Edinburgh Review for 1815.

THE LIFE

OF

HUGH JAMES, M.D.

THE BLIND PHYSICIAN OF CARLISLE.

" Oh ! lost and lamented, whose steps knew the door,
Whose hand dropt life's balm in the wounds of the poor,
Tho' darkness came o'er thee, that darknees enshrin'd
Religion's pure lamp, the strong light of the mind."

HUGH JAMES, M.D. youngest son of the Rev. John James, D. D. Rector of Arthuret, and Kirkandrews, in Cumberland, was born at St. Bee's in the same county, in July, 1771. Having completed his education, and finished his medical studies in London and Edinburgh ; in the spring of 1796, he settled in Whitehaven, as a surgeon. Two years afterwards he had a very severe illness, attended with excruciating pain in his head, and violent inflammation in his eyes, which so impaired his sight, that he was obliged to give up all ideas of practising as a surgeon. After several years of much suffering, which he bore with exemplary patience and fortitude, his sight was so far improved as to enable him, in 1803, to graduate in Edinburgh, and then to fix in Carlisle as a physician. Still, however, he was subject to violent attacks of inflammation in his eyes, which induced him several times to go to London, for the purpose of consulting the first oculists there. But the disease baffled all their skill; and in the winter of 1806, his sight was totally lost. But, notwithstanding this great privation, he pursued his profession even with increased success. By the eye, it is true, the physician learns the attitude of his patient, the expression of the countenance, the state of the tongue, and the colour of the skin; and these signs often indicate the nature of the disorder. How, then, can a blind man be a good physician? A blind physician can acquire a tolerable knowledge of all these signs, with the exception of the colour of the skin, by the sense of touch; and this sense being in him more acute and refined, he is perhaps able to judge more correctly of the state and condition of the skin, which is considered a matter of great importance in the practice of the profession. External diseases, particularly cutaneous diseases, are seldom attended with danger, and are chiefly distinguished by the eye, internal complaints, on the other hand, which are very numerous and more dangerous, are frequently discovered by the sense of feeling; a blind physician has the advantage of a more acute sense of feeling, and is able to form a very correct opinion of the seat and nature of these complaints

Dr. James practised in Carlisle many years, during which, his skill was manifested on many important occasions. But, however important the station he occupied in society, the grand sphere of his usefulness, was in his capacity of physician. Disregarding personal emolument, he was ever as ready to hasten to the relief of the poor as to the rich, and thousands can testify how carefully, how anxiously, he enquired into their maladies and necessities; and how readily relief followed his knowledge of distress; and if his patients were unable to go to him, no sooner was the intimation given, than they found him at their bedside. It was in his attendance on a poor patient, that he contracted the malignant distemper which terminated his valuable life in a few days. A monument was erected to his memory by his fellow citizens with the following inscription.

"To the memory of Hugh James, M. D. who practised physic with eminent skill, for many years, in this city. Providence largely recompensed the loss of sight in early life, with talents which raised him to distinguished reputation in his profession, and more abundantly blessed him with a disposition ever prompt to succour poverty and pain. The study of his art, which shewed him the weakness and uncertainty of life, taught him to meditate deeply on the works of God, and animated his faith in a merciful Redeemer.

He died the 20th of September, 1817, in the 45th year of his age, and was interred in the parish church of Arthuret in this county."

AUTHORITY:
The Carlisle Patriot for 27th September, 1817.

THE LIFE

OF

ALEXANDER DAVIDSON,

THE BLIND PHILOSOPHER OF DALKEITH.

But Oh! instead of Nature's face,
Hills, dales, and woods, and streams combin'd,
Instead of tints, and forms, and grace,
Night's blackest mantle shrouds the Blind.

The many bright examples that have already been given of individuals who, in this state of blindness, have distinguished themselves by their eminence in the severest exercises of the mind, particularly in the acquisition of knowledge, evince how strong must be the natural love of knowledge in the human mind, when, even in the midst of such impediments, its gratification has, in so many instances, been so eagerly sought, and its end, so largely attained.

Alexander Davidson, A.M. was born at Dalkeith, a village in the neighbourhood of Edinburgh, of humble, but respectable parents, who sent him early to the village school. Here, before he could number his seventh year, he had been taught to read with facility and interest, the Sacred Volume, which imparts to the peasantry of Scotland the virtue and intelligence that distinguish them among nations, which, by its doctrines and precepts, addresses itself to man as ignorant and erring ; while, by its consolations and supports, it regards the ever-varying conditions of his changeful life.

Soon were the parents of young Davidson doomed to prove the strength of these consolations. Their son was seized with a violent fever from which he recovered, but with the loss of both his eyes. Light, colour, the fair scene of nature, and the beautiful objects to which the organ of vision renders us alive, seem to have been cherished by him with the fondest recollections ; and in his lecture on the structure of the eye, and the inestimable pleasures and benefits we enjoy by means of it, his voice and language partook of a tenderness and pathos which were inexpressibly affecting. The precocity of young Davidson's powers, and the ardent attachment for learning he discovered before that sad calamity befel him, aided perhaps by the anxious desire of gratifying the inclination of a being now doubly indeared to their affection, determined his parents to continue his education. In the attachment of his playmates he found a ready resource for conducting him to and from school, while the assiduity of the family circle enabled him to acquire the tasks, now become incalculably more laborious, which his teacher prescribed to him. In the same way, but with the assistance of a lad who was engaged to attend him constantly, he proceeded through the Latin classics ; committing to memory the text of each author, as well as the arrangement of syntax, and the vernacular translation. Laborious and unceasing were the toils he had thus to undergo; but his powers seemed to expand with an elasticity proportioned to the burden they had to sustain, while he soon began to experience an ample reward for all his labours, in the access which they gave him to the finest models of literature and taste, to examples of the most fascinating creations of the imagination, to the most delicate application of the powers of language, and to the exhibition of common objects, through the splendid medium with which genius alone can invest them.   On leaving the grammar school he went to the University of Edinburgh, and became a pupil of the late Dugald Stewart; and it is certain that the full flowing periods which distinguished Mr. Davidson's composition, had their prototype in the elegant prelections of that philosopher.

Mr. D.'s studies had hitherto been conducted with the view of qualifying himself for the ministerial office in one of our dissenting establishments, and having gone through all the previous exercises and trials which are usual for candidates requiring license, some warm debates arose among the judges, whether the misfortune he laboured under did not altogether disqualify him for any active charge.   Struck with dismay at the complete subversion of all his fondly cherished hopes, his feelings may be more easily imagined than described : suffice it to say, that they were of the most acute and poignant kind.   What was now to be done ? to what employment of his talents was he to look, for that future maintenance which it is the indispensable and therefore the proper duty of every one to endeavour to procure ?   A different denomination of Christians, with a liberality and humanity which do

them credit, offered him a license, but this he could not
accept, without breaking through the prejudices of his
early education, instilled into his mind and woven
about his heart, by objects endeared to him by more
than filial affection. From medicine, that friendly resource of the divinity student who feels all hope of
success in his intended profession die within him, he
was, by his peculiar circumstances, entirely excluded.
In this dilemma, it fortunately occurred to him to direct his attention to natural philosophy and chemistry,
and his determination was confirmed by the successful career of a gentleman who had precisely the
same difficulties to overcome, I mean the celebrated
Dr. Moyes.

Mr. Davidson enjoyed the great advantage of pro-
secuting his chemical studies under the instruction of
that eminent philosopher Dr. Black, whose zeal for
a science, rapidly advancing in interest and importance, under his own investigations, as well as those
of his contemporaries, he had the happy talent of
communicating to the minds of his students.   The
mind of Davidson, naturally ardent, and now stimulated by the most powerful motives that can call forth
exertion, fully responded to the Doctor's incitements,
and his acquirements were proportionably great.

Mr. Davidson's lectures were characterized by
two very distinctive features; the one, the sublime
and magnificent conceptions they conveyed of the
wisdom and beneficence which may be traced in the
arrangements of nature, the other, the simplicity
with which the explanation of any doctrine was commenced, and the light which, with gradually increas-

ing intensity, was thrown upon it, till the whole appeared in the full blaze of truth, carrying conviction
to the most scrupulous mind. The former of those
qualities may be safely referred to his previous pursuits, but the latter, I have no hesitation in affirming,
was the natural result of the recommendation and example of Dr. Black, and could proceed only from
the profound investigation of his subject, in all its
bearings. The theory of latent heat, the discovery
of which forms so remarkable an æra in the history of chemical science, and crowns the pyramid,
of Dr. Black's fame, was not, it may be expected,
overlooked by his scholar; and accordingly his explanation of that interesting doctrine, would do no dis-
credit to its illustrious author.

Mr. Davidson commenced his career as a public
lecturer in Edinburgh, amidst the numerous circle,
which his peculiar condition, his previous history and
college reputation, had drawn around him, and which
gradually removed a natural timidity and diffidence in
his own powers, which threatened to obscure their
lustre. He set out from Edinburgh to make the
tour of Scotland, in the course of which he visited the
principal cities and towns of that kingdom, and in eac
of those places he delivered one or two courses of lectures, to numerous audiences, who uniformly bore testimony to his profound views and fascinating eloquence. Let not my readers suppose that Mr. Davidson's peculiar condition disqualified him for being of
practical utility : many experiments, instituted under
his direction, had practical and most beneficial results.
Of these we may mention an example. Happening in

the common course of his progress, to rest at a village
near which was a pit, whose workings were impeded,
and sometimes interrupted for days together, by the
copious production of choke damp, the carbonic acid
gas of chemistry, the proprietor applied to our philosopher for aid. On enquiry Mr. D. found that the
mode of ventilating the mine, was by means of a wide
pipe, after which being carried partly along the floor,
ascended by the shaft, and had its upper end terminating in a cast iron cylinder. This cylinder was introduced into the middle of a furnace, the heat of which
by expanding the air produced a current which ultimately removed the annoyance. Mr. Davidson immediately proposed an alteration in this arrangement;
namely, to substitute for the furnace a large smith's
bellows, which was accordingly done. The whole
village emptied itself of its inhabitants, to witness
the "blin' philosopher blawin' awa' the win'," as
they termed it, and many jokes and sarcasms were
freely vented on the occasion. But, unmoved as the
rock amidst the dashing waves, he calmly proceeded
to connect the pipe with the valve of the bellows, and
directing the nozzle away from the wind, he set the
gaping multitude to work; and after some time to
mark the progress of the experiment, caused a bucket
with burning coals to be let down into the shaft. The
pitmen's scoffing was now changed into the most un-
bounded admiration of our philosopher's sagacity, when
they perceived by this unequivocal test, the rapidity
with which their formidable foe was dragged forth
from his lodgement, and that too by a contrivance
so simple. Two bellows of a lighter construction, and

capable of being wrought with less effort, were afterwards employed.

This amiable and accomplished philosopher was
now drawing near the end of his earthly pilgrimage;
he had long suffered from a nervous disease which ended in apoplexy. A friend who saw him a few weeks
previous to his death writes thus,—" I have seen poor
Davidson, but Oh ! what a change. Of his vigorous
intellect nothing now appears to remain but a melancholy ruin, in which I can scarcely recognise the out-
line of those stately proportions which so often filled
me with admiration and delight." He died at the latter
end of the year 1826.

Mr. Davidson was twice married, his first wife was
Isabella Dods, by whom he has one surviving daughter, and his second the daughter of the late Rev. Dr.
Young, of Harwick, whose children arrived only at
that age at which they begin to attract a father's notice.
The assaults of these family afflictions had doubtless
an unfavourable effect in accelerating the progress of
the nervous disease under which he then laboured.
Both ladies managed his experiments with a neatness
and grace, which excited general admiration and put
to shame the clumsy manipulations of us male prac-
titioners. As a public lecturer Mr. Davidson was
much admired. The following extract from one of his
manuscript lectures will be read with interest, and is
no unfavourable specimen of his style.

" For what purpose was the great volume of creation
unfolded to the view of mankind ? and why were the
perfections of its infinite author, there delineated in
characters so legible, that they cannot possibly be
mistaken ? if it was not meant for our instruction to

afford us an opportunity of fulfilling in part the great design of our being. The man who can enttertain a doubt that the stupendous fabric of the universe was built by a being whose wisdom, power, and goodness, shine with undiminished lustre in every part of his works, is either one who never possessed a rational faculty, or who in the course of his enquiries has given it such violent exercise as to render it absolutely unfit for discharging its proper functions. Such an accident, however, although it is the misfortune of of some, is by no means the consequence of their researches into the works of nature; for while the interests of society are promoted by such researches, they are calculated at the same time, to strengthen the powers of the mind, to conduct the man of science by sure and uninterrupted steps, to the fountain of existence in general, and to the absolute dependence of every link in the great chain of causes and effects, on the will of that Almighty Sovereign who regulates the whole by fixed and invariable laws; and on whose awful scale hangs the determination of every event. The more, in short, he indulges in this study, the greater pleasures will he receive ; for in the great laboratory of nature, he meets with every thing, that can either gratify his curiosity, excite his admiration, enlarge his understanding, add to his humility, soften his disposition, or awaken the very finest sympathies of his soul."

AUTHORITIES :

MACOME's Life of DAVIDSON,—The Mechanics Magazine, Manuscript Lectures of Mr. D.

MILITARY, GOVERNMENT,
AND LAW

Military

THE military is one of the world's most hazardous occupations in terms of the potential for sight loss. Apart from physical injuries suffered in battle, loss of sight often occurs during captivity because of unsanitary living conditions, poor nourishment, or a lack of medical treatment. Exposure to poor conditions while in battle also poses a threat to soldiers' vision.

Blinding was an ancient practice performed to reduce able-bodied warriors to objects of pity and ridicule. Samson, mentioned by Wilson in his first edition, is a well-known biblical figure whose life and military exploits against the Philistines are recorded in the Book of Judges (14–16). Frederick Blodi's 1986 book, *The Eye, Vision, and Ophthalmology on Postage Stamps,* recounts that after Samson is bewitched by Delilah and falls asleep, Delilah cuts his hair, the secret of his strength. Following his capture he was blinded by the Philistines, led in chains to the temple, and chained to the pillars. His former strength briefly returned, allowing him to knock down the pillars so that the roof fell, killing Samson and his enemies. Wilson tells Samson's story using a soliloquy by John Milton entitled "On the Putting Out of His Eyes."

John, the Blind King (1296–1346), to whom Wilson refers as "king of Bohemia" and who is most often known in history as Jean l'Aveugle,

John of Luxembourg, the Scholarly King of Bohemia, or John the Blind Count of Luxembourg, was a remarkable military leader. According to Blodi, John fought and campaigned all over Europe, in Poland, Lithuania, Silesia, Italy, and France. Around 1330 the king was blind, but he continued to lead an active life, fighting in many places. John was killed in the battle of Cresy on August 26, 1346. Wilson reports, "Anxious to know how the battle went, he commanded his attendants to lead him forward; for this purpose, he was placed between two of them, and their bridles were tied to his, so that in the heat of the action they might not be separated, and next morning, they were all three found dead together."

John de Trocznow (1350–1424), or Zisca the "Bohemian reformer," as Wilson refers to him, was a great Bohemian revolutionary and general. His biographer, Frederick G. Heymann, spells his name Zizka. There is some disagreement on how he lost sight in his left eye: Wilson says he lost it during military services; Blodi says it was due to an accident as a young boy while playing with friends. He was a follower of Jan Hus (1369–1415), became a leader of the Hussites, and organized an army and trained soldiers, leading them to incredible victories. He lost his right eye at the siege of Rabi Castle, Prague, in 1420. Wilson mentions that like Samson of old, Zisca was more dreaded by enemies of his country after he became blind. According to Heymann, Zisca reinvented the war chariot and rode on it as a blind leader swinging an iron bludgeon.

Timoleon (?–337 B.C.), the Greek general and statesman, is included in Wilson's fourth edition. Like many others, he became blind later in life, and like Zisca, he continued to command military forces.

The welfare of the blind took focus in Europe, Ishbel Ross mentions in her 1950 book, *Journey into Light: The Story of the Education of the Blind*, when Louis IX, known as Saint Louis, opened L'Hôpital des Quinze in Paris in 1254 to take care of returning blind Crusaders. Battle conditions such as the devastating gas attacks and shell and bullet wounds during World War I also caused blindness in thousands of soldiers. The first guide dogs were trained to assist German soldiers blinded during World War I, while organizations such as St. Dunstan's were established to rehabilitate blinded veterans. During World War II in the United States Richard Hoover and C. Warren Bledsoe developed the long cane method while working at the Valley Forge Army General Hospital with newly blinded veterans. Many consider the long cane method to be the most important innovation in blind travel.

As mentioned by Wilson, many blind and visually impaired soldiers continued to function in the military. In more recent times, blinded veterans have gone on to successful civilian careers and those related to assisting fellow blinded veterans.

Government

ISHBEL ROSS notes that a succession of blind lawyers and statesmen exercised influence in Rome while the Empire flourished. An example is Marcus Livius Druscus, who used to walk without hesitation in a straight line through the Forum and implore patronage for the blind.

Modern government officials have also risen to prominence in various positions. Thomas Pryor Gore (1871–1938), who was blind as a result of two childhood accidents, served for twenty years as a U.S. senator from Oklahoma. In an address to a 1914 Conference on the Blind in Washington, D.C., his approach was hard-headed and unsentimental. "It is a mistake to tell the sightless that their loss is insurmountable or that it is inconsequential. It is neither. The sightless confront a situation and not a theory."

Thomas D. Schall (1877–1935) from Minnesota became blind at the age of thirty following an accident with an electric cigar lighter. He served five consecutive terms in the U.S. House of Representatives before going on to the Senate. In 1929 he became the first senator to have a guide dog. Peter Putnam states in his article

"Four Blind Lawmakers" *(AAWB Blindness Annual,* 1974–75) that Schall made a positive virtue of his blindness.

Ian Fraser was blinded by a sniper's bullet during World War I. After the war, he served as chairman of St. Dunstan's and in 1924 he was elected to the British Parliament.

Gore, Schall, and Fraser's successes in government stand as an example of blind people who have triumphed over prejudice and helped eliminate attitudinal barriers. Physical barriers and barriers to information, other than by print, are slowly being removed. Furthermore, legislation such as the Americans with Disabilities Act (1990) has broadened opportunities for the blind by requiring that public services and resources be made accessible to all who are disabled.

Law

NICHOLAS BACON, who lived at the end of the fifteenth century, became blind at the age of nine from a crossbow arrow. Throughout his early life he was ridiculed by both friends and professors. As Wilson mentions, "They admitted him into their schools, rather under the impression that he might amuse them, not that they should be able to communicate much information to him." He obtained his law degree at the University of Brussels and became a highly successful lawyer.

In the eighteenth century, an age when most

blind people were employed in begging, Sir John Fielding (1722–80) surmounted this role and achieved success in the field of law. After becoming blind at age nineteen, he went on to serve as a magistrate at the Bow Street Court in London. He was a progressive lawyer interested in promoting civil causes. The founder of what is now the London Metropolitan Police Force, he became known and respected for his sagacity as a justice. Nelson Coon, in his article in *The New Outlook for the Blind* (March 1958), states that Fielding was a man far ahead of his time and that he had a great vision of justice for the downtrodden. "[He] stood as the great example of the fact now recognized, that the physical handicap has no true relationship to accomplishment." An illustration of Sir John in his Court at Bow Street in 1779 appears in Patrick Pringle's 1956 book, *Hue and Cry: The Story of Henry and John Fielding and Their Bow Street Runners.*

Many blind people since Wilson's time have gone into law and become successful lawyers and judges. In 1995 the American Blind Lawyers Association estimated that there are at least six hundred blind and visually impaired lawyers, nearly half of them women, in the United States. More and more blind people are gradually being accepted into a profession that offers numerous career choices.

AN INTERESTING ACCOUNT

OF

S A M S O N,

The Blind Hero of Israel.

~~~~~~~~~~

'O ! what is strength without a double share
Of Wisdom ? vast, unwieldy, burdensome ;
Proudly secure, yet liable to fall
By weakest subtilties, not made to rule,
But to subserve where Wisdom bears command.'

~~~~~~~~~~

Of all the books, which are at present in use,
there is not one, in my opinion, to which the mind
can turn, either for amusement or instruction, like the
Bible.   Laying aside for a moment its Divine authority, and viewing it as a common history, it presents to
the reader a fund of the most valuable information.
But this is not its only claim to our regard ; it rests
not on human authority, for in the words of one of the
acutest masters (Locke,) in the great science of human
understanding, as well as in Christian philosophy.—
'It has God for its author, Salvation for its end, and
Truth, without any mixture of error, for its matter. '

The character of the divinely inspired Hero, which I am now about to consider, is taken from that Sacred Book, and will not, I hope, be thought obtrusive here.

SAMSON flourished, according to the best commentators, about 2848, A. M. He was a Nazarite of the tribe of Dan. We are informed by the sacred Historian, that he was endued with uncommon strength, and that the seat of that strength was in his hair. The Philistines were at that time a powerful and warlike nation, and held the Israelites in bondage; but Sampson, by his heroic achievements, soon taught his own, and his country's enemies to fear and respect him. He made frequent incursions into the country of the Philistines, laid waste their fields and desolated their cities. At length this illustrious Patriot and Bulwark of his country, was betrayed by a perfidious harlot, who while he was asleep, cut off his hair, and 'delivered him into the hands of his enemies; who treated him with every species of cruelty and insult. And to complete their barbarous work, they put out his eyes, and made him use that strength which had been so nobly employed in the defence of his country, in grinding at a Mill. Milton in describing Samson's situation, makes his hero break out into the following SOLILOQUY, which for pathos and sublime sentiments cannot be surpassed in ours or any other language :—

A SOLILOQUY

On the putting out of his Eyes.

~~~~~~~~~~~~

' Made of my enemies the scorn and gaze,
I grind in brazen fetters under task
With this Heaven-gifted strength !—
O glorious strength, put to the labour of a beast;
Debased lower than bondslave ! promise was
That I should Israel from Philistian yoke deliver:
Ask for this great deliverer now, and find him
Eyeless in Gaza at the mill with slaves,
Himself in bonds under Philistian yoke.
But chief of all !—
O loss of sight, of thee I must complain !
Blind among enemies, O worse than chains,
Dungeon or beggary, or decrepit age !—
Light, the prime work of God, to me's extinct,
And all her various objects of delight
Annulled, which might in part my grief have eas'd;
Inferior to the vilest now become,
Of man or worm—the vilest here excel me ;
They creep, yet see ; I dark in light exposed
To daily fraud, contempt, abuse and wrong,
Within doors, or without, still as a fool,
In power of others, never in my own ;
Scarce half I seem to live, dead more than half:
O dark, dark, dark ! amid the blaze of noon ;

Irrecoverably dark, total eclipse
Without all hope of day !—
O first created Beam, and thou great Word,
Let there be light, and light was over all ;
Why am I thus bereav'd thy prime decree?
The Sun to me is dark
And silent as the Moon,
When she deserts the night,
Hid in her vacant interlunar cave.
Since light so necessary is to life,
And almost life itself, if it be true,
That light is in the soul,
She all in every part ; why was the sight
To such a tender ball as th' eye confin'd,
So obvious, and so easy to be quench'd ?
And not as feeling through all parts diffus'd,
That she might look at will through ev'ry pore ;
Then had I not been thus exil'd from light,
As in the land of darkness, yet in light,
To live a life half dead, a living death,
And bury'd ; but yet more miserable !
Myself, my sepulchre, a moving grave
Bury'd, yet not exempt
By privilege of death and burial
From worst of other evils, pains and wrongs,
But made hereby obnoxious more
To all the miseries of life ;—
Life in captivity
Amongst inhuman foes.

In this state of degradation, and every day exposed to some new method of torture, he continued for
some time. At length his hair began to grow again,
and his strength to return with it. On a day which
had been appointed by the Philistines, as a festival to
their God, (Dagon) for delivering them from the
power of Samson, he was ordered to come to the
feast to play, and show his strength before the
lords and and the people. The theatre or building
in which this exhibition was to take place, wss supported by two main pillars,(1) and between these was
Samson placed, in order that they might have a distinct view of his movements. Being almost exhausted
with fatigue, he requested the lad who held him by
the hand, to permit him to lean on the pillars ;—

  ‘ That to the arched roof gave main support.—
He unsuspicious led him ; which when Samson
Felt in his arms, with head, awhile inclined,
And eyes fast-fixed, he stood, as one who prayed,
Or some great matter in his mind revolved :
This finished, straining all his nerves, he bowed.
As with the force of winds and waters pent,
When mountains tremble, those two massy pillars
With horrible convulsions to and fro,
He tugg’d, he shook, till down they came & drew
The whole roof after them, with burst of thunder
Upon the heads of all who sat beneath ;—
Lords, ladies, captains, counsellors and priests,
The choice nobility and flower, not only
Of this, but each Philistian city round,
Met from all parts to solemnize this feast.

Samson with these inmixed inevitably
Pulled down the same destruction on himself;
The vulgar only 'scaped who stood without. '

~~~~~~~~~~

AUTHORITIES.

Judges, chaps. 13, 14, 15, & 16...Brown's Dictionary of the Bible...Wood's Dictionary of the Bible...Milton's Works, vol. 2nd.

NOTE TO SAMSON.

(1)Milton has finely accounted for this dreadful catastrophe, and obviated the common objection. It is commonly asked how so great a building, containing so many thousands of people, could rest on two pillars so nearly placed together; and to this it is answered, that instances are not wanting of far more large and capacious buildings than this, supported only by one pillar or pin, or hinge, though many thousands of people did sit in it together. *See Poole's Annotations.*

Mr. Thyer further adds, that Dr. Shaw in his travels, observing on the eastern method of building, says, ' that the place where they exhibit their diversions at this day, is an advanced cloister, made in form of a large pent-house, supported only by one or two contiguous pillars in front, or else at the centre, and supposing that in the house of Dagon there was a cloistered structure of this kind, the pulling down the front, or centre pillars only which supported it, would be attended with the like catastrophe.' *See Shaw's Travels, page* 283.

TIMOLEON,
THE CELEBRATED GRECIAN GENERAL.

TIMOLEON was a celebrated Grecian General, who was born about four hundred years before the christian era. He was a native of Corinth, and descended from one of the noblest families in that city. His military talents first became conspicuous, in an expedition of which he was appointed commander, and which was sent into Sicily by the Corinthians, against Dionysius, tyrant of Syracuse. After a series of almost uninterrupted successes continued through a number of years, Timoleon was enabled to expel the tyrant from his throne, and had the satisfaction of seeing peace and prosperity restored in the island, where he spent the remainder of his days.

After so much prosperity, when he was well advanced in years, his eyes began to fail him, and the defect increased so fast, that he entirely lost his sight. Not that he had done any thing to occasion it, nor was it to be imputed to the caprice of Fortune, but it seems to have been owing to a family weakness and disorder, which operated together with the course of time.

It is not to be wondered, that he bore his misfortune without repining ; but it was really admirable, to observe the honour and respect which the Syracusans paid him when blind. They not only visited him constantly themselves, but brought all strangers who spent

some time amongst them to his house in the town, or
to that in the country, that they too might have the
pleasure of seeing the deliverer of Syracuse. And it
was their joy and their pride that he chose to spend
his days with them, and despised the splendid reception which Greece was prepared to give him, on account of his great success.   Among the many votes
that were passed, and things that were done in honour
of him, one of the most striking was that decree of the
people of Syracuse, " That whenever they should be
at war with a foreign nation, they would employ a
Corinthian General." Their method of proceeding,
too, in their assemblies, did honour to Timoleon. For
they decided smaller matters by themselves, but consulted him in the difficult and important cases.   On
these occasions, he was conveyed in a litter, through
the market-place to the theatre; and when he was
carried in, the people saluted him with one voice, as
he sat. He returned the civility ; and, having paused
a while to give time to their acclamations, took cog-
nizance of the affair, and delivered his opinion. The
assembly gave their sanction to it, and then his servants carried the litter back through the theatre ; and
the people, having waited on him with loud applauses,
despatched the rest of the public business without him.

With so much respect and kindness was the old
age of Timoleon cherished, as that of a common father;
and at last he died of a slight illness, co-operating with
length of years. Some time being given the Syracusans to prepare for his funeral, and for the neighbouring inhabitants and strangers to assemble, the whole
was conducted with great magnificence. The bier,

sumptuously adorned, was carried by young men, selected by the people, over the ground where the palace
and castle of the tyrants stood, before they were de-
molished. It was followed by many thousands of men
and women, with the most pompous solemnity, crowned
with garlands and clothed in white. The lamentations
and tears, mingled with the praises of the deceased,
showed that the honour now paid him was not a matter of course, or compliance with a duty enjoined, but
the testimony of real sorrow and sincere affection.

AUTHORITY.
Plutarch's Lives.

AN ACCOUNT OF THE DEATH OF

JOHN, THE BLIND KING OF BOHEMIA,

Who was slain in the memorable Battle of Cressy, August 26, 1346.

" The Prince succeeds, and, on the brazen prow,
The noble Edward raised his princely brow ;
In sable arms he marched, while o'er his head,
Bohemia's triple plume its glories shed,
Soft as the new-formed wreath of Alpine snow,
White as the feath'ry surge that foams below.
The sword that widowed France on Cressy's day,
Again to conquest cuts its wonted way."

SWIFT says, that " blindness is an inducement to courage, because it hides from us the danger which is before us." How far the Dean may be right in his opinion, I shall not pretend to judge, but that blind men possess this virtue, (if a virtue it may be called,) as much as any of those endowed with sight, may be inferred from the following anecdote.

Many of them have braved all the dangers of the field, in some of the greatest battles that ever were fought in Europe, viz. the siege of Constantinople, by the Venetians ; the battle of Falkirk ; and the memorable battle of Cressy. This last engagement commenced at three o'clock in the afternoon, and continued till night put an end to the carnage. The greater part of the nobility of France and Germany fell in the contest ; and, among the slain were two kings, James of Majorca, and John of Bohemia. The death

of the latter, who had for a long time been blind, was
attended by some remarkable circumstances. Anxious to know how the battle proceeded, he commanded
his attendants to lead him forward ; for this purpose, he
was placed between two of them, their bridles being
tied to his, so that in the heat of the action they might
not be separated, and next morning they were all three
found dead together. Barnes, in his life of Edward
III., gives a more particular account of the circumstance than any other historian I have met with, and
I will give it in his own words.

"Marquess Charles, emperor elect, resisted the
prince with great courage ; but his banner being
beaten to the ground, his men slain about him, and
himself wounded in three places, he turned his horse
and rode out of the field, though not without much
difficulty, having cast away his coat-armour, that he
might not be known. Meanwhile, his father, John,
King of Bohemia, now blind with age, when he understood how the day was like to go, asked of his captains, what was become of the lord Charles, his son;
they told him, they knew not, but that they supposed him somewhere in the heat of action. Then
the good old king, resolving by no means to disgrace
his former victories, or to cancel the glory of his youth
by a degenerate old age, said unto them :—' Gentlemen, you are men, my companions and friends in this
expedition ; I only now desire this last piece of service
from you, that you would bring me forward so near to
these Englishmen, that I may deal among them one
good stroke with my sword.' They all said, they
would obey him to the death, and lest by any extremity

they should be separated from him, they all, with one
consent, tied the reins of their horses one to another,
and so attended their royal master into battle.   There
this valiant old hero had his desire, and came boldly
up to the Prince of Wales, and gave more than one,
four, or five good strokes, and fought courageously,
as also did all his lords, and others about him ; but
they engaged themselves so far, that they were all
slain, and next day found dead about the body of their
king, and their horses' bridles tied together.   Then
were the arms of that noble king, (being the ostrich
feathers, with the motto, " Ich Dien," signifying, I
serve,) taken and worn by the Prince of Wales, in
whose memory they have been ever since called the
Prince's arms ; being also from that time worn by his
successors, the Princes of Wales, eldest sons of the
Kings of England."

AUTHORITIES.

Barnes's Life of Edward the III.—Hume's England, vol. ii.

THE LIFE

OF

ZISCA,

THE BOHEMIAN REFORMER.

"Huss, mild and firm, next dares the tyrant's fire;
And sweet tongu'd Jerome, skilful to persuade;
And Zisca whom fair liberty inspires,
Blind Chieftain, waves around his burnish'd blade;
Unwearied pastor, with unbating zeal."

THIS distinguished patriot was a native of Bohemia. His real name was John de Trocznow; but in
the course of his military services he lost his left eye,
from which circumstance he was called Zisca, that
word, in the Bohemian language, signifying one-
eyed. He served for some time in the Danish
and Polish armies, but on the conclusion of the
war, he returned to his native country. Bohemia was, at that time, greatly agitated by the cru-
sade which the Pope was then carrying on, against
what were called the new opinions; the council of
Constance which met in the year 1414, for the pur-

pose of rooting heresy out of the church, cited John Huss and Jerome of Prague before them; who were both found guilty of heresy, and were burned at the stake. This cruel and unjust sentence filled the public mind with horror and indignation. Their blameless lives, their peaceful spirit, and the opinions for which they suffered, endeared them to their countrymen so much, that July 5th, the day of their martyrdom, was observed throughout Bohemia as a day of solemn fasting and prayer. The persecution against their followers still continued, however, with great severity; and the dungeon, the gibbet, and the stake were daily employed.

The people, at last, became exceedingly exasperated against the Pope and the Emperor, on account of their cruelties; they were obliged to take up arms in defence of their lives, and chose Zisca as their general, who soon found himself at the head of forty thousand patriots. He had laid siege to the town of Ruby, which he had almost reduced to extremities, when, as he was viewing a part of the works where he intended an assault, an arrow, shot from the wall, struck him in his remaining eye. The wound being thought dangerous, the surgeons of the army proposed his being carried to Prague, where he might have the best advice; in reality, however, they were afraid of being cut to pieces by the troops, if he should die under their hands. When his removal to the capital was resolved on, it was difficult to check the contest among the soldiers, who strove for the honour of carrying their wounded general. At Prague the arrow was extracted, which, being barbed, tore out the eye with it, and it was feared the fever which succeeded might prove fatal; his life, however, though with difficulty, was saved. By this severe stroke he was consigned to total darkness for the remainder of his life; but, like Sampson of old, he was more dreaded by the enemies of his country after he became blind, than he had been before that accident occurred. His friends were surprised to hear him talk, after his recovery, of setting out for the army, and did what was in their power to dissuade him from it, but he continued resolute; "I have yet," said he, "my blood to shed for the liberties of Bohemia. She is enslaved; her sons are deprived of their natural rights, and are the victims of a system of spiritual tyranny, as degrading to the character of man as it is destructive of every moral principle; therefore, Bohemia must and shall be free." Zisca was so beloved by the army, that the soldiers threatened to lay down their arms, unless their general were restored.

In the mean time, the emperor Sigismond had been making preparations for war during the summer, at Nuremburg. Here he assembled the states of the empire in full convention, opened to them his embarrassed circumstances, and intreated them, for the sake of their sovereign, for the honour of the empire, and in the cause of their religion, to put themselves in arms. His harangue had its effect; proper measures were concerted, and the assembly broke up, with an unanimous resolution to make this audacious rebel feel the full weight of the empire; and that the blow might fall more unexpectedly, it was resolved to defer it till the end of the year, when it was hoped

that Zisca might more easily be surprised, as great
part of his troops left him in the winter and returned
again in spring.

The campaign, as that chief imagined, was now
over, when he was suddenly alarmed with the report
of these vast preparations, and soon after, with the
march of two powerful armies against him; one of
which was composed of confederate Germans, under
the Marquis of Brandenburgh, the Archbishop of
Mentz, the Count Palatine of the Rhine, and other
princes of the empire; the other of Hungarians and
Silesians, under the emperor himself. The former
was to invade Bohemia on the west, the latter on the
east; they were to meet in the centre, and, as they
affected to give out, crush this handful of vexatious
sectaries between them. At the head of such a force
the emperor was very sanguine; but they who are
acquainted with the nature of armies intended to
march in concert, know the difficulty of making such
unwieldy bodies observe those exact laws of motion,
which are traced out by prudent generals in councils
of war; some unforeseen events generally create
unavoidable difficulty, and so it happened on the
present occasion. Sigismond, disappointed in a con-
tract for forage, was obliged to defer his march; he
was likewise retarded by the Austrian and Hungarian nobility, who had entered as volunteers into his
service, and, being suddenly called upon, had not
their equipages and dependants in perfect readiness
for the field. The confederate princes had now begun
their march, and were already advanced a considerable way into Bohemia, before they heard of the

emperor's disappointment. Sigismond gave them hopes that he would presently join them, and advised them to form the siege of Soisin; accordingly they intrenched themselves, and began an attack, for which they were not in the best manner provided, against what was esteemed one of the strongest fortresses in Bohemia. The besieged laughed at their vain efforts, and maintained only their usual guard; while wet trenches, the want of provision, the severities of an inclement winter, and above all, the emperor's delay, introduced mutiny into the tents of the besiegers, and dissension into their councils. In this situation they were ready to catch any alarm, when Zisca approached with his army. The very sight of his banners floating at a distance was sufficient; they struck their tents, and retreated with precipitation, burning the country as they fled, and cursing the emperor's breach of faith.

About the end of December, a full month after the appointed time, the emperor began his march, and as he entered Bohemia, he received the account of the retreat of the confederates. He determined, however, to proceed; he was at the head of an army, the flower of which was 15,000 Hungarian horse, esteemed at that time the best cavalry in Europe, and led by a Florentine officer of great experience; the infantry, which consisted of 25,000 men, was provided, as well as the cavalry, with every thing proper for a winter campaign. This army spread terror throughout all the east of Bohemia; wherever Sigismond marched, the magistrates laid their keys at his feet, and were treated with severity or favour, according as they were well or ill affected towards his cause.

His career, however, was presently checked. Zisca, who had been pursuing the Germans in the west, approached, with speedy march, and threw a damp upon him in the midst of his success; he resolved, however, to try his fortune, once more, with that invincible chief, and chose his ground as well as he was able. No general paid less regard to the circumstances of time and place than Zisca; he seldom desired more than to come up to his adversary, and the enthusiastic fury of his soldiers supplied the rest. There was not a man in his army, who did not meet the enemy with that same invincible spirit with which the martyr meets death; who did not press to be foremost in that glorious band of heroes, whom the Almighty should destine to the noble act of dying for their religion. Such were the troops which Sigismond had now to encounter.

On the thirteenth of January, 1422, the two armies met on a spacious plain near Kamnitz. Zisca appeared in the centre of his front line, guarded, or rather conducted, by a horseman on each side, armed with a pole axe. His troops, having sung a hymn, with determined coolness drew their swords, and waited for the signal. Zisca stood not long in view of the enemy, and when his officers had informed him that the ranks were well closed, he waved his sabre round his head, which was the signal of battle. Historians speak of the onset of Zisca's troops, as a shock beyond credibility; and it appears to have been such on this occasion. The imperial infantry hardly made a stand, and in the space of a few minutes, they were disordered beyond possibility of being rallied.

The cavalry made a feeble effort, but seeing themselves unsupported, they wheeled round and fled upon the spur. Thus was the extent of the plain, as far as the eye could reach suddenly overspread with disorder, the pursuers and the pursued mingling together, in one indistinct mass of waving confusion; here and there might be seen a few parties endeavouring to unite, but they were broken as soon as formed. The routed army fled towards the confines of Moravia; the patriots, without intermission, galling their rear. The river Igla, which was then frozen, opposed their flight, and here new disasters befel them. The bridge being immediately choked, and the enemy pressing furiously on, many of the infantry, and the whole body of cavalry, attempted the river; the ice gave way, and not fewer than two thousand were swallowed up in the water. Here Zisca sheathed his sword, and returned in triumph to Tabore, laden with all the trophies which the most complete victory could give.

The battle of Kamnitz having put Zisca in peaceable possession of the whole kingdom of Bohemia, he had now leisure to pay a little more attention to his designed establishment of a church. He began to abolish in all places the ceremonies of the Romish worship; he erased the Pope's name from all public instruments, and denied his supremacy. "Merit alone," he said, "should give distinction among the clergy of Bohemia; and they should gain the reverence of the people by the sanctity of their lives, not by their luxurious manner of living." From these things we may judge how much farther Huss would, in all probability, have carried reformation, if he had had it in his power; for we may consider Zisca as doing nothing but what was consonant with his express doctrine, or might by fair inference be deduced from it. We have no reason to suppose this military reformer had any bigotry in his temperament, as he seems not to have shewn an inclination to force the consciences of differing sects, but to have left men at liberty to like or dislike, to unite with him, or leave him, as they thought best; nor was he by any means arbitrary in his impositions, but consulted his friends, and fixed on nothing but what met with their general concurrence.

At this time Zisca was in full credit with his party, and was earnestly requested to assume the crown of Bohemia for himself, as a reward for the eminent services he had rendered his country. No one in the kingdom, they assured him, had the power, if he had the inclination, to make the least opposition; as for the emperor, they hoped he would soon be induced to drop his claim. But Zisca, whom even his enemies do not tax with avarice or ambition, steadily refused; "while you find me of service to your designs," said the disinterested chief, "you may freely command both my counsels and my sword, but I will never accept any established authority ; on the contrary, my most earnest advice to you is, when the perverseness of your enemies allows you peace, to trust yourselves no longer in the hands of kings, but to form yourselves into a republic, which species of government only, can secure your liberties."

In the mean while, Sigismond had made great

preparations for what proved to be his final effort, and intended to enter Bohemia with two separate armies. With this view, he placed the Marquis Misnia at the head of a considerable body of Saxons, who were to penetrate by the way of Upper Saxony; while he himself, at the head of another army, should enter Moravia, on the side of Hungary.

Zisca also made the necessary preparation for opening the campaign, and sent Procop, an excellent young officer in whom he had entire confidence, to command in Moravia, to whose management he wholly intrusted the military affairs of that country, recommending to him particularly a cautious behaviour, and measures merely defensive. Zisca was in little fear about Moravia, hoping that Procop would be able to keep the Emperor employed, till he himself should return from the frontiers of Saxony, whither he marched with all his forces, upon the first notice of the enemy's movements. The Marquis, however, had not yet taken the field; Zisca, to strike terror into his troops, ravaged his borders, and, in the face of his army, boldly sat down before Ausig, a strong town situated upon the Elbe, near where that river leaves Bohemia, This place had always shewn a particular attachment to the emperor, and was recommended by him in strong terms, to the protection of the Marquis ; it was sensible mortification, therefore, to that general, to see an enemy already at the gates, and he determined to risk all, rather than leave it a prey. Zisca, who carried on the works with his usual vigour, had brought the siege to its last stage, when the Marquis appeared at the head of a great army, and offered him battle; his maxim being never to decline fighting, he accepted the challenge, though he had many difficulties to encounter. The Marquis had a superior army, and Zisca was obliged to thin his troops, by leaving a large detachment to observe the town; the Saxons were advantageously posted, having taken possession of a rising ground, which secured their flanks, while a strong wind blew in the face of the Reformers, which greatly weakened the flight of their arrows, adding new force to those of the enemy. Zisca, however, had little confidence in missive weapons; his whole line, in their accustomed manner, with pole-axes and sabres, made an impetuous attack upon the enemy, but the Saxons receiving them in good order, stood firm, and gave them a very severe check. This was a reception wholly unknown to the Reformers, who had ever been used to bear down all before them; in these new circumstances they were at a loss how to act, and retreated some paces, as if astonished at the novelty of their position. This critical moment the Saxons should have seized, while the blast, yet fluttering in the sail, seemed to hesitate on which side to give the swell. Had they moved forward at this instant, it is probable the patriots would never have recovered from their surprise; but instead of a general charge, they stood motionless, looking upon the enemy, as if they had done enough in not suffering themselves to be beaten. Zisca, as if almost inspired, had a complete idea of the state of affairs, and being conducted to the front line, which stood yet unbroken, he cried out as he rode along, "I thank you, my fellow soldiers, for all your past services; if you have done your utmost, let us retire." This noble rebuke stung them to the soul; every veteran gnashed his teeth with indignation, grasped his sword, and pressed forward, closing hand to hand with the enemy, in the true temper of determined courage. The combat, thus renewed, soon became unequal; for some time the Saxons still maintained a feeble fight, but four of the principal officers, endeavouring to restore the battle, were cut to pieces at the head of their dismayed battalions, and the whole army soon after gave way in every part, and retreated. A rout and massacre succeeded; the carnage was terrible, not fewer than nine thousand Saxons being left dead upon the field.

From this scene of blood he recalled his troops to new fields of glory; "we must sleep to night," cried he, "within the walls of Ausig." Thither the triumphant army carried the news of their victory. Zisca would grant no conditions; the governor was allowed half an hour to deliberate whether he would surrender at discretion, or take the consequence; he chose the safer measure, and the Reformers were quietly quartered in Ausig before the close of the evening. The next day Zisca ordered the town to be dismantled, that it might no longer be a receptacle for his enemies; he broke down likewise the stately bridge over the Elbe, to cut off as much as possible all communication with Saxony. These two great events consecrated the 22nd of April, for many years, in Bohemia.

Having thus settled every thing in the east of Bohemia, where he had been kept longer than he expected, and having freed that country from even

the apprehension of danger, he returned with his
victorious army to the assistance of Procop. The
news of Sigismond's retreat met Zisca near Prague.
As the troops, having made forced marches from Ausig, had been harrassed with intolerable fatigue, he
thought it proper to give them a few days' rest, and
encamped therefore within three leagues of Prague

Sigismond was now reduced to the greatest extremities; the battle of Ausig had greatly shaken that constancy which had thus far supported him; six times,
in three campaigns, he had been vanquished in the
open field, his towns had been ravished from him,
and his provinces laid waste. He acknowledged the
superior talents of his adversary, and was quelled by
that noble and unconquered spirit which animates the
cause of liberty. Every ray of hope being now excluded, he submitted to his hard fate, and resolving
to procure peace for his bleeding country on any
terms, sent deputies to Zisca, requesting him to
sheathe his sword and name his conditions; offering
him at the same time, for himself, what might have
satisfied the most grasping ambition. Zisca was
equally desirous of reconciliation, as he had taken up
arms only with a view to obtain peace, and was heartily glad of an occasion to lay them down: he therefore
returned a message to the Emperor, full of respectful
language, though at the same time breathing that
spirit which became a chief in the cause of liberty.
After a few couriers had passed between them, a
place of congress was appointed, and Zisca set
out to meet the Emperor, attended by the principal officers of his army. It gave Europe a
subject for various conjecture, when this great man,

whom one unfortunate battle would have reduced to the condition of rebel, was seen passing through the midst of Bohemia, to treat with his sovereign, upon equal terms.

But Zisca lived not to put a finishing hand to this treaty. His affairs obliged him to take his route through a part of the country, in which the plague at that time was raging; at the castle of Priscow, where he had engaged to hold an assembly of the states of that district, the fatal contagion seized him, and put an end to his life, on the sixth of October, 1424, at a time when all his labours were ended, and his great purposes almost completed. Such was the course of Providence, which permitted him to enjoy but for a short time, those liberties, and that tranquillity, which his virtues had so nobly purchased. The remains of this great man were deposited in the church at Craslow, in Bohemia, where a monument was erected to his memory, with an inscription to this purport; "Here lies John Zisca, who, having defended his country against the encroachments of Papal tyranny, rests in this hallowed place, in despite of the Pope."

The capacity of Zisca was vast; his plans of action were extensive; and the vigour of his mind, in executing those plans, astonishing. Difficulties with him, were motives that roused up latent powers, proportioned to the emergency, and even blindness could not check the ardour of his soul. His military abilities were equal to what any age has produced, and they are indeed acknowledged to be so by all historians. He was also equally to be admired as a politician; if the great man was seen in the conduct and courage which he discovered in the field, it was equally seen in governing a land of anarchy, by his own native authority, and in drawing to one point, the force of a divided nation. Nor was the end which he proposed unworthy of his great actions; utterly devoid both of ambition and avarice, he had no aim but to establish, upon the ruins of ecclesiastical tyranny, the civil and religious liberties of his country.

AUTHORITIES.

GILPIN'S Lives of the Reformers, vol. 1st.—Encyclopædia Britannica.

DR. NICHOLAS BACON.

"Men by whom impartial laws were given."

Dr. NICHOLAS BACON, a blind gentleman, descended from the same family with the celebrated Lord Verulam, was created Doctor of Laws, in the city of Brussels with high approbation.

He was deprived of sight at nine years of age, by an arrow from a cross-bow, whilst he was attempting to shoot it. When he had recovered his health, which had suffered by the shock, he pursued the same plan of education, in which he had been engaged; and having heard that one *Nicasius de Vourde*, born blind, who lived towards the end of the 15th century, after having distinguished himself by his studies at the University of Louvain, took his degree as D. D. in that of Cologne, he resolved to make the same attempt; but the public, cursed with prejudices for which the meanest sensitive nature might blush, prejudices equally beneath the brutality and ignorance of the lowest animal instinct, treated his intention with ridicule; even the professors themselves were not far from being of the same sentiment; for they admitted him into their schools, rather from an impression that it might amuse him, than become of any use to him. He had the good fortune, however, contrary to their expectations, to obtain the first places among his condisciples. It was then said that such rapid advances might be made in the preliminary branches of

his education, but they would soon be effectually checked in studies of a more profound nature. This, it seems,
was repeated from school to school, through the whole
climax of his pursuits; and when, in the course of
academical learning, it became necessary to study
poetry, it was the general voice that all was over, and
that at length he had reached his *Ne plus ultra.*

But here he likewise disproved their prejudices,
and taught them the immense difference between
blindness of soul, and blindness of body. After continuing his studies in learning and philosophy for two
years more, he applied himself to law, took his degree
in that science, commenced pleading counsellor, or
advocate, in the council of Brabant, and had the
pleasure of terminating almost every suit in which he
engaged, to the satisfaction of his clients.

AUTHORITY.

Encyclopædia Britannica.

SIR JOHN FIELDING,

THE BLIND THIEF CATCHER.

Sir John Fielding was brother to the celebrated Henry Fielding, and his successor in the office of Justice for Westminster, in which capacity, although blind from his youth, he acted with great energy and sagacity for many years. He kept in his mind the description of many hundred thieves, and was never mistaken when they were brought before him. On receiving information of the place where any stolen property was concealed, so unwearied was he in his exertions, that he was never known to give up the pursuit till he recovered part or all of the property that he was in search of. In short, the name of Blind Fielding was a terror to evil doers, and his death was not only a loss to the city of Westminster, but to the country in general. He was knighted in 1761, and died at Brompton, in 1780.

Sir John Fielding published various tracts on the penal code, and was the author of a miscellaneous publication, entitled, the "Universal Mentor." He was also an active and benevolent promoter of the Marine Society. It is related that he had a tube fixed in the carriage, communicating with the coach box, through which he could converse with the coachman, without being heard by others. When his chariot was interrupted by any obstruction in the streets, he inquired of the coachman what kind of vehicle oc-

casioned it, and would then put out his head, and
shout in his peremptory tone, " take that cart out of
the way ;" or, " you, sir, in that chaise, drive on !"
This used to occasion great astonishment to others,
who wondered that one who was blind could perceive
the cause of the stoppage, and was a source of much
amusement to Sir John.

———

AUTHORITY.

The Gentleman's Magazine, for 1781.

TRADES

By the time Wilson published his books, the pattern of employment for blind people had been well established: if the blind were not beggars they would learn a trade. Sebastian Guille (?–1851), director of the school for the blind in Paris, in his *Essay on the Instruction and Amusements of the Blind* (1819) details the trades that blind students were taught. Each chapter describes and shows pictures of his students learning knitting; spinning; weaving; rope making; basket weaving; and making purses, shoes, carpets, whips, and mats. Wilson, at the school for the blind in Belfast, was taught upholstering.

Thomas Wilson (1750–1825), whom James Wilson mentions as "Blind Tom, the Bell-Ringer of Dumfries," was also a skillful woodturner by trade. Blind from smallpox at an early age, he was only twelve years old when he was appointed chief bell ringer. Margaret Caldwell, in an article about him in the *New Beacon* (November 1964), notes that "it seems that he was thoroughly domesticated, for we are told that his house was a model of cleanliness, that he made his own bed, fetched his water, and not only did his own cooking but grew and lifted his own potatoes and cut the peats for his fire."

Nathaniel Price, a bookbinder, was a notable exception to the many blind people who must change careers after becoming blind in adulthood. Wilson notes that Price was "still capable of binding books." Wimprecht, to whom Wilson refers as "The Blind Bookseller of Augsburgh," was born blind. He was known for his remarkable ability to remember the books he acquired and where they were located in his shop after handling them only once.

William Kennedy (1768–?) became blind at the age of four, and, according to Berthold Lowenfeld in his 1975 book, *The Changing Status of the Blind: From Separation to Integration,* showed musical talent at an early age. He became a cabinetmaker and learned how to construct and repair musical wind and stringed instruments, including Irish bagpipes, clocks, and watches.

John Kay, the Blind Mechanic of Glasgow (1784–1816), became blind at the age of ten from a firearm accident. Like other members of his family he learned carpentry. He was a skilled craftsman, making a wide variety of furniture. It is said that he had the ability to travel through Glasgow without a sighted guide. His "facial vision" was so good that he "found a difference of air on his face, when near any particular object."

Henry Hatsfield, blinded from smallpox as a youth, lived in Pennsylvania and made a living weaving baskets. He carried out every step in the manufacturing process: he found the saplings, cut them, and brought them home to prepare for weaving. Like Kay and others he was an independent traveler who went out alone to sell his wares.

John Macguire lived in Invernesshire, Scotland. Although blinded at age fifteen, he continued to work in the family business as a tailor. He was supposedly able to tell all of the colors of a tartan by touch.

Wilson also mentions a blind Scottish woman who assisted her husband in his weaving trade. She, too, could distinguish colors by touch.

Samuel Gridley Howe (1801–76), first director of Perkins School for the Blind in Boston, tried to change the system that directed the blind primarily into trades. "You must not think because you are blind," he advised students, "that you cannot learn as much as other children." Yet he was faced, as other educators of the blind had been, with the fact that society was not willing to accept the educated and trained blind into its ranks. Howe had to set up a workshop to employ some of his former students.

Slowly there was change—the blind did indeed become teachers, often in schools for the blind. Many were taught trades and skills and were able to find work. Yet society's attitude toward blind workers was difficult to change. Helen Keller (1880–1968) wrote in the January 4, 1906, issue of *The Youth's Companion:* "Ignorant of what blind men can do and have done [the blind person] looks about him for work, but he looks in vain. Blindness bars every common way to usefulness and independence. Almost every industry, the very machinery of society, the school, the workshop, the factory are all constructed and regulated on the supposition that every one can see." Organizations of blind people are working to change these attitudes, which for so long have limited blind and visually impaired persons to a few trades or professions or to working in sheltered employment.

THE LIFE

OF

THOMAS WILSON,

THE BLIND BELL RINGER OF DUMFRIES.

"Then, while on Britain's thousand plains,
One unpolluted Church remains,
Whose peaceful bells ne'er sent around
The bloody tocsin's maddening sound,
But still upon the hallowed day,
Convoke the swains to praise and pray."

It is humiliating to the pride of man to trace the helplessness of his nature, but at the same time gratifying to consider the goodness of providence, in the provision made for his wants and infirmities. In no situation, perhaps, is this better exemplified, than in the case of those who, like the subject of this memoir, condemned to perpetual darkness, are left to grapple with the difficulties of life, and to make their way through its mazy windings, under a privation which, of all others, is the most appalling.

Thomas Wilson was born on the 6th of May, 1750, and lost his eye sight by the small pox, at so early an age, as to have no subsequent recollection of ever having gazed on the external world. When a child, like other boys, he was very fond of visiting the venerable mid-steeple of Dumfries; and, at the age of twelve, was promoted to the office of chief ringer. Being of industrious habits, he also, after much labour and perseverance, succeeded in gaining a pretty correct notion of the trade of a wood turner, which enabled him to support himself, without becoming a burden to any one, and honest Thomas's *Beetles* and *Spurtles* are still held in high repute, by the good wives of both town and country. Although this business requires a considerable number of tools, he had them so arranged, that he could, without the least difficulty, take from his shelf the particular one he might be in want of, and was even able to sharpen them himself when necessary. He moreover excelled in the culinary art, cooking his victuals with the greatest nicety; and priding himself on the architectural skill he displayed in erecting a good ingle or fire. In his domestic economy, he neither had, nor required an assistant. He fetched his own water, made his own bed, cooked his own victuals, planted and raised his own potatoes; and, what is more strange still, cut his own peats, and was allowed by all to keep as clean a house, as the most particular spinster in the town. Among a hundred rows of potatoes, he easily found the way to his own; and, when turning peats, walked as carefully among the hags of lochar moss, as those who are in possession of all their faculties. At raising potatoes, or any other odd job, he was ever ready to bear a hand; and when a neigh-

bour became groggy on a Saturday night, it was by no
means an uncommon spectacle to see Tom conducting
him home to his wife and children.

As a mechanic, he was more than ordinarily ingenious, and with his own hands made a lathe, with
which he was long in the habit of turning various articles, both of ornament and general utility. In making
cocks and pails for brewing vessels, potatoe beetles,
tin smith's mallets, and huckster's stands, for all the
country round, blind Tom was quite unrivalled. Many
a time he has been seen purchasing a plank on the
sands, raising it on his shoulders, even if ten feet long,
and carrying it to his house, without coming in contact with obstruction on the way. He also constructed
a portable *break* for scutching lint, which he mounted
on a nice little carriage, by the means of which he
readily transported himself to any farm house where
his services were required. His sense of touch was
exceedingly acute, and he took great pleasure in visiting the work-shops of ingenious tradesmen, and handling any curious article they had formed. At the
time the Scotch Regalia were recovered, the good old
man seemed quite beside himself with joy; and never,
to the last, did he cease to regret, that circumstances
prevented him from visiting Edinburgh, and feeling
the ancient crown of Scotland.

After his appointment as chief ringer in the mid-
steeple of Dumfries, blind Tom's first visit every morning was to the bell-house; and he tripped up stairs
with as much agility and confidence as if he had possessed the clearest vision, generally inserting the key
into its proper place at the first trial. Never was a

ringer more punctual; for more than half a century Tom was at his post three times a day, without, we believe, a single omission, at the very minute required, whether the clock pointed right or no. The coldest morning, or the darkest night in winter, foul or fair, sunshine or storm, were all one to Tom, and though sluggards might excuse themselves on the score of the weather, his noisy clapper never failed to remind them that there was, at least, one man in the town up and at his duty. Indeed, such was his punctuality, that he was never known to commit a mistake except once, by ringing the bell at eleven, instead of ten at night. A friend calculated, that he had rung the bell more than one hundred thousand times. The lapse of sixty years produces many changes on men and things, and it may be mentioned as a curious proof of the progressive rise of the wages of labour, that his salary at first was only thirty shillings yearly; it was then advanced to two pounds; from two to three, three to five, five to ten, and so on, till at last he received, what to him was a little independency, the high salary of twenty pounds per annum.

About fifteen years before his death, the mid-steeple was thoroughly repaired, and a splendid new weather cock substituted in the place of the former old and clumsy one. This was a great event to blind Tom; the steeple was, in a great measure, his domicile, and he who had so much to do with the base, could not be inattentive to the capital. Up, therefore, he would go to the top; and though repeatedly warned against the danger he would incur, he actually accomplished the perilous enterprize, threw his arms round the bonny

bird, and bestowed on him a benediction to this effect;
that he might long, long continue to indicate as
truly the four winds, as he himself indicated the
time of day. On rejoicing days, during the war,
the bell-man was ever forward to evince his loyalty,
by mounting the bastion of the steeple, and discharge-
ing an old rusty fowling piece which he kept for the
purpose. During the life time of George III., Tom
was a most loyal subject; every returning fourth of
June, he made it his constant practice to ascend to
what are called the high leads of the steeple, and there
fired several rounds in honour of his Majesty's natal
day; performing the operations of priming and loading with admirable precision.

The knowledge he possessed of every part of the
town and neighbourhood of Dumfries was truly wonderful; he could walk to any quarter of the town, without ever deviating in the least from his route, and,
indeed, has been known to take strangers to places
they were in quest of, with the utmost exactness.
Being much in the streets, he was often employed as
a guide, and many laughable stories are told of the
astonishment of persons whom he has conducted to
the very extremities of the town, or even a good way
into the country, on discovering that they had been
led by a blind man. His local knowledge was indeed
very great, and his memory retentive to an uncommon degree. Once he had occasion to call at a shop,
and in crossing the threshold, it was remarked that
he paused, and lifted his foot very high. On this he
was told there was no step, but the old man's memory
was very faithful, and he immediately remarked,

"just four and twenty years ago, I was in this shop, and I am *gye* sure there was a step then." At another time, returning home one evening, a little after ten o'clock, he heard a gentleman, who had just alighted from the mail, enquiring the way to Colin, and Tom instantly offered to conduct him thither. His services were gladly accepted, and he acted his part so well that, although Colin is three miles from Dumfries, the stranger did not discover his guide was blind, until they reached the end of their journey.

Tom was also as well acquainted with persons as with places; if he heard any one speak, although he might not have met the individual for some time, yet he soon recognized him by his voice, when his usual remark was, "Eh! mon, 'tis lang sin I've seen ye." If he was asked the hour, such was his fine sense of feeling that, on touching the hands of his watch, he could inform himself in a moment.

Tom Wilson and another blind man in Dumfries, in order to beguile their leisure hours, contrived to invent a game somewhat similar to draughts, with which they very often amused themselves; and it was quite a treat to hear them, in a dark corner, discussing the probable issue of the game, and sometimes detecting each other in a false move.

Blind Tom had a taste for music, and was particularly fond of attending concerts; for many years he was a member of a musical institution, where the innocent cheerfulness of his manners, and his hearty laugh when any thing arose to please him, rendered his presence always acceptable.

The death of this honest and really ingenious man

happened in a very melancholy way, on the 12th of March, 1825. On that night being in the belfry, he was struck with something like an apoplectic fit, and staggering, as it was supposed, against an old chest which cut his head slightly, sunk on the floor, and remained all night in this forlorn and pitiable situation, without a friend to help him. For some time previously, a person had assisted him in ringing the bells on Sundays, and when this individual visited the steeple, at seven o'clock in the morning, he had to force the inner door of the belfry, before the fate of the deceased could be ascertained. Though he still breathed, he was unable to speak, and was immediately carried to his home, in a state of utter insensibility. Thus died poor Thomas Wilson, the oldest bell ringer, we believe, in Scotland, and who, for the long period of sixty three years, summoned the lieges to labour and repose, with all the regularity of the clock itself.

AUTHORITY.

Dumfries Paper.

WILLIAM KENNEDY,

THE FAMOUS BLIND MECHANIC OF TANDERAGEE.

" Full many a gem of purest ray serene,
The dark unfathom'd caves of ocean bear;
Full many a flower is born to blush unseen,
And waste its sweetness on the desert air."

THE privation of sight is perhaps more easily endured, and less prejudicial, than that of most of the
other senses. Poets, the foremost in renown, have
been incapable of the perception of external objects·
The two finest heroic poems, (the Iliad, and Paradise
Lost) are the immortal productions of the blind. The
eyes of Homer and Milton "rolled in vain, and
found no dawn:" yet, in the forcible expression of the
latter, were their minds "inly irradiated,' and they
have sung " of things invisible to mortal sight." The
contemplation, however, by the blind, of abstract
ideas, which depend not on vision, is by no means
extraordinary, nor of those objects that relate to the
other senses; for the privation of one sense quickens
the perception of the rest; while sensibility in general, and strength of natural reason, appertain to the
blind, as well as to those who are blest with the full
perfection of the senses. It remains for me to record
the powers of another of the blind, who, though he
has no claim to the genius of poesy, nor has ever
expatiated in the regions of philosophy, yet has he,
by the delicacy of touch, arrived at unexampled
perfection in the execution of various pieces of
mechanism, which, in others, would require all the
aid of sight.

The subject of this short narrative, is William Kennedy, of Tanderagee, in the county of Armagh, who has been blind from his infancy. The best account of his extraordinary progress in mechanics, is to be found in his own simple narrative, which the author of this article procured from his dictation. " I was born near Banbridge, in the county of Down, in the year 1768, and lost my sight at the age of four years. Having no other amusement, (being deprived of such as children generally have,) my mind turned itself to mechanical pursuits ; and I shortly became projector and workman for all the children in the neighbourhood. As I increased in years, my desire for some kind of employment that might render me not burthensome, though blind, induced me to think of music ; at the age of thirteen, I was sent to Armagh, to learn to play the fiddle ; my lodging happened to be at the house of a cabinet maker ; this was a fortunate circumstance for me, as I there got such a knowledge of the tools, and manner of working, as has been useful to me ever since : though these things engaged my mind, and occupied a great part of my time, yet I made as decent a progress in music as any other of Mr. Moorhead's scholars, except one. After living a year and a quarter there, I returned home, where I made, or procured tools, so as to enable me to construct different pieces of household furniture.

" Not being satisfied with the occupation of cabinet maker, I purchased an old set of Irish bagpipes, and without instruction, it was with difficulty that I put them into playing order. I soon, however, became so well acquainted with the mechanical part of them, that instruments were brought to me from every part of the neighbourhood, to be repaired. I found so many defects in this instrument, that I began to consider whether there might not be a better form of it than any 1 had yet met with; and from my early instruction in music, and continual study of the instrument, (for indeed I slept but little,) in nine months time, (having my tools to make,) I produced the first new set. I then began with clock and watch-making,* and soon found out a clock-maker in Banbridge, who had a desire to play on the pipes, and we mutually instructed each other. From this time, I increased in musical and mechanical knowledge, but made no more pipes, though I repaired many, until the year 1793, when I married, and my necessities induced me to use all my industry for the maintenance of my wife and increasing family; my employment for twelve years, was making and repairing wind and stringed instruments of music. I also constructed clocks, both common and musical, and sometimes recurred to my first employment of a cabinet maker. I also made linen looms, with their different tackling. My principal employment,

---

* William Huntly was born blind; or, at least, never had the recollection of seeing. He was bred by his father, who was a clock and watch maker, to that business; in which employment he carried on a successful trade at Barnstaple. He was considered by the inhabitants as very superior in his profession, particularly in repairing musical clocks and watches, and seldom met with any difficulty, even in the most complicated cases: in fact, it often occurred, when others failed in repairing a watch or clock, that Huntley discovered its defects.

however, is the construction of the Irish bagpipes, of which I have made thirty sets in the little town I live in, within these eight years past." Thus ends the simple sketch of the life of William Kennedy, in his own unadorned style. His modesty, however, has induced him to suppress several particulars, very much to his credit, as one of the most ingenious improvers of the Irish bagpipes. This imperfect instrument, (as it is a national one,) deserves, together with the harp, the peculiar cultivation of those who can feel the musical strains of their own island ; whether melancholy or gay ; whether amorous or martial, its modulation is, in general, delightful. We are all acquainted with the sympathetic effect of national music on the Swiss, when engaged in foreign warfare, far from his native mountains ; one air, in particular, has been known to occasion an intense desire to return to his country.

The effect of the bagpipes in rallying Frazer's regiment at Quebec, and the victory gained by general Wolfe, over the French, has been recorded in the anecdotes of that battle. The inspiring airs of the wounded piper in the glorious victory of Vimiera, is a fact too recent to require repetition ;—would, that the Scotch General, Dalrymple, had felt the electric inspiration of the Highland piper and his pibroch.

Pennant derives the Irish pipes from a period of very remote antiquity ; and the observation of that most indefatigable antiquary, is confirmed by the early testimony of Aristides Quintilianus. The compass of the Highland bagpipes, is confined to nine notes, while that of the Irish extends to more than two octaves. The modesty of our blind mechanic, as I have said before, has prevented him from enlarging on several points, which I shall here beg leave to notice, illustrative of his ingenuity as an improver of this instrument. In this respect, indeed, he deserves the character of an inventor, as his additions to the Irish pipes will do away many of their imperfections; and his invention has the great merit of simplicity; for the management of the instrument is nearly as easy now as formerly. To the chaunter he has added keys, by which some flats and sharps, not capable of being before expressed on the instrument, are now produced with ease. He has also added E in alt. being one note above the original compass of the instrument. Two additional notes are given by him to the organ stop, and some of its notes are now capable of being varied from naturals to sharps, according to the key on which the tune is played.

The basses, or drones, as they are commonly called, were formerly only in correct tune when playing on some particular keys, but are now so constructed, that their notes can be varied as the key varies on which the tune is played. There is also another alteration worthy of notice; by the addition of two large keys, managed with the wrist, a part of the basses, or all of them, can be stopped or opened at pleasure. The particulars of these most ingenious alterations would require terms too technical to be introduced here. In short, this blind mechanic, at the time this account was written, was unequalled, in the elegance of his workmanship, and the perfection of his scale, in

our favourite national instrument. From a rude block
of ebony, a fragment of an elephant's tooth, and a
piece of silver; having first formed his lathe and his
tools, he shapes and bores the complicated tubes,
graduates the ventage, adapts the keys, and forms
an instrument of perfect external finish and beauty,
" that discourses most eloquent music," capable of
expressing the finest movements in melody, and by
no means deficient in harmony; and all this by the
exquisite sensibility of touch, for he is stone blind,
and quite incapable of distinguishing the black colour of ebony, from the white of ivory.   Under
poverty, therefore, and physical privation of the
most overwhelming kind, he has gradually brought
his mechanical powers to this pitch of comparative
perfection !   What an incentive to perseverance under difficulties much less insuperable !   It is hoped
that the readers of this article, will be induced to
inquire into the actual authenticity of the statement,
and be led to encourage such extraordinary application and ingenuity.

AUTHORITY.—Belfast Monthly Magazine, vol. 1.

JOHN KAY,

THE BLIND MECHANIC OF GLASGOW.

> "The chamber, where the good man meets his fate,
> Is privileged beyond the common walk
> Of virtuous life;—quite on the verge of Heaven."

THE subject of this memoir was a native of Carriden, near Borrowstounness. He spent his early years, like most children, in the keen pursuit of amusement, while at the same time he became acquainted with the elementary parts of education. He was generally the leader of his companions at their various diversions; but, in the tenth year of his age, the following unfortunate accident happened to him. A loaded musket had been carelessly placed where he and his companions were amusing themselves; one of them inconsiderately took it up, not knowing it was loaded, and fired off the contents, and John Kay being close by, was in a moment deprived of his sight. Not long after this melancholy event, his relations left their native parish, and he accompanied them to Glasgow. Confined now to more sedentary employments, he often amused himself by making various articles of wood, which he executed with great ingenuity. For several years before his death, he assisted his brothers, who were carpenters, in their trade, at which he wrought constantly, and finished his work so well as to astonish those who saw it. He worked in mahogany and other sorts of fine wood, and made various kinds of furniture.

When going about the town, he needed no person to guide him, as he could find his way himself; and, what was very remarkable, if taken to any particular house, though even in a close, or up a stair, he could easily return again, without any person conducting him. He has taken his friends sometimes to places, in the evening, which they could scarcely find out when they had occasion to call again, even in day-light. It was not unusual for him to take a journey to Paisley, and other neighbouring towns, and to be the guide of any stranger who might accompany him. Walking one day in the streets of Glasgow with a friend, who warned him of being near a horse, he said there was no need of that, as he could perceive it himself; being asked how, he replied, that he found a difference in the current of the air on his face, when near any particular object, and that from this feeling, he could even avoid a lamp-post when he approached it, which he was frequently observed to do, while walking alone.

I am not able, from any information which I have received, to point out the exact time when he began to pay serious attention to religion. The accounts which were read to him of the success of missionaries, among heathen nations, gave him the most unfeigned pleasure. His heart was also much engaged in the religious instruction of youth, and he was one of the teachers in a Sabbath evening school. A great number of the scholars were considerably beyond the age of those who usually attend such schools; they highly respected him, and derived much improvement from his instructions. Many of them were remarkably instructed in the word of God, and their conduct in general, was very regular and becoming. Besides being so useful in his own school, he took much interest in others; he was grieved when any of them fell away, and used all his endeavours to keep the scholars together, or to collect them again. Those persons whom he thought qualified for instructing youth, he urged to come forward and take a part in this good work. He perceived with regret, that the business of the schools, in the city and neighbourhood with which he was connected, did not go forward, for some time, with that activity which he could have wished. This led him and one or two more to inquire into the cause, and, if possible, to apply a remedy. They were induced, in consequence, to propose another plan for conducting those schools, which was universally approved, and has since been acted upon, with great efficiency. His zeal in this important work did not fall away, after the commencement of his last illness; he went to meet his young friends, even when he was scarcely able to address them; and they frequently called upon him in his sick chamber, to receive his pious instruction. The words which he spoke, and the prayers which he offered up in behalf of the scholars and teachers of his school, a short time before death, will not soon be forgotten. I beg leave, in connexion with this, to mention a little incident related by a friend who was present, which happened upon a Wednesday evening, when he was accustomed to meet his more advanced pupils for religious instruction. One of them had been idling, and disturbing some of the rest, when he was calling upon them in the most affectionate manner, to persevere in the ways of *truth* and *godliness*. He quickly perceived it, and naming the scholar, said, " I cannot see you, but remember God sees you, and will not forget what you do ;" and, when concluding the exercise with prayer, he prayed for her in the most fervent and affectionate manner. Indeed, whenever he spoke on religious subjects, it was with a pathos peculiar to himself.

He was a zealous friend to the Religious Tract Society. He aided its funds as far as his ability reached, and at the same time, used his utmost endeavours with those who were rich, for the same purpose. He took every opportunity of distributing tracts, both in town and country, and has been known to convey them into families, where he thought they might be useful, and, when he dared not put them into their hands, to leave them under their doors. It was usual for him, when on a journey from home, to have a parcel of tracts always in his pocket, that he might bestow them in the places he visited, or give them away to persons whom he might meet with on the road ; such was his zeal for the propagation of the Gospel, and so indefatigable was he in his efforts for the good of his fellow creatures. When engaged in his daily work, he was seldom to be found without tracts, and was accustomed to distribute them among the servants where he was working. Upon an occasion of this kind, he had been employed for several days in a gentleman's house, where he had frequent opportunities of conversing with the servants. One of them appeared particularly trifling, and quite unwilling to enter upon any serious conversation. He one day put into her hands some suitable tracts, and requested her to read them, which she promised to do. It was not long before he saw a considerable change in her behaviour, and she listened with more attention when he spoke to her upon religious subjects; she also enquired what church he attended, and expressed her astonishment, that one who was blind could know so much about the Bible.

The deceased will live long in the remembrance of those who were benefited by his salutary counsels. Many who were in perplexity concerning the path of duty betook themselves to his advice, and he frequently was the means of restoring peace to the troubled mind. He entered into all the feelings of others, in the most sympathising manner; he wept with those who wept, and rejoiced with those who rejoiced, and frequently pointed out the path of duty, and removed difficulties which appeared, to the dejected mind, wholly insurmountable. He was particularly affectionate in waiting on the sick, and frequently sat at their bed-sides, speaking to them the words of consolation, and praying with them. He was very faithful in the case of any of his brethren, who had forgotten their duty to God and his people. It is much to be lamented, that this duty is too much neglected by brethren in the church-fellowship; they see others fall, and are not careful to help them, and point out the evil of their conduct. The deceased, however, was an eminent pattern of faithfulness to his brethren;

he set the evil of their conduct in so prudent, and at the same time, in such a forcible manner, before them, that he had often the comfort of reclaiming them from the error of their ways, while at the same time, he cleared himself of the blood of those who would obstinately go on in a course of sin. We would not, however, be considered as holding up the subject of this memoir as faultless; far from it. None was readier than he to confess sin; but it may with truth be affirmed that his faults, so far as they were known to man, were few, and his virtues many.

I now hasten forward to speak of the wondrous love of God manifested towards him, at the period when he was near the termination of his earthly career. He had been nearly six months afflicted with a disease, which was supposed to be an affection of the stomach, and was quickly wasting away; during a great part of that time he was confined to his room. I should mention, that in the prayers I have already referred to, he was particularly mindful of his own school, and he afterwards expressed a particular desire that the Christian friend whom he had procured to teach in his place, would continue in the school; he also desired his sister to collect what tracts he had, and give them to Mr. A——, to go on with in the school, and to hope for the divine blessing, as the Lord would certainly countenance his own ordinances, though, perhaps, not immediately. It may surprise some, that he was able to speak so much when he was so weak, and near his dissolution. All his friends who visited him that day, were astonished at it: they had formerly seen him when he could scarcely reply to them, but now, when, in reality, he was on the verge of eternity, he spoke as he was accustomed to do when in health. Surely we must see in this the hand of God, and that he himself spoke truly, when he said, "the Lord hath opened my mouth, that I might speak to his praise." He was enabled to converse until within a short period of the great change, which took place about seven o'clock, on the morning of the 16th of December, 1809, when he breathed his last, aged thirty-two years.

———

AUTHORITY.

The Life of Kay. Glasgow, 1816.

THE BLIND SCOTCH WOMAN.

A poor woman, the wife of a weaver, at Cambusbarron, in Scotland, died in 1822, who had lost the use of her eyes many years before; but who, notwithstanding, employed herself, during her blindness, in winding the woof of her husband's web, as well as that of others; but, what was more singular with her, was, that she was able to discriminate the different colours used in the worsted which went through her hands, so that the loss of vision seemed to give her but little inconvenience.

AUTHORITY.—Scotch Paper.

HENRY HATSFIELD,

In 1825, resided in Pott's Grove, Pennsylvania, who had been blind from his youth, caused by the small-pox. He was a respectable citizen, and kept a public-house ; was married, and had several children. Besides attending to the public-house, he made baskets of all sizes and descriptions, of a superior quality. What was most singular in him, he would go alone, as far as six miles from his home, with his axe, into a wood, where he would single out saplings of small trees, such as answered his purpose of making splits, &c.; he would cut them down to such lengths as suited him; he would then hide his axe in the leaves or branches of trees, and start off to a neighbouring farmer ; employ his waggon and horses to carry his wood home; and then return and take his axe from the place where he had hid it : and this he would do without any living soul near him. He has been seen repeatedly a considerable way from home, travelling on the public road, and if he was asked where he was, or where he was going to, he always answered correctly. He was the best player on the violin in those parts, and could keep the instrument in as good repair as any person. He was a subscriber to the Pottsgrove Paper, and often called at the office for it.

THE BLIND BOOKSELLER

OF AUGSBURGH.

Perhaps one of the greatest curiosities in the city of Augsburgh, is a bookseller, of the name of Wimprecht, who had the misfortune to be born blind, but whose enterprising spirit has enabled him to struggle successfully against the melancholy privation he is doomed to sustain, and to procure, by his industry and intelligence, a respectable and comfortable support for a large family, dependent upon him. His stock consists of more than 8,000 volumes, which are subject to frequent change and renewal. When he receives new books, the particulars of each are read to him by his wife, and his discrimination enables him to fix its value ; he recognises it by his touch, at any future period, however distant, and his memory never fails him, in regard to its arrangement in his shop. His readiness to oblige, his honesty, and information on books in general, have procured him a large custom ; and under such extraordinary natural disadvantages, he has become a useful and, probably, will become a wealthy member of the community to which he belongs.

AUTHORITY.
A London Newspaper.

THE BLIND TAILOR.

The following account of Blind Macguire, is no less wonderful than true, and will show that the privation of sight does not always impede the exercise of mechanical skill. "The late family tailor of Mr. M'Donald, of Clanronald, in Invernesshire, lost his sight fifteen years before his death, yet he still continued to work for the family as before, not indeed with the same expedition, but with equal correctness. It is well known how difficult it is to make a Tartan dress, because every stripe and colour (of which there are many,) must fit each other with mathematical exactness; hence, even very few tailors, who enjoy their sight, are capable of executing that task. Blind Macguire having received orders to make for his master's brother, who had lately returned from India, a complete suit of Tartan within a given time, proceeded to work without delay. It so happened, that that gentleman passed at a late hour, at night, through the room where the blind tailor was working, and hearing some low singing, he asked, ' Who's there?' To which the poor blind tailor answered, 'I am here, working at your honour's hose !' ' How,' said he, forgetting that Macguire was blind, ' can you work without a candle?'

O! please your honour,' rejoined the tailor, ' midnight darkness is the same to me as noon-day !' " It was said that Macguire could, by the sense of touch, distinguish all the colours of the Tartan.

AUTHORITY.

Philosophical Transactions of the Royal Society.

NATHANIEL PRICE,
A BLIND BOOKSELLER.

NATHANIEL PRICE, was a bookseller at Norwich, who, giving up business in that city, went out with goods to a considerable amount, from London to America. On his voyage thither, he lost his sight in consequence of a severe cold, and having suffered much distress and fatigue, he at length returned to his native country, after an absence of nearly five years.

This remarkable man could make every part of his dress, from the shoes on his feet, to the hat upon his head. After his loss of sight, he followed the employment of a bookbinder, and bound several books in the first style; being the first instance of a blind man who was capable of such an employment. As a proof of his abilities, there is a quarto Bible, elegantly bound by him, now in the Marquis of Blandford's library, at Sion-hill, in Oxfordshire. Strange as this may appear, to those unacquainted with the extraordinary capabilities possessed by many of the blind, this account has been confirmed by several respectable people, with whom the author is acquainted, and in whose veracity the reader may place implicit confidence.

GENTLEMEN AND LADIES

Gentlemen

JAMES HOLMAN (1786–1857), a wealthy young lieutenant in the Royal Navy, became blind at the age of twenty-five. Having a "great passion" for travel, he toured the world—Europe, Asia, Africa, America, and Australia—accompanied by a servant. He published accounts of his travels in six volumes. Ishbel Ross's 1950 book *Journey into Light: The Story of the Education of the Blind* mentions that he was accused and arrested in Siberia as a "blind spy." After ascending Adam's Peak in Ceylon (Sri Lanka), he observed, "I could not see this glorious sight with visual orbs, but turned toward it with indescribable enthusiasm. I stood upon the summit of the Peak, and felt all its beauties rushing into my heart of hearts." He lived in London and was a Fellow of the Royal Society.

Adam Mond lived in county Antrim, Ireland, and was the very opposite of Holman. His is a sorry tale of a man born on a small farm, whose father died when Mond was quite young, leaving the mother with a number of young children to rear. When his mother was unable to take care of the farm and was evicted, Mond sought the aid of a local "lawless bandit" to help the family regain the farm from the new occupant. This endeavor failed, and Mond was brought before a magistrate and sentenced to death. On being sentenced, "he resigned himself to despair … and he wept without intermission." His landlord, "knowing that he had acted through ignorance and impetuosity of youth," appealed on his behalf and obtained his pardon. But before it arrived, Mond actually "wept out his eyes." He returned to his own neighborhood and eventually became an unhappy miser.

In the chapter "The Biter Bit, An Interesting Anecdote," Wilson reprints an article from *The Universal Magazine* for 1768 about blind people who have "the senses of hearing, smelling, and feeling, more fine and exquisite." Although the assumption is still held by some today that blind people are compensated with heightened senses, recent research shows that this is not the case. Blind children show no greater natural acuity in hearing and touch, but the senses can be improved by developing them.

Ladies

WILSON mentions just a few blind women: Theresa Paradis (Maria von Paradis) (1759–1824), Anna Williams (1706–83), Joan Wast (?–1553), and Mademoiselle de Salignac (1741–63). Berthold Lowenfeld, in his 1975 book, *The Changing Status of the Blind: From Separation to Integration,* claims that Salignac became famous because Diderot wrote about her in his *Addition to the Letter on the Blind* of 1780. Salignac was a highly gifted, charming, and independent person. "She could calculate the size of a circumscribed space," Diderot says, "by the sound which her feet produced, or by that of her voice." She died when she was only twenty-two years old.

Some other women, including the Blind Lady of Geneva, the Blind Scotch Woman (?–1822), and another Mademoiselle Salignac (1745–?), of Xaintonge, are only briefly mentioned by Wilson. However, he dedicated his first edition in 1821 "To the Ladies Directresses of the Molyneaux Asylum for Blind Females."

In some areas of the world, conditions for women have changed little from Wilson's day. At the First International Conference on the Situation of Blind Women, held in Belgrade in 1975, Fatima Shah, representing the International Federation of the Blind, reported:

"In almost any present-day society, especially in the rural East, loss of sight for a female is almost always accompanied by loss of status, privileges, and rights both in the society and within the family. In society discrimination against women in general reaches its peak against blind women in particular, and, coupled with prejudice, makes her an object of false pity and mindless charity. In the family she is deprived of her normal role because of the belief that her disability renders her incapable of performing it."

As discrimination issues against blind women are resolved, more blind women may come to hold prominent roles, not just in organizations of the blind, but in all areas of society as well.

MADEMOISELLE DE SALIGNAC,

A BLIND FRENCH LADY.

THIS distinguished individual was born in 1741, and was deprived of her sight when about three years of age. M. Diderot has given an interesting account of this accomplished young lady, and from his narrative we will give a few extracts, and allow the author to speak for himself.

"She had," says M. Diderot, "an unusual fund of good sense, the utmost mildness and sweetness of disposition, uncommon penetration, and great simplicity of character. In her dress and person, there appeared a neatness, which was the more extraordinary, as not being able to see herself, she could never be sure that she had done all that was requisite to avoid disgusting others with the opposite quality. From her earliest youth it had been the study of those around her to improve her other senses to the utmost; and it is wonderful to what a degree they succeeded. By feeling, she could distinguish peculiarities which might be easily overlooked by those who had the best eyes; her hearing, and sense of smell, were also exquisite. She knew by the state of the atmosphere whether it was cloudy or serene; whether she was in an open place or a close street; also, whether she was in the open air or in a room; or if in a room, whether it was large or small. She could calculate

the size of a circumscribed space, by the sound produced by her feet or her voice. When she had once
gone over a house, she so well knew the plan of it,
that she was able to warn others of any danger; she
would say, 'Take care, the door is too low'; or, 'Do
not forget that there is a step.' She accurately observed varieties of voices, and when once she had
heard a person speak, she always knew the voice
again: she was neither sensible to the charms of youth,
nor shocked by the wrinkles of age, and said that she
regarded nothing but the qualities of the heart and
mind. She was much disposed to confide in others,
and it would have been no less easy than base to have
deceived her; it was an inexcusable cruelty to make
her believe that she was alone in a room, when any
one was concealed there. She was not, however, subject to any kind of panic terrors; seldom did she feel
ennui, for solitude had taught her to be every thing
to herself. Of all the qualities of the heart and mind,
a sound judgment, mildness, and cheerfulness, were
those which she prized the most. She spoke little,
and listened much; 'I am like the birds,' said she,
'I learn to sing in darkness.' In comparing things
which she heard one day, with those that she heard
another, she was shocked at the inconsistency of our
opinions; and it seemed to her a matter of indifference, whether she was praised or blamed by beings so
variable. She had been taught to read, by means of
letters cut out. She sung with taste, having an
agreeable voice; she also learned to play on the violin,
and this latter was a great source of amusement to herself, by drawing about her the young people of her

own age, whom she taught the dances that were most
in fashion. Mademoiselle de Salignac was exceedingly beloved by all her brothers and sisters; 'This,'
she said, 'is another advantage which I derive from
my infirmity,—people are attached to me by the so-
licitude they feel for me, and by the efforts I make
to deserve it, and be grateful for it; added to this, my
brothers and sisters are not jealous of me. Indeed, I
have many inducements to be good; what would become of me, if I were to lose the interest I inspire!'
She was taught music by characters in relief, which
were placed in raised lines, upon the surface of a large
table; these characters she read with her fingers, then
executed the air upon her instrument, and, after a
very little study, could play a part in a concert, however long or complicated. She understood the elements of astronomy, algebra, and geometry. Her
mother sometimes read to her the Abbé De Caillè's
book, and, on asking her whether she understood it,
she replied, 'Oh, perfectly!' 'Geometry,' she said,
'is the proper science for the blind, because no assistance is wanting to carry it to perfection: the
geometrician passes almost all his life with his eyes
shut.' I have seen the maps by which she studied
geography; the parallels and meridians were of brass
wire; the boundaries of kingdoms and provinces were
marked out by threads of silk or of wool, more or less
coarse; the rivers and mountains by pin-heads, some
larger, others smaller; and the towns by drops of
wax, proportioned to their size. I one day said to
her, 'Mademoiselle, figure to yourself a cube.' 'I
see it,' said she. 'Imagine a point in the centre of

the cube.' 'It is done.' ' From this point draw lines
directly to the angles ; you will then have divided the
cube'—' Into six equal pyramids,' she answered,
' having every one the same faces; the base of the
cube, and the half of its height.' ' That is true,
but where do you see it ?' ' In my head, as you do.'
I will own that I never could conceive how she
formed figures in her head without colour. She wrote
with a pin, with which she pricked a sheet of paper,
stretched upon a frame : on this were placed two
moveable metal rods, having a sufficient space between
them, in which to form the letters. The same mode
of writing was adopted in answering her letters, which
she read by passing her fingers over the inequalities
made by the pin, on the reverse of the paper. She
could read a book printed only on one side, and
Priault printed some in this manner for her use. The
following fact appears difficult to be believed, though
attested, not only by her own family, but by myself
and twenty other persons still alive. In a composition of twelve or fifteen lines, if the first letter of every
word was given her, with the number of letters of
which each word was composed, she would find out
every word, how oddly soever the composition might
be put together. I made the experiment with some
poems of Collè, and she even sometimes hit upon an
expression much happier than that used by the poet.
There was no sort of needle work that she could not
execute. She made purses and bags, plain, or with
fine open work, in different patterns, and with a variety of colours ; garters, bracelets, and collars for the
neck, with very small glass beads sewed upon them

in alphabetical characters. The following conversation, in which I am the interlocutor, will shew the learness of her conceptions on the arts of drawing, engraving, and painting. She said, ' If you were to trace on my hand the figure of a horse, a mouth, a man, a woman, a tree, I certainly should not be mistaken, and if you were to trace the profile of a person I knew, I should not despair of naming the individual, if the likeness were exact ; my hand would become to me a sensible mirror, but great indeed is the difference between this canvas and the organ of sight. I suppose, then, that the eye is a living canvas of infinite delicacy ; the air strikes the object ; from this object it is reflected towards the eye, which receives an infinite number of different impressions, according to the nature, the form, and the colour of the object, and perhaps the qualities of the air ; these are unknown to me, and you do not know much more of them than myself ; it is by the variety of these sensations that they are painted to you. If the skin of my hand equalled the delicacy of your eyes, I should see with my hand, as you see with your eyes ; and I sometimes figure to myself, that there are animals which are blind, and are not the less clear sighted.' 'But explain,' said I, ' the mirror.' ' If all bodies,' she replied, ' are not so many mirrors, it is by some defect in their texture, which extinguishes the reflection of the air. I adhere so much the more to this idea, since gold, silver, and polished copper, become proper for reflecting the air ; and troubled water and streaked ice lose this property. It is the variety of the sensation, and consequently the various property of reflecting the air in the matter you employ, which distinguishes writing and drawing, a drawing from an engraving, and engraving from a painting. Writing, drawing, engraving, painting, with only one colour, are so many cameos.' ' But when there is only one colour', I inquired, ' how can any other colour be discerned ?' ' It is apparently', she answered, 'the nature of the canvas, the thickness of the colour, and the manner of employing it, that introduces in the reflection of the air, a variety corresponding with that of the forms ; for the rest, do not ask me any thing more, I have gone to the utmost extent of my knowledge.' ' And I should be giving myself a great deal of very useless trouble,' I replied, ' in endeavouring to teach you more.' "

Thus ends M. Diderot's account of Mademoiselle De Salignac. She died at the early age of twenty-two. With an astonishing memory, and a penetration equal to it, what a progress might she have made in the paths of science, if Providence had granted her a longer life.

AUTHORITIES.

M. Diderot's Letters.—Memoirs of Baron De Grimm.

EXTRAORDINARY ACCOMPLISHMENTS.

WE have now to introduce to our readers another
young lady named Salignac, who, like the one of
whom we have previously given some particulars, was
blind from an early age, and was likewise distinguished by attainments extraordinary in one labouring under that severe privation.

Mademoiselle Salignac was a native of Xaintonge,
in France, and lost her sight when only two years old,
her mother having been advised to lay pigeons' blood
on her eyes, to preserve them in the small-pox, whereas, so far from answering the end, it caused an inflammation, which destroyed sight.   Nature, however,
may be said to have compensated for that unhappy
mistake, by beauty of person, sweetness of temper,
vivacity of genius, quickness of perception, and many
talents which certainly softened her misfortune.   She
played at revertis (a game of cards) without any direction, and often faster than others of the party.
She first prepared the packs allotted to her, by pricking them in several parts, yet so imperceptibly that
the closest inspection could scarcely discover her in-
dexes; at every party she altered them, and they were
known only to herself; she also sorted the suits and
arranged the cards in their proper sequence, with
the same percision, and nearly the same facility,
as they who have their sight.   All she required of those who played with her, was to name every

card as it was played, and these she retained so
exactly, that she performed some notable strokes at
revertis, such as showed a great power of combina-
tion and a strong memory. A very wonderful circumstance was, that she learned to read and write ; she
regularly corresponded with her elder brother, whom
some mercantile affairs had called to Bourdeaux, and
from her he received an exact account of every thing
that concerned them. The mode adopted by her
friends in writing to her was, to prick the letters
down on the paper, and by the delicacy of her touch,
feeling each letter, she followed them successively,
and read every word with her finger ends.* A person scratched, with the point of a pair of scissors, on a
card, " Mademoiselle de Salignac est fort aimable,"

---

* The important art of printing for the blind, has, we are
happy to perceive, been practically carried into effect in Scotland. Practically, we say, for though it has been introduced
both in Vienna and Paris, yet from the faulty nature of the
alphabet employed in those places, it has been found of very
little utility. " At a meeting of the managers of the Edinburgh Blind Asylum, on the twenty-sixth of January, 1828,
after some routine business, they proceeded specially to examine the nature and efficiency of the books lately printed for
the use of the blind. Some of the boys belonging to the asylum
were introduced, who, though the books had been in their possession only a few weeks, and they had had no regular teaching
were yet able readily to distinguish all the letters, and easily
distinguished those which were most like each other. They
were then, by Dr. Gordon and others of the directors, made
to take isolated words in different pages of the book, which
they at once knew, and they afterwards read slowly, but correctly, the different parts. From repeated trials, and varying
the exercises, the directors were of opinion that the art pro-

and she fluently read it, although the writing was small and the letters very ill-shaped. In writing, she made use of a pencil, as she could not know when her pen was dry; her guide on the paper was a small thin ruler, of the breadth of her writing. On finishing a letter, she moistened it, which fixed the traces of the pencil, so that they should not be obscured or effaced; she then proceeded to fold and seal it, and write the direction, all without the assistance of any other person. Her writing was very straight and well cut, and the spelling no less correct. To teach this singular mechanism, the indefatigable cares of her affectionate mother were long employed, who, accustoming her daughter to feel letters cut out of card or pasteboard, taught her to distinguish an A from a B, and thus

---

mised to be of the greatest practical utility to the blind, who, it evidently appeared, would be able to use these books with increasing facility. Mr. Gall also stated, that the writing apparatus for the blind, was in a state of considerable forwardness; the principles had been completely settled, and found efficient. The letters were easily formed upon common post letter paper, by one motion of the hand; and being submitted one after another to the pupils, were correctly and invariably distinguished by them."—*Scotsman.*

The benevolent Mr. Taylor, vicar of Bishop Burton, whose surprising success in cultivating the faculties of the blind is well known, has published " The Diagrams of Euclid's Elements of Geometry, in an embossed or tangible form, for the use of blind persons who wish to enter upon the study of that noble science." It is a very happy idea, and admirably calculated to add to the enjoyments of those afflicted with the loss of sight, by opening for them, in their dark state, a new and interesting source of employment and mental gratification. The plan is as simple as it is effectual.

the whole alphabet, and afterwards to spell words;
then, by the remembrance of the shape of the letters,
to delineate them on paper, and lastly, to arrange
them, so far as to form words and sentences. She
learnt, almost without instruction, to play on the
guitar, sufficiently for her little companions to dance
to, and had even contrived a way of pricking down
her tunes, as an assistance to her memory; but,
being in Paris with her father and mother, a music-
master observing the way used in writing to the young
lady by pricking, taught her the common musical
characters; and to distinguish the open notes, they
were made larger. She learnt to sing, and, so accurate was her ear, that in singing a tune, though new
to her, she was able to name the notes, whilst singing,
for them to be pricked down. In figured dances, she
acquitted herself extremely well, and in a minuet,
with inimitable ease and gracefulness. She was very
clever in both fancy and plain work, she sewed very
well, and in her work threaded her needles for herself,
however small. She never failed telling, by the touch,
the exact hour and minute by a watch.

AUTHORITY.
Encyclopædia Britannica.

THE BITER BIT,

AND OTHER ANECDOTES.

" Gold, too oft, with magic art,
  Subdues each nobler impulse of the heart!"

Blind persons, not being subject to have their attention distracted by the number of objects which the sense of sight presents, must have the senses of hearing, smelling, and feeling more refined and exquisite. This we find confirmed by several facts; and we may add, that the habit of exercising one sense, in default of another, makes that one more acute.

It is said of a person born blind at Puiseaux, in France, that he judged of the fulness of vessels by the sound of the liquors while they were decanted, and of the nearness of bodies by the action of the air on his face. By constant practice he had made very exact balances of his arms, and almost infallible compasses of his fingers. The varieties in the polish of bodies were distinguished by him with great facility, and he was also very expert in perceiving variations in the sound of the voice. He judged of beauty by feeling, and also by pronunciation and the tone of voice. He was very sure of the exact spot from whence a voice or noise came; it is reported, that he once had a quarrel with his brother, whose eye-sight was of no advantage to him in avoiding his blows; and that, vexed at his taunts, and at something he took to be ill usage, he laid hold of the first object at hand, threw it at him, struck him in the middle of the forehead, and knocked him down. This adventure, and some others, caused him to be cited before the Lieutenant of the police, in Paris, where he then lived. The external signs of power that affect others in so sensible a manner, make, however, no impression on the blind. He appeared before the magistrate, as before his equal, and his menaces did not in the least intimidate him. "What will you do to me?" said he to the magistrate. "I will cast you," answered the magistrate, "into a dungeon." "Ah! good sir," said the blind man, "I have been in one these five and twenty years past."

It may be perhaps thought that one born blind has no idea of vision. Of this we may judge by the answer of the same blind person, when asked, "What are eyes?" "Eyes," said he, "are organs on which the air has the same effect as my stick has on my hand. This is so true," added he, "that, when I place my hand between your eyes and an object, my hand is present to you, but the object is absent. The same thing happens to me, when I seek for a thing with my stick, and meet with another thing." He defined a looking-glass to be a machine that gives things an existence, far from themselves, if placed conveniently relatively to them. "Just as my hand," said he, "which I need not place near an object in order to feel it." "How many renowned Philosophers," says a modern author, "have shewn less subtility, in endeavouring to prove the truth of notions, which have been equally false!"

Some blind men are distinguished by peculiar sagacity. One of this character, who was possessed of two hundred guineas, hid them in a corner of his garden ; but a neighbour, who had taken notice of what he did, dug them up and carried them away with him. The blind man, not finding his money, suspected who was the thief. What did he do to obtain his money again ? He went to his suspected neighbour, and said that he came to him for advice; that he had four hundred guineas, the half of which he had hidden in a safe place, and that he was thinking with himself, whether he should deposit the rest in the same place. The neighbour advised him to do so, and conveyed back, in all haste, the two hundred guineas he had taken away, in hopes of being soon master of four hundred. But the blind man having found his money, secured it effectually ; and, calling upon his neighbour, told him, " that the blind saw more clearly than he did, who had two eyes."

Tho' darkness still attends me,
    It aids internal sight ;
And from such scenes defend me,
    As blush to see the light.

No weeping objects grieve me ;
    No glittering fop offends ;
No fawning smiles deceive me;
    Kind darkness me befriends.

Then, cease your useless wailings,
    I know no reason why ;
Mankind to their own failings,
    Are all as blind as I.

On a very dark night, a blind man was seen walking the streets, with a light in his hand, and a large bottleful of some liquor on his back. Some one going along, knowing him, and surprised at the light, said, " What a simpleton thou art ! What need hast thou of a light ? are not day and night the same to thee ?' " It is not for myself that I carry the light," answered the blind man ; "it is rather that such bodies as yours should not jostle against me, and break my bottle."

———

AUTHORITY.

The Universal Magazine for 1768.

Mr. JAMES HOLMAN, R.N.

THE WONDERFUL BLIND TRAVELLER.

"Hither he wandered, anxious to explore
Antiquities of nations now no more;
To penetrate each distant realm unknown,
And range excursive o'er the untravell'd zone."

This sightless and enterprising individual is a native of Exeter; he lost his sight at the age of twenty-five years, while on service on the coast of Africa, as a lieutenant in the royal navy, in the year 1811. He was subsequently appointed one of the Naval Knights of Windsor. In 1820, strange as it may appear, he travelled through France and Italy, and, in 1822, favoured the public with an account of his interesting travels; which work was favourably received. In the same year, he undertook an arduous journey through Russia, Siberia, Poland, Austria, Saxony, Prussia, and Hanover; these travels he published in 1825, in 2 vols. 8vo. His proposed objects in travelling were of so extensive a character, as to startle us in the outset, especially when we recollect his blindness. He was unfortunately prevented from executing his plan, by his being apprehended as a spy, after travelling some thousands of miles, and spending some months in the midst of Siberia, and was conducted from thence a state prisoner, to the frontiers of Austria. Indeed, in Russia, Mr. Holman was called the

" blind spy;" rather a whimsical and paradoxical appellation, for a person totally deprived of the use of his visual organs. The object which Mr. Holman had, in undertaking this arduous journey, is developed by himself in the following words: "On the 19th of July, 1822, I embarked in the Saunders Hill schooner, commanded by Captain Courtney, then lying in the London docks, and bound for St. Petersburgh, with the ostensible motive of visiting the Russian empire; but my real intention, should circumstances prove propitious, was to make a circuit of the whole world. My motives for concealing so important a part of my views, it will not be difficult to explain; they are attributable to the opposition my kind friends have always been inclined to make against what, under my peculiar deprivation, they are disposed to regard as quixotic projects; a feeling on their parts which I am desirous to suppress, since, on various occasions, I have to charge it with the disappointment of my most anxious wishes. Alas! how little are they able to appreciate my true sentiments and powers, as developing themselves in an intense desire to occupy the mind, to acquire solid information, and triumph over those difficulties which others might deem insurmountable. That my views are not chimerical, may be inferred from the success which, as far as my own powers are concerned, has hitherto attended my exertions."*

---

* The following brief notice of this extraordinary man appeared in one of the St. Petersburgh newspapers, during his stay in that city.

" Mr. Holman, a blind gentleman, about thirty-five years of age, and possessed of an agreeable countenance, arrived in

Mr Holman gives a most interesting account of the manners and customs of the Russians; their buildings, shipping, commerce, &c. Being obliged to leave Moscow, his mind was soon seriously occupied with various reflections: " my situation," says he, " was now one of extreme novelty, and my feelings corresponded with its peculiarity. I was engaged under circumstances of unusual occurrence, in a solitary journey of several thousand miles, through a country, perhaps the wildest on the face of the earth, and whose inhabitants were scarcely yet accounted within the pale of civilization, with no other attendant than a rude Tartar postilion, to whose language my ear was wholly unaccustomed; and yet I was supported by a feeling of happy confidence, with a calm resignation to all the inconveniences and risks of my arduous undertaking; nay, I even derived a real inward gratification, in the prospect of retirement from the

---

this city, (Petersburgh,) in July last; and we understand that he intends to visit a great part of the world. He enquires into every thing, and examines most bodies by the touch; which astonished us so much, that we could not have believed it, had we not seen it with our own eyes. When he visited my cabinet, without saying a word, I took him to the bust of the Emperor, by Orlovskii; after feeling it a short time, he exclaimed, 'This is the bust of the Emperor Alexander.' It ought to be observed, that he had previously examined a bust of his imperial majesty, in which, as he remarked, the forehead was more covered with hair; he also very justly observed, that the right ear was more perfect than the left, in the bust by Orlovskii. Mr. Holman also recognized the busts of Peter the Great, Catherine II. Suvarof, &c.

Soinin's Russian Journal.

eternal round of pleasure and social enjoyments, in which I had been participating, to a degree of satiety that began to be oppressive. Again and again I interested myself, by contrasting my voluntary exile, with the constrained banishment of the numerous unfortunate wretches, who have been known to languish away in the inhospitable wilds I was about to traverse, the remnant of a protracted existence; aggravated by an eternal separation from all the blessings that they have deemed most dear to them in life." Having passed through Poland, Prussia, Hanover, &c. our author ultimately landed at Hull, on the 24th of June, 1824, after an absence of two years and one day from his native country.

In January, 1827, Mr. Holman visited Lichfield, and seemed greatly interested with the various objects which that ancient city presented to his notice; but more particularly with the beautiful monument by Chantry, so deservedly deemed one of the brightest ornaments of the cathedral, and which he examined with great attention. His accurate taste and critical judgment, respecting the delicacies of sculpture, excited general admiration and surprise.

AUTHORITY.

Holman's Travels, London, 1825.

THE LIFE

OF

ADAM MOND,

A BLIND MISER.

" 'Tis true as witty poets sing,
That avarice is a monstrous thing;
By antient bards and modern rhymes,
'Tis painted as the worst of crimes.
   Old Plautus, in his comic scene,
Seizes the miser by his chin,
Holds up his face to public view,
For laughter and for hatred too.
Philosophers have all agreed
No vice has less excuse to plead.
   Not all the labours of the pen
Can cure this plague in aged men;
Like aged trees, the deeper shoot,
In grossest earth their worthless root;—
Then where such characters are found,
Let ridicule and mirth go round;
By jeers and pointing fingers tell,
Where such detested monsters dwell.
   The avaricious will not spare,
To rob the orphan—cheat the heir—
Nor honesty, nor honor rests
Within such sordid culprit's breasts;
This truth to view in clearest light,
Attend while I my tale recite."

Some men have had their names handed down to
posterity, on account of their vast skill in military

tactics, their dauntless courage in the field of battle, and their extensive knowledge of political science. Others have been famed for their great learning, their deep researches into the hidden recesses of nature, and the good which their useful discoveries have produced to mankind. Some have left a lasting memorial behind them, by their superior piety and useful labours in the church; while not a few have been recorded in the pages of history, merely on account of some enormous vice, or vices, to which they were obstinately addicted. From this it appears, that mankind are willing to allow any one a place in their records, who is particularly distinguished from his fellow men. Among the various vices to which human nature is subject, none is more detestable than avarice. It petrifies the finer feelings of the soul, fastens the affections to this world " by strong and endless ties," blinds the understanding in relation to that which is to come, and leaves the wretched individual who is overcome by it, without any other God to trust in for happiness or help, but the mammon of pelf. The principle is the same in the nobleman and the peasant, in him who dotes on countless thousands, and him whose soul is engrossed by a few paltry pence. It debases its miserable captive, not only below the dignity of his nature, but reduces him to the meanest shifts and artifices, strains his every nerve, and racks his ingenuity in accumulating wealth, which it dooms never to be enjoyed by its owner, and very often leaves to be squandered by a prodigal heir. These remarks are illustrated by the following singular and well attested relation.

Adam Mond, (the subject of this memoir) was a
native of the county of Antrim, in Ireland. His
mother was left a widow when he was very young,
with a number of children besides, and a very small
property, in the neighbourhood of Ballycastle. A
horse and two ewe sheep constituted their live stock,
and as much pasturage as served them for grazing,
with a little arable ground, was their entire landed
estate.

The mother being destitute of that energy of
mind which her circumstances required, her family
gradually became insubordinate, and regardless of her
authority. The consequences were soon visible, and
severely felt. The little farm was ill laboured, the
cattle neglected, and every thing managed so badly,
that by the time Mond came to man's estate, they
were ejected from their house and farm, by a sheriff's
order for non-payment of rent.

The time in which this disaster happened, was
very unfortunate; for young Mond, as there was then
in the north of Ireland, a lawless banditti, who, to
express the soundness of their principles, and inspire
their adherents with confidence, termed themselves
Hearts of Steel. Their professed object was not only
to redress wrongs, remove grievances, and administer
justice, but also to renovate the government of the
country. Mond, finding himself now destitute of those
means whereby he formerly indulged his slothful
inclinations and lazy habits, and being still strongly
possessed of those associations which attach man to
his natal spot, instead of reflecting on the justice and
legality of the decree, had recourse to the *Hearts of*

Steel. His case being peculiarly adapted for a display of their self-constituted authority and nightly depredations, they espoused it with all that enthusiasm which is common to those who are led by their bewildered imaginations, to form themselves into secret associations for illicit purposes. A paper was accordingly written and signed by their chief, in behalf of the whole body ; warning the person who succeeded Mond, in the occupation of the farm, to resign it immediately in his favour, or *Captain Firebrand* would pay him an unexpected visit, and consign him, his family, and effects, to the flames.

The person thus addressed was not intimidated, and, instead of obeying the unlawful mandate of this midnight cabal, he had recourse immediately to a neighbouring magistrate, swore against Mond, had him apprehended, and conveyed to the county gaol, for serving him with such an unlawful paper. At the ensuing assizes he was tried, convicted, and in fact sentenced to death, and delivered into the hands of the sheriff to be executed on a certain day. The unexpected sentence of the law, the fear of death, and the love of life, now operated so sensibly on his mind, that he resigned himself up to despair and extreme grief.—Every degree of fortitude forsook him, and he wept without intermission. The gentleman who was his landlord, knowing that he had acted through ignorance and the impetuosity of youth, made immediate and personal application to the executive government, and obtained a full pardon ; but before it arrived, he had actually wept out his eyes. He now returned to his own neighbourhood completely blind,

which no doubt was the leading cause of his afterwards becoming one of the most wretched misers that
ever lived.

The peculiar circumstances leading to, and flowing
from Mond's trial and sentence, rendered him an
object of charity. Losing his sight, which he had so
long enjoyed, made him extremely awkward, until he
became acquainted with, and inured to his new situation. He had therefore no other resource left but to
live on the bounty of others. Incapable of any manual
labour, he was led from house to house to seek a supply of bread, generally abiding with some of his more
liberal neighbours, so long as a disposition remained
to entertain him. Getting acquainted, however, with
the art, and no doubt with the profits of begging, he
became in a short time a complete proficient, and
made active application to all who came in his way :—
perhaps in this respect, he has been outdone by
few; his industry, perseverance, and ingenuity, became proverbial ; although he had no heartfelt affection for religion, he has often attended the church,
the Presbyterian meeting-house, and the Catholic
chapel, in the same day, which were all at a
considerable distance from each other, that he might
receive from the liberality of their congregations.

The gentleman who obtained his liberation, after
some time taking compassion on him, gave him a little
house, rent free, and employed hi 1 s a bailiff. In
this department he acted occasionally for more than
forty years. When he travelled at any considerable
distance from home, the compassionate ear was distressed in listening to his lamentable tale, concerning

some disaster which had happened to his house or property. When he begged in the immediate neighbourhood, he was always in need of, and in the way of getting, some article of dress. Part of the price of a pair of shoes, a shirt, &c. he had always in possession, and was now making application for the remainder, that he might be somewhat comfortable.

The promised hour of comfort and indulgence, however, he never suffered to arrive; for that sun never rose for more than forty years after his blindness, that ever saw him in possession of shoe, shirt, or stocking. His whole wardrobe he continually carried on his back, which consisted generally of an old tattered coat and waistcoat, a woollen cap, which served him at least twenty years, and a pair of small clothes, which he was very careful to keep whole for a reason to be explained in the sequel. The reader may be ready to imagine he is in possession of the reason at once, when he is informed, that for more than twenty years, Mond appeared to be severely afflicted by a well-known disease in the abdomen; but, in this he is mistaken, as well as Mond's most intimate observers were for the above period.

Although apparent disease, added to his blindness, excited the compassion of the beholders, there was no primary intention of deception in this respect. There is no doubt, however, that he congratulated himself on the adoption of a lucky project, which served the double purpose of securing and increasing his unsuspected treasure at the same time. His art in hiding and retaining what he once got in possession, was fully equal to his industry in acquiring.

At one time he had almost raised suspicions by keeping a dram shop without license, but he soon gave this up, exclaiming ever after that it broke him, and that he never was master of a penny since. In short, his asseverations concerning his distress, and his continual applications, completely blinded all who knew him, while his house and person presented one of the most wretched pictures of abject poverty ever displayed to the human eye.

In this miserable state, the winter of 1817 overtook him, the inclemency of which was severely felt in Ireland. In his despicable hovel he had neither clothing, food, nor fire. Still, he would not accept the friendly invitation of a neighbour, who offered him a good fire and lodging, free of any expense, during the cold. This offer he declined on pretence of not being troublesome, but the real cause arose from a fear of losing his money, or having it discovered. Finding the cold extreme, he resided by day in his own hut, receiving whatever food was sent to him, and retired at night to a corn kiln in the neighbourhood, where he slept snugly at the fire left by the last occupier. Had he accepted the benevolent proposal now mentioned, perhaps he might have concealed what was dearer to him than life itself, and dragged on his miserable existence a few years longer; whereas, by his niggardly caution, his purposes were defeated in the following singular manner, and his misery so increased as to render life a burden.

Whatever occupies the mind intensely, and captivates the affections by day, is likely to become the subject of our dreams at night. It was so with Mond

Money was his favourite object, whether awake or asleep. Hence, in the presence of a person who was occupying the kiln, Mond, while asleep, made mention of the spot where he had concealed a part of his treasure. The curious individual resolved upon a trial, and so repaired quietly to the secret place ; here there was no disappointment. Ten pounds sterling, in silver, were found concealed ;—and, the conscience of the person being as fast asleep as Mond was at the time, it was deemed a virtue to pocket it, since its wretched owner was not disposed to use it. When Mond awoke in the morning, he speedily directed his steps to pay his morning devotions to his only deity ; but how great was his grief and disappointment when he found the beloved of his soul was gone ! he could by no means contain himself. He vociferated a most hideous yell, that alarmed his neighbours to a considerable distance. On their arrival, so poignant was his grief, that he could not conceal the cause. He informed them of his loss. The report soon circulated, and strong suspicions were now entertained that he was still in possession of more.

To ascertain this fact was now the prevailing desire of those who had long known him. A few of his neighbours therefore one day entered his hut suddenly, and found him busily employed in counting money on the cover of a chest which had served him for the different purposes of table, chair, and treasure-desk. Perceiving he was caught, he threw himself immediately over his money, and although he knew his visitors were his best friends, he could not be con-

strained to rise but by violence. They now reckoned it over for him, and found the amount only £12
in silver.

On their leaving the house, imagining from the
bustle that they were about to look for more, he
bawled out vehemently not to meddle with some old
bottles which stood in a wall-cove, as they belonged
to one of his neigh'ours. A contrary effect was produced. They returned, and examined the bottles,
finding silver in each of them. This induced a general
search; when, to their great astonishment, they found
better than £100, all in silver, concealed in different
parts of the house. Mond now became the subject of
conversation in all places where he was known, and
though the sum in itself is comparatively small, yet,
considering the means used by him to gather it, and
the impression relative to his poverty, which had been
left on the minds of the people, it did not fail to
astonish all on their coming to a knowledge of it.

Application was now made to the gentleman
already mentioned, as he had previously interested
himself in behalf of Mond. He advised the applicants
not to return the money again to Mond, but to put it
to interest, and have him comfortably clothed out of
the principal. About twenty-six shillings were laid
out for this purpose, certainly contrary to Mond's
inclination: for on hearing the decision given, which
robbed him of the pleasure of counting his coin, and
involved the loss of so much, (for so he deemed it) it
threw him into one of the most dreadful paroxysms of
grief that language can describe. He continued three
days and three nights without either food or sleep.

No argument whatever could prevail with him. Those who were most attentive to him, and interested themselves most in his behalf, he deemed his greatest enemies. His grief was only equalled at the time he laboured under sentence of death, and there is little doubt, that had he possessed another pair of eyes, he would now have wept them out at the irretrievable loss which he conceived he had sustained. On the fourth day, however, his grief was assuaged. He summoned up a little courage, and appeared to feel a temporary repose. It was indeed but temporary, for on the arrival of his new clothes it was renewed in the most pungent and sensible manner.

Being requested to strip, that he might be washed and dressed, he complied only in part, for he peremptorily refused a change of small clothes. His tattered coat and waistcoat, on examination, were found to contain none of the sacred treasure; but it was imagined that he refused a change in the other parts of his dress from motives of delicacy. It may here be observed, that a few days previous to the discovery of his wealth, his neighbours had subscribed and bought a flannel shirt or frock, for the making of which, he paid the tailor with one shilling instead of eighteen pence, asserting, with horrid imprecations, that he was not master of a single penny more. On removing this article, how was every feeling shocked on beholding a hard cord (suspended round the neck, and supposed to be attached to his truss-band,) which had sunk into his flesh in a most miserable manner! His attendants now attempted to remove the cord, but he declared in the most solemn and violent language, that he would die before it should be disturbed.

Prompted however by their humanity, they paid no attention to his denunciation, and forcibly took it away; when, to their utter astonishment, instead of its being attached to a truss-belt, they found a pewter pint measure (no doubt, the one he had used in his dram-shop,) fastened to the end of it, hammered closely together at the mouth and so weighty, that it sufficiently indicated that it was not barren in contents. This singular depository contained no less than one hundred and seven guineas, in gold. For better than twenty years he had carried it in this manner, with the utmost patience and composure. It was the appearance of this, which caused all who saw him to imagine he was diseased.

When we consider that this affection for money was so strong, that he endured, for a long series of time, without any apparent uneasiness, the laceration of his flesh, which must have produced considerable pain continually; we need not wonder that the removal of his idol proved the cap-stone of his woes; grief now preyed upon his vitals like a vulture; wasted his strength, and sunk him shortly into a kind of stupor, from which he never recovered. He lived only seven months after this event, died unexpectedly, and went into a world of spirits, grieved on no other account but because he could not carry a portion of his treasure along with him.

AUTHORITY.

Imperial Magazine. Vol. 2.

THE BLIND LADY OF GENEVA.

THIS lady lost her sight when she was but a year old, by being too near a stove that was too hot; there remained on the upper part of her eye, so much sight, that she distinguished day from night; and, when any person stood between her and the light, she could distinguish, by the head dress, a man from a woman; but, when she turned down her eyes, she could not see. She played well on the organ and on the violin, and wrote legibly; in order to her learning to write, her father furnished her with masters, who ordered letters to be carved in wood, and by feeling the characters, she formed such an idea of them, that she wrote them very legibly; she had a machine that held her papers, and kept her writing always in line.

———

AUTHORITIES.
Travels through France and Switzerland.

INSTANCES OF ACUTENESS IN THE SENSES OF
HEARING AND FEELING.

The following interesting anecdotes are related by
Dr. Abercrombie. In speaking of the blind, he observes; "There is something exceedingly remarkable
in the manner in which the loss or diminution of one
sense, is followed by increase of the intensity of others,
or rather, perhaps, by an increased attention to the
indications of the other senses. Blind persons acquire
a wonderful delicacy of touch ; in some cases, it is
said, to the extent of distinguishing colours. Two instances have been related to me, of blind men who
were much esteemed as judges of horses. One of
these, in giving his opinion of a horse, declared him
to be blind, though this had escaped the observation
of several persons who had the use of their eyes, and
who were with some difficulty convinced of it. Being
asked to give an account of the principle on which he
had decided, he said it was by the *sound* of the horse's
step in walking, which implied a peculiar and unusual
caution in the manner of putting down his feet. The
other individual, in similar circumstances, pronounced
a horse to be blind with one eye, though this had also
escaped the observation of those concerned. When
he was asked to explain the facts on which he formed
his judgment, he said, he *felt* the one eye to be colder
than the other.

" Dr. Rush relates another instance, not less extraordinary, of acuteness in the sense of hearing.   Two blind young men, brothers, of the city of Philadelphia, knew when they approached a post in walking across a street, by a peculiar sound, which the ground under their feet emitted in the neighbourhood of the post and they could tell the names of a number of tame pigeons, with which they amused themselves in a little garden, by only hearing them fly over their heads."

AUTHORITY.

Abercrombie on the Intellectual Powers, p. 52, 3.

APPENDIXES

BIOGRAPHICAL INDEX

JAMES WILSON'S INTRODUCTION

TO

BIOGRAPHY OF THE BLIND

EDITIONS 2, 3, AND 4

INTRODUCTION.

———

THE branch of biography which the following pages exhibit, has not, until now, been entered on as a distinct subject. In all preceding works, the lives of the blind have been classed and confounded with those of others; and though individuals have been pointed out as objects of admiration and astonishment, yet no work has appeared in which they have been considered in a proper point of view, as a class of men seemingly separated from society; cut off from the whole visible world, and deprived of the most valuable faculty that man can possess; yet, in many instances, overcoming all those difficulties which would have been thought insurmountable, had not experience proved the contrary.

In the pursuit of knowledge, the blind have been very successful, and many of them have acquired the first literary honours, that their own, or foreign universities could confer. If they have not excelled, they have equalled many of their contemporaries, in the different branches of philosophy, but more particularly in the science of mathematics, many of them having been able to solve the most abstruse problems in algebra. In poetry, they have been equally distinguished. Two of the greatest men that ever courted the muses, laboured under the deprivation of sight— Homer, the venerable father of epic poetry, and Milton, the inimitable author of "Paradise Lost." In philosophy, Saunderson and Euler were eminently distinguished. The former lost his sight when only twelve months old, but was enabled, by the strength of his comprehensive genius, to delineate the phenomena of the rainbow, with all the variegated beauty of colours, and to clear up several dark and mysterious passages, which appeared in Newton's Principia. And though the latter did not lose his sight until he arrived at the years of manhood, yet, after that period, he was able to astonish the world by his labours in the rich fields of science, where he earned those laurels which still continue to flourish in unfaded bloom. He had the honour of settling that dispute which had so long divided the opinions of philosophers in Europe, respecting the Newtonian and Cartesian systems, by deciding in favour of Newton, to the satisfaction of all parties. The treasures of his fertile genius still enrich the academies of Paris, Basle, Berlin, and St. Petersburgh.

In mechanics, the blind have almost surpassed the bounds of probability, were not facts supported by evidence of unquestionable authority. Here, we find architects building bridges, drawing plans of new roads, and executing them to the satisfaction of the commissioners. These roads are still to be seen in the counties of York and Lancaster, where they have been carried through the most difficult parts of the country, over bogs and mountains. Indeed, there are few branches of mechanics in which the blind have not excelled.

It was of trifling importance to me, at what time of life or by what cause, the subjects of these memoirs lost their sight, provided they distinguished themselves after they became blind. My principal object was, to exemplify the powers of the human mind, under one of the greatest privations to which man is exposed in this life. It was partly with a view of rescuing my fellow sufferers from the neglect and obscurity in which many of them were involved, that I was induced to commence the present work,—an undertaking attended with immense toil and laborious research. This will readily be allowed, when it is considered that I had often to depend on the kindness of strangers, for the loan of such books as were requisite for my purpose, and also to supply the place of a reader or amanuensis. However, after surmounting the various difficulties with which I had to contend, the work made its appearance in 1820, in one volume, 12mo. The reception it met with from the public, was gratifying to my feelings, and far exceeded my expectations.

The present edition is very much improved and enlarged; many new and interesting subjects being added, which I hope will meet with the approbation of my kind friends, and generous subscribers.

JAMES WILSON.

SOURCES FOR FURTHER READING

American Foundation for the Blind. *Directory of Services for Blind and Visually Impaired Persons in the United States and Canada,* 24th ed. New York: American Foundation for the Blind, 1993.

Anderson, Robert. *The Life of Samuel Johnson, LL.D, with Critical Observations on His Works,* 3d ed. Edinburgh: Doig and Sterling, 1815.

Artman, William, and L. V. Hall. *Beauties and Achievements of the Blind.* Dansville, N.Y.: William Artman and L. V. Hall, 1856.

Bauman, Mary K. and Norman M. Yoder. *Placing the Blind and Visually Handicapped in Professional Occupations.* Washington, D.C.: Department of Health, Education, and Welfare, 1962.

Bhalerao, Usha. *Blind Women's Emancipation Movement: A World Perspective.* New Delhi: Sterling Publishers, 1986.

Bird, John. *Essay on the Life, Character, and Writings of James Wilson, as Well as on the Present State of the Blind.* London: Ward and Lock, 1856.

Bledsoe, C. Warren. "History and Philosophy of Work for the Blind." In *Social and Rehabilitation Services for the Blind.* Edited by Richard E. Hardy and John Cull. Springfield, Ill.: Thomas, 1992.

Blind Authors. *The St. James's Magazine* (August 1866): 91–110.

Blodi, Frederick. *The Eye, Vision, and Ophthalmology on Postage Stamps.* Bonn: J. P. Wayenborgh, 1986.

Butterworth, Hezekiah. *The Great Composers*. Boston: Lothrop, 1884.

Cardwell, Margaret. "Henry Moyes." *New Beacon* 49 (March 1965): 63.

———. "Joseph Strong, Blind Mechanic and Musician of Carlisle." *New Beacon* 46 (April 1962): 98–99.

———. "Professor Nicholas Saunderson." *New Beacon* 45 (December 25, 1961): 322–23.

———. "Thomas Wilson." *New Beacon* 48 (November 1964): 634–35.

Clarke, George. *The Life and Sketches of Curious and Odd Characters*. Boston: Clarke, 1833.

Collingwood, Francis. "Handel and His Blindness." *New Beacon* 43 (March 25, 1959): 59–60.

Coon, Nelson. "George Eberhard Rumph." *New Outlook for the Blind* 52 (April 1958): 147–48.

———. "Sir John Fielding." *New Outlook for the Blind* 52 (March 1958): 95–96.

Courtney, Abram V. *Anecdotes of the Blind; by Abram V. Courtney Himself Totally Blind with a Memoir of the Author*. Boston: Abram V. Courtney, 1835.

Eaton, Allen H. *Beauty for the Sighted and the Blind*. New York: St. Martin's Press, 1959.

French, Richard Slayton. *From Homer to Helen Keller: A Social and Educational Study of the Blind*. New York: American Foundation for the Blind, 1932.

Gostin, O. Lawrence, and Henry A. Beyer. *Implementing the Americans with Disabilities Act: Rights and Responsibilities of All Americans*. Baltimore: Paul H. Brookes, 1993.

Heymann, Frederick G. *John Zizka and the Hussite Revolution*. Princeton, N.J.: Princeton University Press, 1955.

Houldey, William E. *Ziska: The Blind Hero of Bohemia*. London: Society for Promoting Christian Knowledge, 1881 (?).

Keller, Helen. "What the Blind Can Do." *The Youth's Companion* (January 4, 1906): n.p.

Kitto, John. *The Lost Senses.* Edinburgh: William Oliphant, 1845.

Lowenfeld, Berthold. *The Changing Status of the Blind: From Separation to Integration.* Springfield, Ill.: Thomas, 1975.

Mell, Alexander. *Encyklopädisches Handbuch des Blindenwesens.* Vienna: Von A. Pichlers Witwe und Sohn, 1900.

Nippon Lighthouse. *The World Encyclopaedia of the Blind* (in Japanese). Osaka: Nippon Lighthouse Welfare Center for the Blind, 1972.

O'Sullivan, Donal. *Carolan: The Life, Times, and Music of an Irish Harper.* 2 vols. London: Routledge and Keegan, 1958.

Platt, I. *A Library of Wonders and Curiosities Found in Nature and Art, Science and Literature.* New York: John B. Alden, 1884.

Pringle, Patrick. *Hue and Cry: The Story of Henry and John Fielding and Their Bow Street Runners.* New York: Morrow, 1956.

Putnam, Peter. "Four Blind Lawmakers." *AAWB Blindness Annual.* (1974–75): 9–15.

Revesz, G. *Psychology and Art of the Blind.* New York: Longmans, Green, 1950.

Ross, Ishbel. *Journey into Light: The Story of the Education of the Blind.* New York: Appleton-Century-Crofts, 1950.

Rovig, Lorraine. "JOB—A Unique Resource with a Realistic Appraisal of Blindness." Speech presented to the National Federation of the Blind, April 7, 1995.

Schoelcher, Victor. *The Life of Handel.* London: Trubner, 1857 (?).

Scholler, Heinrich. *Enzyklopädie des Blinden- und Sehbehindertenwesens.* Heidelburg: C. F. Muller, 1993.

Smiles, Samuel. *Life and Labor: Characteristics of Men of Industry, Culture, and Genius.* Chicago: Donohue, Henneberry, 1922 (?).

Thomas, Mary G. *Edward Rushton.* London: Royal National Institute for the Blind, 1950.

Todd, Henry J. *Illustrations of the Lives and Writings of Gower and Chaucer.* London: F. C. and J. Rivington, T. Payne, Cadell and Davies, and R. H. Evans, 1810.

Trevor-Roper, Patrick. *The World through Blunted Sight: An Inquiry into the Influence of Defective Vision on Art and Character.* New York: Bobbs-Merrill, 1970.

Van Landeghem, Hippolyte. *Exile and Home: The Advantages of Social Education for the Blind.* London: Hippolyte Van Landeghem, 1865.

Wilson, James. *The Life of James Wilson, Who has Been Blind from His Infancy.* Birmingham, England: J. W. Shotwell, 1842.

FRIENDS OF LIBRARIES FOR BLIND AND PHYSICALLY HANDICAPPED INDIVIDUALS IN NORTH AMERICA

OFFICERS

Dr. Kenneth Jernigan, Maryland, President
Dr. Euclid Herie, Ontario, Canada, Vice President
Peggy Elliott, Iowa, Secretary/Treasurer

BOARD MEMBERS

Daniel Boyd, South Dakota
Geraldine Braak, British Columbia, Canada
Paul Edwards, Florida
Duane Gerstenberger, Maryland
Sharon Gold, California
Mary Ruth Halapatz, Virginia
Marc Maurer, Maryland
Barbara Pierce, Ohio
Priscilla Hudson, Colorado

EX OFFICIO MEMBERS

Director, National Library Service for the Blind and
Physically Handicapped, Library of Congress
Frank Kurt Cylke

Executive Director, Library for the Blind,
Canadian National Institute for the Blind
Rosemary Kavanagh

EXECUTIVE DIRECTOR

Keith R. Krueger

Colophon

JAMES WILSON'S *Biography of the Blind* was first printed in 1821 by D. Lyons in Belfast, Ireland. Three subsequent editions, printed by J. W. Showell in Birmingham, England, followed in 1833, 1835, and 1838. Wilson's biographies and introductions are reproduced here in facsimile and are taken, for the most part, from the later English editions.

The editorial commentary for this new comprehensive edition of *Biography of the Blind* was composed in Monotype Bulmer, based on types cut by William Martin for the Shakspeare Printing Office of William Bulmer. Dedicated to the ideals of fine typography, Martin and Bulmer collaborated on the nine-volume "Boydell Shakspeare" (1792–1802), as well as *Poems of Goldsmith and Parnell* (1795) and *The Chase* by William Somerville (1796).

Martin's font combines beauty with functionality, anticipating the modern style of Bodoni while retaining qualities from the transitional style of Baskerville. The type is characteristic of its era and similar to the fonts used in the original English editions of *Biography of the Blind*. The digital version of Bulmer used in this book was first released in 1994 and redrawn in the Monotype Type Drawing Office by Ron Carpenter following a study of Bulmer's printed works and extensive research into the hot metal versions of the 1930s.

Biography of the Blind was designed and composed by Robert L. Wiser of Archetype Press, Inc., in Washington, D.C., and printed by The Stinehour Press in Lunenburg, Vermont, on 60-pound Glatfelter Offset.